AN ACCOUNT OF THE ISLAND OF CEYLON

AN ACCOUNT OF THE ISLAND OF CEYLON

CONTAINING
ITS HISTORY, GEOGRAPHY, NATURAL HISTORY, WITH THE MANNERS AND CUSTOMS OF ITS VARIOUS INHABITANTS

TO WHICH IS ADDED

THE JOURNAL OF AN EMBASSY TO THE COURT OF CANDY

ILLUSTRATED BY A MAP AND CHARTS

ROBERT PERCIVAL

GYAN

Published by

Gyan Publishing House
5, Ansari Road
Daryaganj, New Delhi-110002
Phone: 011-47034999, 9811692060
E-mail: books@gyanbooks.com

Distribution Network
gyanbooks.com
India, USA, Canada, UK, Australia, France

ISBN : 978-81-212-3013-1 (PB)
First Published, 1803

2nd Impression 2020

Printed at: Gyan Press, Delhi.

An Account of the Island of Ceylon
Author: Robert Percival

AN

ACCOUNT

OF

THE ISLAND OF CEYLON,

CONTAINING

Its History, Geography, Natural History, with the Manners and Customs of its various Inhabitants;

TO WHICH IS ADDED,

THE JOURNAL OF AN EMBASSY TO THE COURT OF CANDY.

ILLUSTRATED BY A MAP AND CHARTS.

BY ROBERT PERCIVAL, ESQ.

OF HIS MAJESTY'S NINETEENTH REGIMENT OF FOOT.

LONDON:

PRINTED BY AND FOR C. AND R. BALDWIN, OF NEW-BRIDGE STREET, BLACKFRIARS.

1803.

TO

HIS ROYAL HIGHNESS FIELD-MARSHAL

THE DUKE OF YORK,

ETC. ETC.

May it please your Royal Highness,

IT is to the Commander in Chief of His Majesty's forces that every soldier naturally looks for protection and patronage, when he has turned his attention towards any object tending to promote the prosperity of his country. To your ROYAL HIGHNESS, however, any individual of the British armies addresses himself with peculiar confidence, since their welfare and encouragement have appeared the principal objects of your life, ever since the attainment of your present exalted situation. When I say that a steady discipline and a spirit of loyalty have been uniformly conspicuous in the army; that the condition of the soldier has in every respect been improved, and that every comfort of which his situation is susceptible is now attained:

when I attribute all these advantages to the regulations and the cares of your ROYAL HIGHNESS, I only speak the sentiments of every officer and every private in his Majesty's service.

While your ROYAL HIGHNESS is occupied with objects of so much greater importance, I should not presume to intrude with the following Work upon your notice, were I not conscious that it was undertaken and completed chiefly with a view to point out to the attention and enterprise of this country a new acquisition of the greatest importance both in a commercial and political point of view.

From the observations I then made, I am enabled to affirm that its retention in our hands must prove of the greatest benefit to our East India trade, and our commerce in general; and is in this view a measure which must reflect the highest honour on the wisdom of his Majesty's Councils.

From the period of my arrival with his Majesty's 19th regt. on the island of Ceylon shortly after its capture, I endeavoured, during my few leisure moments from military duty, to obtain as much useful information as an officer in my situation had it in his power to collect.

Having had an opportunity of seeing different parts of the sea-coast, and also some of the interior, while serving with the escort which accompanied General Macdowal in his embassy to the Court of Candy, I was enabled to notice the many advantages to be derived from this valuable possession, as well as to acquire a knowledge of its actual state, a subject hitherto but superficially treated of: and it struck me that the observations I had made might afford some information to the public, and perhaps might not be altogether useless in respect to more important considerations. All the merit, however, which I can lay claim to in the following volume, is an authentic relation of facts; and I hope that your ROYAL HIGHNESS, with your usual goodness, will excuse the want of elegant and scientifick composition in one who has spent his life in a military career.

Whatever may be the fate of this publication, the condescension of your ROYAL HIGHNESS, in allowing it to be ushered into the world under your august patronage, has impressed the most lively and lasting gratitude on the mind of

Your ROYAL HIGHNESS'S most humble

and ever devoted servant,

ROBERT PERCIVAL.

CONTENTS.

CHAPTER V.

CHAPTER VI.

CHAPTER VII.

CHAPTER VIII.

CHAPTER IX.

CHAPTER X.

CHAPTER XI.

CHAPTER XII.

CHAPTER XIII.

CHAPTER XIV.

CHAPTER XIV *

CHAPTER XV.

CHAPTER XVI.

CHAPTER XVII.

CHAPTER XVIII.

AN
ACCOUNT
OF
THE ISLAND OF CEYLON.

CHAPTER I.

Introduction—History of the Island previous to its being taken possession of by the English—The successive conquests of the Portuguese, Dutch, and English.

ON my arrival in Ceylon with his Majesty's forces, in the year 1797, I was induced by curiosity, and the contradictory and romantic accounts I had heard of this island, to make particular enquiries with regard to its present state; and I found an agreeable amusement in taking notes of such facts and objects as appeared to me remarkable. In the prosecution of my enquiries, however, I found that they might be rendered conducive to objects of infinitely greater importance than temporary amusement. The accounts hitherto published of this island had been extremely imperfect; as the watchful jealousy of the Dutch both excluded the researches of strangers, and prevented their own people from publishing any observations which they might have made during their stay in the island. Few, indeed, of that nation were anxious to inquire into the history either of the country, or its inhabitants. The desire of increasing their wealth was with them the ruling passion; and while they could carry on their commerce in the towns on the sea-coast, they concerned themselves very little with the interior of the island. Many Dutchmen, even of the better sort, had resided on Ceylon for a considerable number of years, without having ever been so much as a few leagues from the coast. Even those sent to command there were seldom men of enlightened minds; and provided they could secure their own interests, they were unwilling to occupy their attention with the prosecution of plans which might have been productive of national benefits.

All these causes conspired to render the accounts which Europeans possessed of this island, exceedingly imperfect; and I was soon convinced that the narrow policy of the Dutch government, and the selfish views of their officers, had made them overlook many things which tended greatly to increase the value of the colony. As it was now in our possession, these ideas made a forcible impression on my mind; and the hope that I might contribute to render this new acquisition more valuable to my country, gave new eagerness to my researches. The vast importance of the island both in a commercial and political view made me confident that it would not be given up at any future peace; for with the exception of Bombay, it contains the only harbour either on the Coromandel or Malabar coasts, in which ships can moor in safety at all seasons of the year; and even before it came into our possession, its internal produce presented several rich articles to commerce. Any attempt therefore to throw light on the present state of the island, and thus to point out the means of improving its internal cultivation, and securing it against the attacks of external enemies, would at least have the merit of aiming at a national benefit.

With these objects in view I continued my enquiries; and was fortunate enough to have every opportunity in the prosecution of them which the present situation of the island affords. During a residence of three years I visited almost every part of the sea-coast; and before I left the island, I was become quite familiar with its general appearance, its natural productions, the present state of its cultivation, and the manners and dispositions of its inhabitants. On an embassy being sent to wait upon the native king of the island, I was also among those officers who were appointed to accompany it; and by this means had an opportunity of observing the interior of the country, into which the jealousy of the natives has seldom permitted any European to penetrate.

The advantages which I derived from personally visiting the greater part of the island, were very much improved by the assistance of Mr. Dormieux, a Dutch gentleman, in the English service, who had resided upwards of twenty years in Ceylon, and had during that period acquired a complete knowledge both of the manners and language of its several inhabitants. By his means, therefore, I was enabled to get over many obstacles which presented themselves to my researches; and the valuable communications of several friends have rendered me essential service in completing my accounts of Ceylon. Still, however, I have been careful not to advance any fact of which I was not either an eye-witness, or which was not derived from information which no one could hesitate to believe. The manners and customs of the inhabitants, I have endeavoured to describe in the manner they impressed my mind at the time I observed them. I have followed the same plan in giving an account of the natural productions of the island; and hence my observations may be thought more calculated for the general reader, than the man of science. But I hope the public will make some allowance for the habits of my profession; and if I succeed in affording either amusement or instruction, I trust they will excuse a little deficiency in systematic knowledge.

Before proceeding to the principal object of this work, a description of the present state of the Island of Ceylon, it will probably gratify curiosity to give a short account of its history, and the successive changes it has undergone, since it came into the possession of Europeans. Such a sketch is even necessary to throw light on its present state, and to point out the way to its farther improvement, by shewing the errors committed by its former possessors.

Previous to the arrival of the Portuguese, little is known of the history of Ceylon. It is said to have been celebrated for its spices even in the earliest ages; and it is hence that Solomon is said to have brought the spiceries and precious stones, for the use and embellishment of his temple. Such vague traditions, however, are nowise to be depended upon; and the wild stories current among the natives, throw no light whatever on the ancient history of the island. The earliest period at which we can look for any authentic information, is the arrival of the Portuguese under Almeyda, in the year 1505. Being accidentally forced by stress of weather into one of the harbours of Ceylon, he was hospitably received by the inhabitants. The situation of the island, and its valuable productions, made him turn his attention to cultivating a closer connection with the natives; and the difficulty which they felt in defending themselves against the attacks of the Arabs, rendered them extremely willing to enter into an alliance with a people, whose daring enterprise and tremendous arms were so well calculated to strike terror into their enemies. Almeyda therefore, on being introduced to the king of Ceylon, had little difficulty in persuading him to pay an annual tribute to the Portuguese, on condition that they should protect his coasts from all external invasions.

The situation in which Almeyda found the island, was not essentially different from its present state; except in those changes which have been introduced into it by its successive European inmates. The inhabitants consisted of two distinct races of people. The savage Bedas then, as now, occupied the large forests, particularly in the northern parts; the rest of the island was in the possession of the Cinglese. The towns of the sea-coast were not as yet ravished from the latter people by foreign invaders; and their king held his court at Columbo, which is now the European capital of Ceylon. Cinnamon was even then the principal product and the staple commodity of the island, as we find by the tribute paid by the king to the Portuguese, which consisted of two hundred and fifty thousand pounds weight of cinnamon.

Such are the few circumstances respecting Ceylon, which can be collected from the narratives of its first Portuguese visitors. The minds of these adventurers were too much occupied with the desire of enriching themselves, and aggrandizing their nation, to make any enquiries into the manners of the natives, or the natural history of the country. The rich harvest which the cinnamon of Ceylon presented to commerce, seems to have been the chief object which attracted the attention of Almeyda; and accordingly we soon find him endeavouring to secure these advantages, by forming a Portuguese settlement on the island. This conduct, as might be expected, roused the jealousy and indignation of the native princes. After a long and bloody struggle, however, the Portuguese succeeded in their object; and under the conduct of Albuquerque, the successor of Almeyda, the whole sea-coast was reduced under their power, and the natives were driven to the mountains of the interior, of which they still maintain possession.

Albuquerque was an excellent commander, and an accomplished politician; but he was deeply tinctured with that insatiable thirst of military glory, which distinguished his countrymen in that age; and dazzled by the glare of extensive conquest, he overlooked the solid advantages to be derived from each of the countries he subdued. Ceylon in particular seemed designed by nature to secure the possessions, and extend the influence of the

Portuguese in the Eastern world. Its excellent harbours could afford protection to their ships at all times of the year, while there was no other station on the same coast which could at all periods afford shelter to the vessels of any other European power: the island was naturally so strong that it could be defended by a comparatively small number of troops: and its situation was so centrical, that troops could with the utmost ease and expedition, be sent from it to any part of India. Albuquerque, however, was too much engrossed with extending his conquests over the coasts of India, to pay due attention to these advantages; and Ceylon, instead of being made the centre and guardian of the Portuguese possessions in India, continued to be cultivated by them chiefly on account of its own natural productions.

The manner in which the Portuguese conducted the government of Ceylon, looked as if it had been their intention to counteract, as much as lay in their power, the advantages conferred on it by nature. Instead of maintaining a friendly intercourse with the natives, and inducing them to assist in promoting the cultivation of the island, every species of insult and barbarity was practised towards them. Not only was any little wealth they possessed seized by the rapacious grasp of avarice: their manners and customs were trampled upon; and their religious opinions, which they could still less give up, were not only insulted, but even persecuted with the most wanton cruelty. The religious bigotry of the Portuguese completely triumphed over their real interests; and to this cause in particular may be ascribed the universal hatred entertained against them, and the eagerness with which the native inhabitants of their conquered countries received and assisted their rivals.

As nothing can be more contrary to the spirit of the Christian religion, than the attempt to impose it on mankind by force, so this method has been uniformly unsuccessful. The Cinglese looked with horror on strange gods, who seemed to delight in blood; and chose rather to leave the sea-coasts to their enemies, and find refuge for themselves and their grotesque idols in the mountains of the interior. The Portuguese government was, however, still weak enough to yield to the arguments of the priests, who maintained, that imposing the Christian religion by means of the inquisition, was the only sure method of securing their dominion. These tyrannical invaders therefore pursued the Cinglese to their forests and fastnesses; and the latter, in their turn, made frequent incursions on the sea-coasts, and often destroyed the richest plantations of the Portuguese. This desultory warfare continued for almost a century with much bloodshed, and no advantage to either party. The internal government of the natives at that time, indeed, enabled the Portuguese to acquire considerable accessions of territory. The jurisdiction of the interior was parcelled out among a variety of petty princes, each of whom was the sovereign of his particular tribe, or separate valley. It was the policy of the Portuguese to stir up animosities between these princes, and to prevent their making a common cause for the deliverance of their country. When any open quarrel broke out between these islanders, their European neighbours were ever ready to lend their assistance to either of the parties who desired it. That prince who solicited their alliance was of course successful; and they had always the prudence to see their own generosity rewarded, by taking possession of the territories of the vanquished prince. By these arts they gradually extended their dominions farther into the interior of the island; and wherever they became masters, their avarice and bigotry prompted them to perpetrate such cruelties, as have ever since rendered the name of European hateful to the ears of a Cinglese.

While the natives of Ceylon were thus daily perishing in fruitless struggles against the regular discipline and concerted plans of the Portuguese, a powerful assistance was offered them, which promised to put a speedy end to their miseries. No sooner had the Dutch succeeded in throwing off the Spanish yoke, than their commercial and enterprising spirit led them to explore every coast of the known world in search of opulence. The inexhaustible riches of the East speedily attracted the adventurous merchants of that nation. In every quarter, however, they found the Portuguese already established; and the jealousy with which these earlier settlers observed the approach of any rival, soon convinced them that it was only by force they could ever hope to carry their commercial plans into effect. The Dutch and Portuguese were actuated by a different spirit, and proceeded in a very different manner in extending their foreign possessions. The former displayed none of that romantic bravery, that rapid attack, and dazzling success, which so much distinguished the first conquests of the Portuguese in India. But they were possessed of that persevering resolution in the pursuit of an object, which is the soul of commercial enterprise; and hence we find them, though often repulsed, gradually wresting one settlement after another from the Portuguese; till at the commencement of the seventeenth century, they had already made themselves masters of the most important islands and settlements, which stretch to the eastward of the straits of Molucca.

The situation and rich productions of Ceylon presented a tempting object to the Hollanders: the extent and strength of the island however, deterred them for some time from hazarding an enterprise of such magnitude. In the year 1603, the Dutch Admiral Spilberg at length ventured to approach the coasts of Ceylon; and the natives, from their hatred of the Portuguese, gave him a very favourable reception. During the constant wars in which they had been engaged, the king of Candy had acquired such a superiority over the other princes, that at the arrival of the Dutch, he was looked upon as Emperor of Ceylon. To this prince, Spilberg was introduced, and soon conciliated his favour, by declaring himself and his countrymen to be the inveterate foes of the Portuguese. He added, that it was their determinate resolution, to expel these cruel invaders from the possessions which they had so unjustifiably seized; and concluded with an offer of his countrymen's assistance to the Ceylonese, in expelling the Portuguese from their island. The king of Candy, as might be expected, received this proposal with the utmost joy: "Tell your countrymen," said he, "that if they will only be willing to build a fort in this island, myself, my wife, and my children, will be the first to supply them with the necessary materials." The Dutch were not long of availing themselves of the advantages which this alliance presented to them. In 1632, they sent a strong armament to act, in concert with the native prince, against the Portuguese. A violent and bloody struggle ensued: the Portuguese seemed to recover a portion of their anciont spirit, and appeared determined to dispute to the last the possession of a country, which had been so easily conquered by their more warlike ancestors. They were, however, overmatched by the resources and the policy of the Dutch. These persevering and prudent republicans were careful to assist their commanders with continual re-inforcements, while the Portuguese government in Europe, feebly trusting to the renown of former exploits, left their valuable colonies to their own unassisted efforts. The consequences were inevitable. The Portuguese of Ceylon had no internal resources to trust to. Their commerce was entirely cut off by the fleets of the Dutch: their cruelties had exasperated the natives to such a degree, that it was impossible ever again to conciliate their minds: and this antipathy, joined to the fair promises of the Dutch, and the hopes of a speedy deliverance, had awakened such a spirit among the Ceylonese, that they in their turn attacked their former tyrants even in their own possessions, and laid waste those plantations from which the only resources of the Portuguese were derived.

The Dutch, however, found Ceylon by no means an easy or a rapid conquest. Every pass, every fortress was disputed with them; and after the Portuguese had been driven from every other station along the coast, they still seemed determined rather to perish than to yield up Columbo, the seat of their government. The Dutch invested the town, and completely cut off the entrance of all supplies, either by sea or land. The courage of the Portuguese, however, seemed to increase with their difficulties: and for some time they baffled all the attempts of their enemies, and rejected all proposals to surrender with disdain. At length, however, they began to be attacked by enemies, against whom all their valour was in vain. The place was ill provisioned for a siege, and as no supplies could be thrown in, famine and disease began to subdue those brave spirits which had despised death in every other shape. After sustaining a siege of seven months, and after braving innumerable hardships, the Portuguese at length surrendered Columbo to the Dutch, in the year 1656; and thus ended their dominion in Ceylon, exactly a century and a half after the first arrival of their countrymen in that island.

The improvements made in the cultivation of Ceylon by the Portuguese, were by no means considerable. Those people, when they first took possession of it, were rather warriors than merchants. Their continual wars with the natives contributed to keep up the same spirit; and their principal attention seems to have been directed to the fortification of a few stations on the coasts, and the erection of some military posts to awe the natives. But the Portuguese appear never to have properly discovered the advantages to be derived from this island, either in a commercial or military point of view. Their dominions extended all around it; and no station could be pointed out more commodious for a depot either of merchandise or military stores. These advantages were overlooked by the Court of Lisbon; and those individuals who were sent to command at Ceylon were more anxious to gratify their pride by conquest, and their avarice by extortion, than to pursue any plan of permanent advantage either to the mother country or the colony. The Portuguese, therefore, by their own misconduct, were deprived of this valuable island, before they were aware of the benefits to be derived from it.

The joy of the Ceylonese, on being delivered from the yoke of these tyrannical invaders, and their gratitude to their deliverers, at first knew no bounds. The king of Candy willingly paid the expences of their armaments in cinnamon; and conferred upon his new allies the principal possessions, from which he had by their assistance expelled the Portuguese. Among these were the port of Trincomalee, and the fortress of Columbo. The former of these, which lies on the north-east part of the island, is that harbour which renders Ceylon the most valuable station in the Indian ocean. Columbo was built originally by the Portuguese in the south-west of the island, in the heart of that tract most celebrated for the production of cinnamon, as the most commodious station for collecting that staple production of the country. Along with this post, the king of Candy also bestowed on the Dutch the towns of Nigumbo and Point de Galle in the same quarter, together with a large tract of rich land adjoining to them.

The Dutch appeared exceedingly grateful to the monarch for all these concessions; they assumed only the humble appellation of *Guardians of his coasts;* and they began to fortify the different stations put into their hands, merely, as they said, for his security; and so well were the Candians convinced of the good intentions of their new allies, that they gave them every assistance in their power to complete their operations. The Dutch took this opportunity to increase the strength of their principal post at Columbo. They greatly enlarged the town; and were at pains to render the fortifications as complete as possible. Their post of Trincomalee, on the other side of the island they also endeavoured to render secure against any attack either from an external or a domestic enemy. Their numbers in the meantime were daily increasing by the addition of fresh adventurers from Europe. The parts assigned to them were the best fitted for cultivation in the island; and they immediately set about turning them to the best account. By means of these prudent measures, and persevering industry, the colony was soon brought into a flourishing state, and was able to depend upon its own internal resources.

While the Dutch were thus strengthening themselves, they kept up the most friendly intercourse with the natives; and this conduct, besides enabling them to pursue their plans of improvement without interruption, was also of very considerable benefit to their commerce. The Ceylonese looked upon them without jealousy, and were eager by their good offices to shew their gratitude to the Guardians of their coasts. The Dutch trafficked with them for the natural productions of the island to great advantage: and had they persisted in the same wise and moderate policy, it is probable that Ceylon would in process of time have become as profitable to them from their intercourse with the natives, as if it had been wholly possessed by Dutch settlers.

The ruling passion of the Dutch however, their avarice, soon began to over-reach itself, and by rapaciously seizing upon every opportunity of gain, quickly disgusted and alienated the natives. They began not only to push their posts farther and farther into the interior, and to seize upon every spot which appeared well adapted to cultivation; they also increased their demands on the king for the protection they afforded him; and he soon found that all the cinnamon which grew in his dominions was insufficient to gratify the *guardians of his coasts*. Enraged at their repeated extortions, he at last fell suddenly upon their settlements, where he committed the greatest devastations. This breach between the Candians and the Dutch was followed by a long course of hostilities, during which much blood was shed, and no lasting advantage gained by either party. The Dutch, however, were the greatest losers by the contest; for though they frequently routed the natives, over-ran their country, and destroyed their villages; yet the hardships which they encountered in forcing their way through a country covered with wood, and every where full of defiles, destroyed so many of their troops, that all their successes were too dearly purchased; and in the end, they were always obliged to abandon their conquests with great loss. The incursions of the natives, on the other hand, into their cultivated possessions on the coasts, although momentary, and in general easily repulsed, frequently destroyed the labours of years. These considerations induced several of the Dutch governors to attempt the restoration of tranquillity, rather by conciliating the natives, than by ineffectual struggles with them. For this purpose they sent ambassadors to them, with a variety of rich presents, and with instructions to gratify the Candian king by all those attentions and tokens of respect which have so great an effect on uncivilized minds. Their letters to him were wrapped up in silks embroidered with gold and silver, and their embassador carried them all the way on his head, the highest token of respect known in that country. In these letters, the king was dignified with all those high-sounding titles which are usually conferred upon an eastern monarch; while the Dutch subscribed themselves his humble and loyal subjects, repeating their former assurances that their only motive for building fortresses was the security of his Majesty's dominions. These conciliatory measures never failed to have considerable effect; but few of the Dutch governors were either sufficiently enlightened or disinterested to persevere in them. As they were usually men of no education and entirely of mercantile habits, they could not extend their views to distant advantages; and if they could accumulate a fortune by acts of extortion on the natives, they little regarded how prejudicial such conduct might prove to the future interests of their country.

The renewed oppressions of the Dutch was the constant signal for the renewal of hostilities between them and the natives. A long course of warfare rendered the Ceylonese both brave and dexterous. The Dutch were frequently repulsed even in close combat; several of their forts were taken; and whenever they attempted to penetrate into the interior parts of the island, they seldom failed to lose large parties of their men in attempting to force the woods and defiles, or by the ambushes with which their vigilant and active enemy every where surrounded them. But European discipline, and Dutch perseverance, frequently surmounted all these difficulties. The king of Candy saw those woods, which he looked upon as impenetrable barriers, burst through; and the Dutch soldiers appeared in those vallies, where indeed there were no fortifications, as their native possessors never supposed they could have been approached by a foe. The king was twice driven from his capital of Candy, and forced to seek for refuge in the mountains of Digliggy, the highest and most impenetrable in his kingdom. Here, however, he found himself secure from the pursuit of the enemy, and contented himself with surprising and cutting off their convoys of provisions and stores sent up from the coast, till they should of their own accord abandon his dominions. This, after all their victories, they were constantly obliged to do, and with the loss of a great number of their men.

I have often heard persons, unacquainted with the interior of Ceylon, express their surprise that a tract of land in the heart of an island, cut off from all external supplies, and every where surrounded by European settlements, should so long have remained in the hands of a people neither strong nor warlike, in spite of repeated efforts to wrest it from them. I own that this circumstance appeared to myself very extraordinary, until I had an opportunity of investigating the causes on the spot. The very appearance of the country, however, made me rather wonder that it ever should have been penetrated by an enemy, than that they were unable to retain possession of it. The whole country is high and mountainous; the approaches are steep, narrow, and scarcely accessible, except by persons on foot. The thick jungles and woods every where obstruct the view; and they are only penetrable by narrow and intricate paths, known but to the natives themselves. Besides the difficulty of clearing a passage through such obstacles, every opportunity is presented to those who know the country, of destroying the assailants without being seen or exposing themselves to the least hazard; and this is the mode of fighting which the native Ceylonese continually practise. They know well that they are unable to cope with the discipline or bravery of Europeans in the open field; their skill in war therefore consists in posting themselves in proper positions among the bushes, suddenly falling upon the enemy, and then hastily retreating from one position to another, before he has an opportunity of observing the course they have taken. By this method of warfare, the Dutch suffered as much after their victories as before; and their communications with the coast, which, from the nature of the country, must at any rate have been difficult, was by this mode of warfare rendered almost impossible, as every convoy would have required an army to defend it.

In addition to these difficulties arising from the nature of the country, and the manner of fighting practised by the inhabitants, the Dutch troops suffered dreadfully from the effects of the climate, which, in the interior parts, is exceedingly unwholesome to Europeans. The immense woods which cover the whole face of the country, naturally render the atmosphere moist and damp; and the heavy dews that succeeded the intense heat of the day, which was not refreshed by any sea breezes, overpowered the constitution even of those who had for years been settled on the coast. The only method by which the Dutch could have obviated the disasters arising from the climate, would have been the employment of native troops, as we do the Sepoys in India; but this measure their own misconduct had rendered impossible. The Ceylonese of the inland parts, like all the other inhabitants of mountainous countries, are exceedingly attached to their native land, and have a proportionable antipathy to a foreign yoke. This attachment, originating in the nature of the country, supplies the place of all other ties; and though they have not the smallest idea of political freedom, yet as their princes seldom violate their customs or the liberty of their persons, they cherish with enthusiasm the pride of immemorial independence, maintain the most inviolable attachment to their native kings, and would sooner die than swerve from their allegiance, or bear arms against them. The behaviour of the foreign nations who have successively invaded their island, has tended greatly to nourish these sentiments; and the cruelties of the Portuguese and Dutch have so exasperated them against all Europeans, that it will require much pains to reconcile their minds so far as that any confidence can be placed in them.

All these causes combined to frustrate the attempts of the Dutch at forming a settlement in the interior of the island; and the difficulties which they encountered, made them affect to despise the advantages which they could not attain. They pretended to look upon the interior as an object of no consequence; a poor and barren country rendered equally useless by the badness of its soil, and the unhealthiness of its climate. Such is the description, which after my arrival, I always heard given of it by the Dutch settlers; but my own observation has since convinced me, that either they were very little acquainted with the country, or that they were unwilling that any other European power should reap those advantages which their own short-sighted policy had made them neglect.

But notwithstanding the Dutch seem to have been convinced that it was impracticable to retain possession of the interior, yet their own misconduct had sown so many seeds of jealousy between them and the Candians, that they were often compelled to have recourse to arms. The last great war which they carried on with the natives, was about the middle of last century. In 1764, they penetrated into the heart of the king's dominions, and made themselves masters of Candy. Their success, however, ended as on former occasions. After having experienced great hardships from the climate, and the activity of the natives, who continually intercepted their convoys and communications with the sea-coast, they were at last obliged to evacuate the capital. Their disasters did not, however, end here. In their retreat, four hundred of their best soldiers were made prisoners and put to death at Cuddavilli and Sittivacca, only two days march from their own chief settlement at Columbo. Notwithstanding this disaster, however, they had many ways left of harassing the king of Candy; and in particular by their power to deprive him of salt at pleasure, they reduced him at last to comply with all their demands. In 1766 he was compelled to accede to a treaty which greatly curtailed his dominions, and left him little better than a prisoner at large in those that remained to him. All those parts of the sea-coast, which had not formerly belonged to the Dutch, were now conceded to them, with the addition of several other tracts which they reckoned advantageous for their purposes. They insisted that the king should have no intercourse with any other power whatever; and that he should deliver up all foreigners or subjects of other princes, who should happen to come into his dominions. All cinnamon which grew on the coasts was to be considered as exclusively Dutch property; and the natives, by way of special privilege, were allowed quietly to cut and carry it to the several Dutch factories on the island. The cinnamon growing in the woods was allowed to be, in some degree, the property of the natives; they were obliged to peel it and sell it to the Dutch at a rix-dollar a pound: this is a coin of a nominal value, and exchanges for about the worth of two shillings sterling of their copper money. But though cinnamon formed the chief article in the stipulations, the other productions of the island were by no means overlooked. The king of Candy was also obliged to stipulate that his subjects should gather the pepper, cardamoms, coffee, and cotton growing in the interior, and sell them to the Dutch at certain very low prices. A certain proportion of elephant's teeth, areka nut, and betel leaf, together with a share of the precious stones found in their country, formed part of the tribute imposed on the natives. The number of elephants to be delivered up, was fifty in the two seasons; these the Dutch transported to the opposite coast of the continent, and sold to the native princes there at very high prices, as the elephants of Ceylon are accounted superior to all others. The pearl fisheries on the west and north-west shores where the pearl-banks are situated, formed another acquisition to the Dutch by this treaty. Several persons from the Malabar coast, and other parts of the continent, had established cotton manufactories in the northern town of the island, particularly at Jaffnapatam: all these were now given over to the dominion of the Dutch.

In return for all these valuable acquisitions, the Dutch acknowledged the king of Candy to be the Emperor of Ceylon, with a long string of other sounding titles, which could only serve by their mockery to aggravate his mortification; and under these magnificent appellations they engaged, as his dutiful subjects, to pay him a tribute, and to send ambassadors yearly to his court. The most valuable condition granted to him, and indeed that for which he had consented to the hard terms of this treaty, was a stipulation on the part of the Dutch to supply his people with salt, free of expence, and in such a quantity as to equal their consumption. The tribute to be paid him was to consist of a certain part of the produce, or its value, of the ceded tracts along the coast: but this article was soon infringed upon, and indeed scarcely one stipulation of the treaty was fulfilled with good faith.

It is evident, that by this treaty the Dutch obtained a monopoly of all the valuable productions of the island; and scarcely any thing was left for the king and his subjects, but quietly to assist them in availing themselves of their acquisitions. But it was not to be expected, that advantages obtained in such a manner could be permament. Such harsh and degrading terms naturally shocked and exasperated the Candians, and fostered in their breasts the most rooted and inveterate hatred to their oppressors. They eagerly catched at every occasion to elude or infringe the terms of the treaty; and the Dutch soon found that in their sanguine hopes of satiating their avarice, they had over-reached themselves, and rather diminished than increased the little benefit they had formerly derived from the interior of the island. Nor was even their tranquillity at all secured by this treaty; the Candians frequently attempted by force of arms to procure better terms, although the Dutch constantly succeeded in repulsing them; not, however, without much bloodshed on both sides. About twenty years ago the Dutch again penetrated into the king's country, but were attacked by the natives with so much spirit, that the present General de Meuron, then a colonel in the Dutch service, narrowly escaped being cut off with a large detachment near Sittivacca, and by accidentally taking a different road from that which the Candians expected he would, he got safe to Columbo.

Both parties at last became wearied out with these constant, ineffectual struggles; and hostilities, as well as all other intercourse, were discontinued as if by mutual consent. The Dutch were chiefly anxious to prevent any connection being formed between the natives and foreigners; and the king of Candy was resolved to prevent any intercourse between his subjects and a nation, which he found ready on every occasion to deprive him of his rights in order to gratify their own avarice. A few articles of no great value, such as betel leaf, areka and cocoa-nuts, were occasionally smuggled by the natives down to the Dutch provinces; but these practices, if discovered, were severely punished by the king.

Such was the situation in which affairs stood between the Dutch and the native Ceylonese, towards the commencement of the late war. It was now about one hundred and forty years since the Portuguese had been finally expelled, and no other European power had since that time been able to acquire a permanent footing on the island. It is not however to be supposed, while the attention of all the nations of Europe was so eagerly turned towards the commerce of the East, and while they maintained so many violent contests among themselves, that so valuable an acquisition as Ceylon could have escaped their notice. Such however was the difficulty of approaching that island, except in a very few points, and such was the strength of the Dutch, and the weakness of most other nations in that quarter of the globe, that very few attempts were made to wrest it from them. Soon after the expulsion of the Portuguese, the French seemed inclined to dispute the possession of Ceylon. They appeared off the island with a large fleet, entered into a treaty with the native prince, and avowed their determination to drive out the Dutch. All these threatening movements however ended in nothing: an enterprise planned without wisdom was executed without spirit, and imaginary obstacles prevented the French from even attempting to gain a footing on the island.

An attempt of the English towards the conclusion of the American war, was likely to prove more formidable to the power of the Dutch in Ceylon. The vigorous enterprise of the English had already procured them a great ascendancy in

India; and they were at this time pursuing their conquests on the Coromandel coast. The station of the Dutch at Ceylon proved a principal obstacle to their enterprises, as their enemies there found a secure shelter to their fleets at all seasons of the year, and could readily transport from thence men and military stores to any part of the continent. A fleet under the command of Sir Edward Hughes, having on board a detachment of land forces, commanded by Sir Hector Munro, was therefore dispatched towards the commencement of the year 1782, to attempt the reduction of this island. On the second of January they sailed from Negapatnam, a Dutch settlement on the Coromandel coast which they had previously reduced, and on the fourth they arrived in the bay of Trincomalee. Next day the troops landed without opposition, and on the following night, while the Governor of the town was considering of terms of capitulation, a company of English marines suddenly made their way through one of the gates, and made themselves masters of the place without resistance. Fort Ostenburg, a strong fort in the neighbourhood, situated on the top of a hill, and commanding the harbour, still continued to hold out. In a few days, however, it was taken by assault; the garrison, consisting of four hundred Europeans, after a feeble resistance, threw down their arms and were made prisoners of war.

Such a prosperous commencement of the enterprise gave the happiest prospect of speedily reducing the whole island; and Lord Macartney, then Governor of Madras, determined to lose no time to secure and improve this valuable acquisition. An officer of experience and judgment was appointed to command the fortress of Trincomalee; and he was charged to endeavour by every means to conciliate the natives to the English, and to neglect no measure which could tend to strengthen the British interest in the island. The most sanguine hopes were entertained of the success of this enterprise; but this fair prospect was soon converted into a striking lesson, that dilatory measures are utterly incompatible with success in military operations. Soon after the capture of Trincomalee, the English Admiral judged it necessary to sail to the roads of Madras for repairs. While these were completing, it was understood that the French Admiral Suffrein had formed a design to retake it; and about two hundred men of the forty-second regiment, under the protection of two ships of war, were dispatched to reinforce the garrison, till the rest of the fleet should be in a condition to join them. The ships, after landing the troops, returned to Madras with information, that they had fallen in with the French fleet off Trincomalee, and had with difficulty made their escape. The English Admiral at last found himself in a condition to sail for the protection of the place, having on board the new commander together with a body of troops. But on arriving off Trincomalee, he discovered the French colours flying on all the forts, and the French Admiral with a fleet of thirty sail of the line moored in the bay. It was in vain that the British fleet, though inferior in numbers, attacked and routed the

French; the latter found a secure retreat under the cannon of those forts, which their activity and the want of precaution on the part of their enemies had suffered to fall into their hands. And thus the attempts of the English to attain possession of Ceylon were for this time frustrated.

The immense accessions of territory which the English have acquired in the East Indies since the conclusion of the American war, have rendered them greatly an over-match for any other European power in that quarter of the world. On the vast peninsula of India in particular, there is scarcely a power either foreign or native that can oppose to them even a shadow of resistance; and they are left at leisure to cultivate the invaluable advantages which this rich country presents to their commerce. The chief obstacle to their enterprises is the want of stations where their ships might be enabled at all times to baffle the violent storms incidental to that climate. As the whole of that large tract, which we possess along the Coromandel coast, presents nothing but open roads, all vessels are obliged, on the approach of the monsoons, to stand out into the open seas; and there are many parts of the coast that can be approached only during a few months of the year. As the harbour of Trincomalee, which is equally secure at all seasons, offered the means of obviating these disadvantages, it was evident that, on the first rupture with the Dutch, our countrymen would attempt to gain possession of it. Accordingly, the junction of the Dutch with the French Republic in the late war was the signal for the commencement of our operations against their colonies in the East. A body of troops was in 1795 detached for the conquest of Ceylon; and this enterprise was crowned with success, after a course of military operations, which I shall detail when I come to describe the several places where they were carried on.

Such is the history of Ceylon previous to its falling into our possession. The mismanagement of the Portuguese and Dutch, and their impolitic conduct towards the natives, prevented them from at all reaping from this valuable colony the advantages which it was calculated by nature to afford. Superstition and the love of tyranny continually stirred up internal enemies to the Portuguese, while luxury and the relaxation of military discipline, made them fall a prey to the first foreign invader. The prudent and persevering efforts by which the Dutch obtained possession, seemed to promise greater stability and longer duration to their power. That thirst of gain, however, which had given vigour to their operations for the reduction of the island, counteracted the national advantages which might have been derived from the acquisition; for being as strong in each individual as in the nation at large, every one was solicitous only for his own private emolument; and provided this was attained, he gave himself little trouble to promote public objects. Rapacious exactions, the want of any regular plan of policy, and a total neglect of military defence were the consequences of this spirit. That fire of patriotism which had once animated the Dutch in Europe was completely extinguished in this colony. During the American war, the French and English fleets successively occupied their harbours, while the Dutch seemed in resigned apathy to await their fate from the fortunes of others.

These errors, and this misconduct which ended in depriving its successive possessors of this valuable island will, it is to be hoped, be avoided by our countrymen; and from my own observation, I can confidently state, that if the care of it be entrusted to such men as the present Governor, and the officers under his command, the advantages to this country must be both speedy and secure.

I now proceed to describe this new acquisition to the British empire, avoiding any circumstances of which I either was not an eye-witness, or had not authenticated in the most indubitable manner.

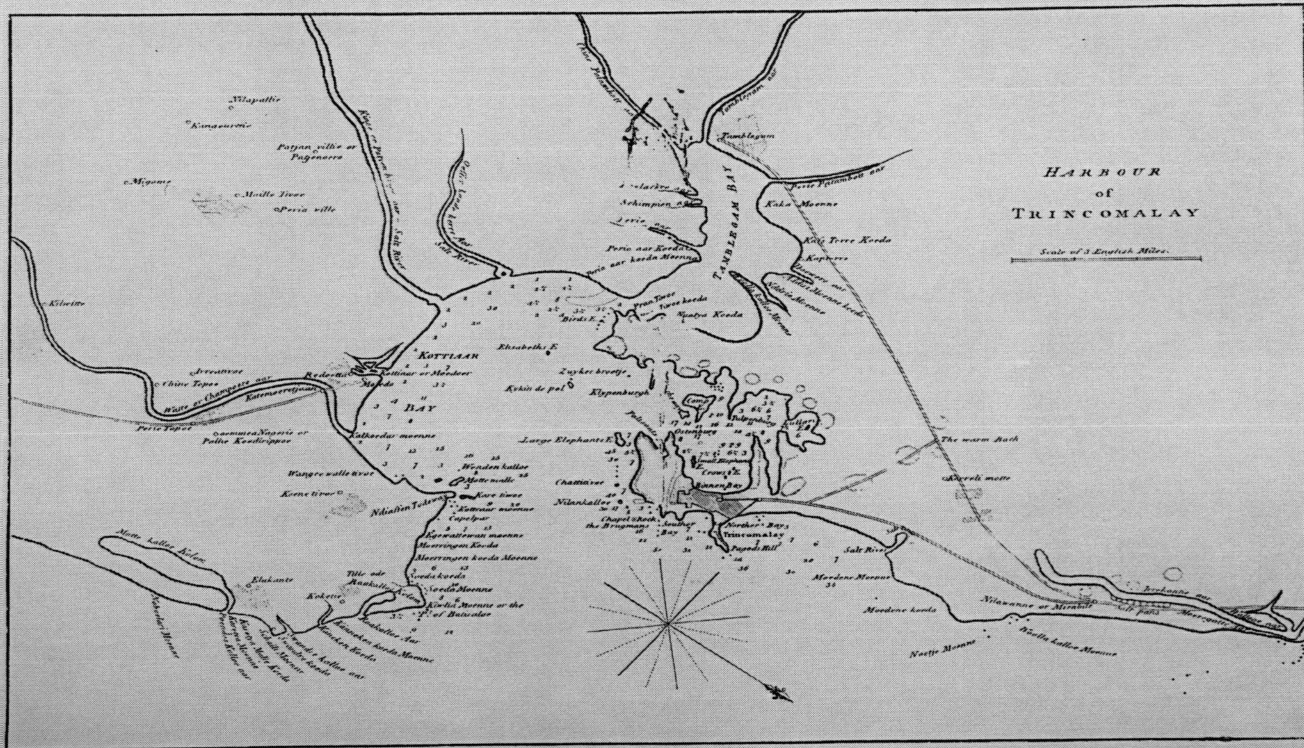
HARBOUR
of
TRINCOMALAY
Scale of 3 English Miles.
TAMBLEGAM BAY
KOTTIAAR
BAY
Tamblegam
Kaka Moenne
Elisabeths E.
Large Elephants E.
Klypenburgh
Ostenburg
Trincomalay
Pagods Hill
Salt River
The warm Bath
Nilawanne or Meraballe
Mordene Moenne
Mordene keeda
Noettie Moenne
Nilapallie
Kangoeruwe
Migame
Moille Tivoe
Peria ville
Kilvette
Perie Topoe
Chine Topoe
Wangre walle tivoe
Koene tivoe
Elakante
Kokettie
Chattiavoe
Nilankallee
Wenden kallee
Motte walle

CHAPTER II.

General description of Ceylon—The harbours—Monsoons—Climate—Rivers—Internal communications—Soil—General divisions—British dominions—Trincomalee—Malativoe—Jafnapatam—Manaar.

THE Island of Ceylon lies between 5° 40′ and 10° 30′ north latitude; and between 79° and 82° east longitude. It is situated at the entrance of the bay of Bengal, by which it is bounded on the north. On the north-west it is separated from the Coromandel coast by the gulph of Manaar, a narrow strait full of shoals, and impassable by large ships. It is distant about sixty leagues from Cape Comerin, the southern point of the peninsula of India, which divides the Coromandel and Malabar coasts. Its circumference is computed to be about nine hundred miles; and its length from Point Pedro at the northern extremity to Donderhead at the southern is about three hundred miles. Its breadth is very unequal, being in some parts only from forty to fifty miles, while in others it extends to sixty, seventy, and even one hundred. Towards the southern parts it is much broader than in the northern, and nearly resembles a *ham* in shape. The peninsula of Jafnapatam has hence received from the Dutch the name of *Hamsheel*, and Point Pedro they call *Hamsheel Point*.

As you approach the island from the sea, it presents a fresher green to the eye, and has every way a more fertile appearance than most parts of the Malabar and Coromandel coasts. This I had an opportunity of observing in nearly every quarter, as on my passage from Madras I almost completely coasted round the island. All the flat tracts on the sea-shore are bounded by beautiful *topes*, or groves of cocoa-nut trees, while the intermediate plain is covered with rich fields of rice; and the prospect usually terminates in woods, which cover the sides of the mountains, and display a verdant foliage through every season of the year. Such a prospect has the most pleasing effect on the eye, after being fatigued with the shores of barren white sand, which every where skirt the Continent.

The appearance of the eastern coast is bald and rocky, and a few reefs of rocks run out into the sea on the south east between Point de Galle and Batacolo. The deep water on the eastern shores admits the approach of the largest vessels in safety; and if that side of the island be the least fertile, its other defects are amply compensated by the harbours of Trincomalee and Batacolo. The north and north-west coast from Point Pedro to Columbo is flat, and every where indented with inlets of the sea, frequently of considerable magnitude. The largest of them extends almost quite across the island from Mullipatti to Jafnapatam on the north-west point of the island; and forms the peninsula of Jafnapatam. Several of these inlets form small harbours; but so full is that coast of sand-banks and shallows, that it is impossible for vessels of a large size to approach them. Small craft however, find stations here sufficiently convenient and secure.

The interior of the island abounds with steep and lofty mountains, covered with thick forests, and full of almost impenetrable jungles. The woods and mountains completely surround the dominions of the king of Candy, and seem destined by nature to defend him against those foreign enemies, whose superior skill and power have deprived him of the open tracts on the sea-coast. The most lofty range of mountains divides the island nearly into two parts, and so completely separates them from each other, that both the climate and seasons on either side are essentially different. These mountains also terminate completely the effect of the monsoons, which set in periodically from opposite sides of them; so that not only the opposite sea-coast, but the whole country in the interior suffers very little from these storms.

The monsoons in Ceylon are connected with those on the Coromandel and Malabar coasts, and very nearly correspond with them; but they set in much sooner on the western than the eastern side of the island. On the west side where Columbo lies, the rains prevail in the months of May, June, and July, the season when they are felt on the Malabar coast. This monsoon is usually extremely violent, being accompanied with dreadful storms of thunder and lightning, together with vast torrents of rain, and violent south-west winds. During its continuance, the northern parts of the island are very little affected, and are even generally dry. In the months of October and November, when the opposite monsoon sets in on the Coromandel coast, it is the north of Ceylon which is affected, and scarcely any impression of it is felt in the southern parts.

These monsoons pass slightly over the interior, and seldom occasion any considerable inconvenience. But this part of the island is not altogether freed from the dreadful storms which so terribly ravage the tropical climates. During its own periodical season, which happens in March and April, the rain pours down in torrents, and the thunder and lightning are awful to a degree almost inconceivable to an European.

From the situation of this island, so near the Equator, the days and nights are necessarily always of nearly equal length; the variation during the two seasons not exceeding fifteen minutes. The seasons are more regulated by the monsoons than the course of the sun; for although the island lies to the north of the line, the coolest season is during the summer solstice, while the western monsoon prevails. Their Spring commences in October, and the hottest season is from January to the beginning of April. The heat, during the day, is nearly the same throughout the whole year; the rainy season however, renders the nights much cooler, from the dampness of the earth, and the prevalence of winds during the monsoons. The climate, upon the whole, is much more temperate than on the Continent of India. For though Ceylon lies so near the Equator, the heat is by no means so oppressive as I have felt it on many parts of the Coromandel coast in a more northerly latitude. This is owing to the constant sea-breezes by which it is fanned, without being subject to the hot and suffocating land-winds, which so frequently annoy the Continent. For this reason, although the perpendicular beams of the sun must of course be intensely hot, the shade and the houses always afford a tolerably cool retreat.

This temperate climate, however, is chiefly confined to the coast where the sea-breezes have room to circulate. In the interior of the country, owing to the thick and close woods, and the hills which crowd upon each other, the heat is many degrees greater than on the sea-coast, and the climate often extremely sultry and unhealthy. This inconvenience, however, might be in a great degree obviated by cutting down the woods and clearing the jungles, as has been proved by a tract in the neighbourhood of Trincomalee, cleared by Colonel Champagne since it came into our possession, and thus rendered much less noxious to Europeans.

The principal harbours in the island for large ships, are Trincomalee and Point de Galle; they also come to anchor, and at certain seasons of the year moor securely in the roads of Columbo. There are several other inferior ports all around the island, which afford shelter to the smaller coasting vessels. These are Batacolo, Matura, Barbereen, and Caltura on the south-east; and on the north and west, are Nigumbo, Chilou, Calpenteen, Manaar, and Point Pedro. At all of those places are rivers of greater or less magnitude emptying themselves into the sea. These rivers, which are for the most part broad, deep, and navigable for some distance by small craft, are of essential benefit to the inhabitants of the parts adjacent to the coast, as they afford a cheap and easy method of conveying their produce and merchandise to those places where European vessels wait to receive them.

But these rivers, although unusually smooth at their immediate outlet into the sea, are seldom navigable to any considerable distance. As soon as they enter the mountains which cover the native kingdom of Candy, they become rocky and rapid; and tumble down with such a headlong course that it is impossible for the smallest canoe to navigate them. This is one great cause of the little intercourse which subsists between the natives in the higher country and those who live under the dominion of the Europeans on the sea-coast, as the way by land is equally difficult, nor have the natives been ever anxious to surmount these obstacles.

The two principal rivers are the Malivagonga and the Mulivaddy. The former takes its rise among the hills to the south-east of Candy, and nearly surrounds that city. After a variety of circuitous windings among the mountains, it at last discharges itself into the sea at Trincomalee. This river is so deep as to be fordable only towards the source; but the rocks which every where break its course prevent it from being navigated. The Malivagonga rises from the foot of a very high mountain, known to Europeans by the name of Adam's Peak, and situated about sixty miles to the north-east of Columbo. This river falls into the sea by several branches:

the largest of these, called the Mutwal River, empties itself about three miles from the fort of Columbo, after having nearly surrounded a large tract of the level country, of which it forms a very beautiful peninsula. The country along the banks of the Mutwal for many miles is extremely picturesque and delightful; and I had an opportunity of experiencing its utility in accompanying an escort from Columbo to Sittivacca in the interior, a distance of thirty-five miles; for while we marched along the beautiful banks, our ammunition and stores were commodiously transported on the river in boats.

Besides the rivers with which Ceylon abounds, there are many lakes and canals communicating with them, particularly in the neighbourhood of Columbo and Nigumbo. They are often of considerable extent, and of very great utility to the inhabitants in their neighbourhood, who have thus an opportunity of readily transporting their several articles of trade; and it is by this means also that the towns on the coast are supplied with the greatest abundance of fresh-water fish.

The internal communications by land through the island have scarcely passed the first stage of improvement. Along the sea-coasts indeed there are roads and stations for travellers; but these roads are in many places rugged and steep, and are not only difficult but dangerous from the numbers of wild hogs, buffaloes, and elephants, which infest them. These animals are met particularly from Chilou to Manaar on the west side of the island, and from Matura to Batacolo on the east; in these roads they sometimes occasion accidents.

Since the island has come into the possession of the English, the roads have been greatly improved. Governor North ordered a general survey of them to be made, and the distances to be ascertained, previous to adopting measures for facilitating the communications. I have been favoured by Colonel Champagne with a chart of the distances around the whole coast of the island, and with his obliging permission I have annexed a copy of it to this work.

The improvements made in the communications by the Dutch, were dictated more by their jealousy, than any plans of liberal policy. At a great expence they built forts and posts at certain distances round the island, with a view to prevent any intercourse between the natives and foreigners. This was what they chiefly feared; and while they fruitlessly spent large sums and much pains in this pursuit, they neglected the means of rendering the island beneficial to themselves, or secure against the intrusion of other nations.

To speak of the soil in general, it is sandy, with but a small mixture of clay. In the south-west parts, however, particularly about Columbo, there is a great deal of marshy ground, very rich, and exceedingly productive. This tract, however, is chiefly occupied with cinnamon plantations, and the rest of the island, in its present state of cultivation, does not produce a sufficient quantity of rice for the consumption of its inhabitants; but requires yearly supplies from Bengal and other places on the continent. I am convinced, however, that this is entirely owing to mismanagement, and that with proper attention, the necessity of importation might be entirely superseded.

The island of Ceylon was originally divided into a number of distinct petty kingdoms, separated by the several rivers and mountains which are dispersed over the face of the island, and subject each to its own independent sovereign. In process of time, however, the whole country was reduced under the dominion of the king of Candy, and divided by him into a few great provinces, from which several of the numerous titles he still retains were derived. These provinces were Candy, Coitou, Matura, Dambadar, and Sittivacca, which included the rich districts on the west coast. The chief of these provinces was Candy; it was situated in the centre of the island, and honoured with the royal residence. The king holds his court there to this day; and though all the other provinces have been more or less encroached upon, no part of Candy has ever been reduced to permanent subjection under a foreign power. These provinces were subdivided into districts, known in that country by the name of *corles*, and corresponding to our shires or counties. These subdivisions are still continued in the parts wrested from the natives by the Dutch; and the government of each of them is given to the civil and military officers who hold posts in their vicinity.

The great divisions of the island now are reduced to two; the one comprehending those parts under the dominion of Europeans, and the other those which still remain to the natives. In the map prefixed to this volume, the boundaries of these two divisions are distinctly pointed out; and it will be observed that the European dominion, like a ring, completely encircles the territories of the king of Candy. Owing to the richness of the country around Columbo, and its size and population, that city has always been accounted the capital of the European dominions in the island; although in regard to all advantages to be derived from it with regard to foreign commerce, Trincomalee is unquestionably of much superior importance.

As the British dominions in Ceylon skirt the coasts quite round in a circle, my description of them must follow the same direction. I shall, therefore, set out from the place where I first landed, and lead my readers completely round the island in the same course in which I travelled it, and endeavour to communicate to them those impressions and observations which occurred to me at the several places I visited.

It was at Trincomalee I first touched the shores of Ceylon. I have already mentioned the motives which must have induced our government to attempt to wrest this important harbour from the Dutch. General Stewart was in 1795 sent for this purpose from Madras. The force under him consisted of the 72d regiment, the flank companies of the 71st and 73d, two battalions of Sepoys, accompanied by a detachment of artillery and pioneers. The vessels conveying this force, came to anchor to the south-east of the fort. Here the Diomede frigate was unfortunately lost by striking on a sunk rock. The General found it most expedient to land the troops at about the distance of two miles from the fort, to which he afterwards laid regular siege. The climate, the nature of the ground, and the situation of the fort occasioned much fatigue, and some loss to our troops. Several, both officers and men, were killed by the fire from it. During the siege a sally was made by a party of Malays in the Dutch service. They contrived to steal unperceived into one of the batteries, spiked the guns, and killed some of our artillery-men, before they were repulsed and driven back into the fort. After a siege of three weeks, a breach was at last effected, and the English were preparing to storm; when the Dutch Governor thought it more prudent to trust his safety to the terms of a capitulation, than the arms of his troops, although they were greatly superior in number to the force acting against them.

The town of Trincomalee lies in latitude 8° 30′. It runs in a north-east direction along one branch of the bay. The country around it is mountainous and woody; the soil uncultivated and rather barren, and the whole appearance wild. The woods, which are very thick, contain abundance of wild beasts of various descriptions; particularly, wild hogs, buffaloes, and elephants. The latter often come down to the lakes in the neighbourhood of the fort, to drink and bathe; they have been often shot within a mile of the town.

Trincomalee from its situation and construction is naturally strong. It occupies more ground than Columbo, but contains a much smaller number of houses, and those inferior in size and appearance to those which are to be met with in several towns on the south-west coast. The circumference of Trincomalee, within the walls, is about three miles: within this space is also included a hill or rising point, immediately over the sea, and covered with a great quantity of thick jungle, in which wild deer and other game find shelter. This rising ground is very little inhabited, most of the houses being close to the landing place, which lies in the lowest part. Even the lower parts of the fort were much incumbered with wood till within these few years.

The fort is strong, and commands the principal bays; and, in particular, the entrance into the grand harbour, or inner bay, which affords at all seasons and in every variety of weather, a secure shelter to ships of all descriptions, being land-locked on all sides, and sufficiently deep and capacious to receive the largest vessel, or any number of vessels. This harbour is also overlooked by Fort Ostenburg, a strong fort standing on a cliff, which projects into the sea; it was originally built by the Portuguese out of the ruins of some celebrated pagodas which once stood here. This fort cannot be attacked by sea, till the fort of Trincomalee be first taken, and the entrance of the harbour forced. In the bay the shores are so bold, and the water so deep close up to them, that it is almost possible to step from the rocks into the vessels that moor alongside of them. At the extremity of the rock on which the fort stands, a strong battery is erected, where the flag-staff of the fort is placed.

This harbour, from its nature and situation, is that which stamps Ceylon one of our most valuable acquisitions in the East Indies. As soon as the violent monsoons commence, every vessel which is caught by them in any other part of the bay of Bengal, is obliged immediately to put to sea to prevent inevitable destruction. At these seasons Trincomalee and Bombay alone, of all the ports on the different coasts of the peninsula of India, are capable of affording a safe retreat. The incalculable advantages to be derived from such a harbour, are increased by its proximity and easy access to our settlements in the bay of Bengal. A vessel from Madras may arrive here in two days, and can at any time make the harbour. These circumstances point out Trincomalee as an object of particular attention to our government, and of far more consequence to retain than the whole of the rest of the island. It will, however, require great encouragement, and many improvements to render the town populous or anywise equal to Columbo. For the country around is not by any means so fertile as to tempt settlers to reside here, nor are the natural productions calculated to attract commerce. The climate has also been looked upon as the hottest and most unhealthy of the whole island; and both the 72d and 80th regiments suffered severely from it on their first arrival. These noxious qualities of the climate were owing in a great measure to the woods and marshes which come up to the very fort, and which the Dutch had never sufficient policy or public spirit to remove. Since the place has been in our possession, a very proper system has been adopted to render the climate wholesome. Colonel Champagne, while stationed here with the 80th regiment, cleared a large tract of ground, in the neighbourhood of the fort, of the jungles with which it was covered; and also drained several of the swamps and marshes. The good effects of these improvements have already been experienced, and the European garrison has since suffered very little from the climate. It is to be hoped that remedies may, in the same manner, be applied to the other defects under which Trincomalee at present labours: its trade is nothing, as there are no valuable natural productions to nourish it; but, from its situation, it is capable of becoming the richest emporium of the East. The want of commerce, and the uncultivated state of the surrounding country, are defects which flow mutually from each other; and the removal of one would soon, in a great measure, do away the other.

As we advance along the coast to the north-west from Trincomalee, little presents itself to the eye but a bold shore, and large tracts of wood stretching into the interior. The country here, as well as in other parts of the island, at first view appears desolate and without inhabitants; but this is more appearance than reality; for the natives are very numerous, although from building their huts in the woods, and avoiding the approach of strangers, they are seen only by those who explore their recesses. The next post to Trincomalee on this side is Malativoe, which lies about half way to Jafnapatam. Here the Dutch had a small factory with a fort, and a house for the commanding officer. It was a subaltern's command, depending upon the garrison of Trincomalee; and was employed chiefly as a post of communication, and to collect provisions for that garrison. For these purposes, and to keep the natives in awe, a few

Malay or Sepoy soldiers, were stationed here; but it was never considered as capable of any defence.

Malativoe lies in a very romantic and delightful situation. Close by the fort is a small village; and a river which here falls into the sea, forms a harbour sufficient to admit small craft. The principal employment of the inhabitants is fishing; and with this article they supply the fort of Trincomalee. Cattle and poultry are here in great abundance, and sell astonishingly cheap. Game is exceedingly plentiful, and the woods abound with wild hog and deer. The manner of procuring these animals is attended with as little expence or difficulty to an European as can well be imagined; for the native peasants are so much at his beck, that he has only to supply them with a little powder and shot, and send them into the woods, and they will be sure to bring him back as much game as he can use, without expecting any return for their services.

As we proceed northward from Malativoe, we find the northern extremity of the island stretched out into an oblong peninsula, almost cut off from the rest by a branch of the sea, which, as we have already mentioned, penetrates almost across the island. This district, which is known by the name of Jafnapatam, looks directly towards Negapatam on the Coromandel coast, and is considered as the most healthy in the island. This is owing to its situation, surrounded by the sea on almost all sides; by which means the violent hot winds from the continent of India are cooled in their passage.

These land winds are to Europeans the most intolerable circumstance in the climate of India. In Bengal, and several other parts in our possession, they prevail almost to suffocation; and it is with pain I recollect the expedients we were obliged to have recourse to in order to diminish their effects. The common remedy is to place, in frames before the windows or doors, *Tatts*, or blinds of straw loosely woven; and these being kept constantly wet by black fellows retained for the purpose, the air which penetrates through the interstices is cooled by the water, and deprived in a great measure of its noxious heat. The violence of these winds indeed, depend on the quantity of moisture they meet with in their passage. In those parts where they blow over tracts of low and marshy grounds, or rice fields, they are much cooled and less sensibly felt at the places which they afterwards meet in their course. I recollect to have observed a very striking instance of this while I was stationed at Trichinopoly. On one side of the fort is an extensive sandy plain, and on the other a large tract of low marshy ground: during the season of the land-winds, that part of the fort which is exposed to those from the sandy plain, is heated almost to suffocation; while that part which receives the winds from the marshy grounds, rather feels refreshed from the breeze. The violence of the land-winds in their hottest state is almost inconceivable. The intense heat cracks every thing which comes in their way: the glass in the windows is often splintered in pieces, on which account Venetian blinds are generally used instead. Unless precautions be employed, even the drinking glasses used at table are apt to split and fall asunder among the fingers of the guests.

The violence of this scourge being broken by the intervening sea before it reaches Jafnapatam, the breezes which afflict the continent serve here rather to agitate and refresh the air; and the fields clothed with verdant pasture are the strongest proof of the temperate nature of the climate. Fruits, vegetables, game and poultry, abound every where in this district. There appears to be something in the atmosphere here different from the other parts of the island; for it is only in the tract which lies between Point Pedro and Jaffna that sheep have ever been reared with success. The articles of foreign commerce produced here are of no great value, for though it affords some cinnamon and pepper. yet they are of an inferior kind to that which grows in the south-west of the island.

The fort and town of Jaffna, the capital of the district, stands at the distance of some miles from the sea, but communicates with it by means of a river navigable by boats. The river falls into the sea near Point Pedro, where there is also a fort and harbour, in which the troops sent by General Stewart from Trincomalee for the reduction of Jaffna disembarked, and met the fifty-second regiment which had been sent over from Negapatam on the opposite coast for the same purpose. The passage from Point Pedro to Negapatam is usually made by boats in a few hours.

The fort of Jaffna was given up by the Dutch to our troops as soon as they appeared before it. It is small, but exceedingly neat and well built. The Pettah, or Black Town without the walls, is larger and more populous than that of Trincomalee. Since Columbo was taken possession of by the English, several Dutch families have quitted it, and taken up their residence in the neighbourhood of Jaffna; as this latter place is much cheaper, and better supplied with all the necessaries of life, several of which are scarcely to be procured in the other parts of the island.

The inhabitants of Jaffna consist of a collection of various races. The greatest number are of Moorish extraction, and are divided into several tribes, known by the names of Lubbahs, Mopleys, Chittys, and Choliars: they are distinguished by wearing a little round cap on their close shaven heads. There is also a race of Malabars found here somewhat differing in their appearance from those on the continent. These different tribes of foreign settlers greatly exceed in number the native Ceylonese in the district of Jaffna. Those I first mentioned were induced many years ago by the encouragements held out to them by the Dutch, to pass over from the Coromandel coast, and carry on here a variety of manufactures, of coarse cloths, calicoes, handkerchiefs, shawls, stockings, &c. These articles were all made from the cotton growing on the island; and to this day the district of Jaffna continues to be the only part of Ceylon where manufactures of this sort continue to be carried on, with the exception of a very few about Columbo.

At Jaffna there are also a number of handicraftsmen, such

as goldsmiths, jewellers, joiners, and makers of all different parts of household furniture. They are very expert in their respective occupations; particularly that race known in this island by the name of Portuguese, who surpass all the rest in the beauty and dexterity of their workmanship.

Dependent upon the district of Jaffna, and at a small distance in the sea to the north-west of Point Pedro, are several small islands, which the Dutch named from their own native cities, Delft, Harlem, Leyden, and Amsterdam. These islands they employed in breeding horses and cattle, as from their excellent pasturage they are better adapted to this purpose than any part of Ceylon. The English government continues the same system. The horses are bred under the superintendance of officers appointed for the purpose, and when at a proper age, are disposed of on account of government. It would be unjust to pass unnoticed the many improvements introduced into every department of this district, by Colonel Barbet of the seventy-third regiment, who has been commander and collector of this district ever since it came into the possession of this country. His conduct has rendered him equally esteemed by his countrymen and the natives.

The woods towards the interior which separate this district, and the others we have hitherto described, from the king of Candy's dominions, are inhabited by an extraordinary race of savages, supposed to be the aboriginal inhabitants of the island, and known by the name of Bedas or Vaddahs. As they never leave the recesses of their woods, and carefully conceal themselves from the eye of every stranger, little is known concerning them; and many Dutchmen have resided for years on the island, who were so far from having seen any of them, that they looked upon the reports handed about of them in much the same light as we in Europe do the stories of fairies and Lapland witches. The exaggerated and improbable tales related of them were indeed enough to make any one who had not actually seen them, look upon the whole as fabulous. There are, however, certain circumstances so well authenticated, that they can admit of no doubt; and these I shall detail, when I come to give a particular account of the several races of people who inhabit this island.

The road to the south-west of Jafnapatam is extremely tedious and disagreeable. The paths are often very narrow, passing through thick woods and heavy sands; and are very much infested with wild hogs, elephants, and buffaloes. These circumstances render a journey by this way very unpleasant; and those who are compelled by business to undertake it, prefer, if the season permit, to coast along in those large passage boats called *Donies*. The narrow sea which lies betwixt this side of the island and the continent, is called the gulph of Manaar, from a small island of that name lying off the coast of Ceylon, about sixty miles south-west of Jafnapatam.

The island of Manaar is separated from Ceylon by an arm of the sea about two miles broad, which, at low water, is almost dry, with the exception of a small channel in the middle not exceeding thirty or forty yards in breadth, and usually called the Straits of Manaar. The passage from this island to Ramiseram on the Coromandel coast is not above twelve or fourteen leagues; but the advantages which might be derived from this speedy communication are in a great measure prevented by the numberless shallows and sandbanks which every where interrupt the passage, and are so high as to be many of them completely dry except during the monsoons. There is in particular a line of sandbanks which runs quite across from Manaar to Ramiseram, known by the name of *Adam's bridge.* The name and situation of these banks are connected with a variety of curious traditions among the natives. It is universally believed among them that Ceylon was either the Paradise in which the ancestor of the human race resided, or the spot on which he first touched on being expelled from a Celestial Paradise. Adam's bridge is with them, the way by which he passed over to the continent; and some imagine that the Gulph of Manaar, like the Red Sea in scriptural history, closed after him to prevent his return. The opinion however, is almost universally received, that Ceylon at a distant period formed a part of the continent, and was afterwards separated from it by some great convulsion of nature. This account, though merely an unsupported tradition, is not altogether improbable; for when we consider the narrowness of the intervening space, and the numberless shallows with which it abounds, it cannot be denied that some violent earthquake, or still more likely, some extraordinary eruption of the ocean, might have placed Ceylon at its present distance from the continent.

The Gulph of Manaar, although too shallow to admit vessels of a large size, is not altogether useless for the purposes of commerce. Sloops, donies, and small vessels of various descriptions, convey goods by this passage from Madras and other places on the Coromandel coast direct to Columbo, instead of taking the circuitous outside passage, and rounding the island by Trincomalee and Point de Galle. This is called the *Inner*, or ***Paulk's Passage***, from a Dutchman of that name, who first attempted it. Adam's bridge, indeed, frequently proves an insurmountable obstruction, and vessels are often obliged to unload or lighten at Manaar before they can make good their passage. It is common indeed to have large boats stationed here to receive the goods and convey them forward to Columbo; so that the obstructions trade meets with here are similar to those which several large cities are subject to, of not being accessible to large vessels, but the articles of trade are obliged to be conveyed to them by lighters and small craft. The Dutch, notwithstanding these obstructions, found means to carry on a constant traffic by this passage between the western coast of Ceylon and their factories of Tutucoran, Vipar, Manapar, Ponicail, and Kilkerre. Coarse cloths and calicoes were the chief articles thus imported by the Dutch, and in return they carried back areka and cocoa-nuts, betel-leaf, fruits, arrack, and coya, or cordage made from the cocoa-tree. All these places are now in the possession of the English, and there is no doubt that this trafficking might be carried on to a much greater extent than formerly.

The shortness of the passage from Ramiseram to Manaar, is particularly useful on account of the speedy conveyance it affords to people on business, and to the communication of intelligence. Small boats continually ply between these two places, and passengers may be ferried over for a trifle. Government has also boats stationed here for the purpose of conveying the *tapal*, or letter bags, between Ceylon and the continent. By means of particular stations appointed for the purpose, letters are conveyed here in a manner wonderfully expeditious, when we consider that there are no roads fit for posting, and that the letter-carriers have to make their way through sands and thickets under the burning heat of the tropic suns. The distance from Columbo to Madras is upwards of five hundred miles, and yet the *tapals* are conveyed between these places in ten days by the *peons*, a cast of people employed for this purpose. Their common rate of travelling is five miles an hour, where the country will admit of it; and they are relieved at certain stages by fresh runners. They usually go from Columbo to Manaar, a distance of one hundred and sixty miles in three days. Here they take boat, and cross over by Adam's bridge to Ramiseram, and then proceed along the Coromandel coast to Madras. When the weather is not so violent as to occasion any delay in crossing the ferry, an express will run this journey in eight days.

The Dutch built a fort on the island of Manaar, with a view to command the passage, and the communication with the continent by Adam's bridge. It was principally intended to prevent the subjects of the king of Candy from smuggling over any of the produce of the island, particularly spiceries; and also to cut off all intercourse between that prince and those of the continent, by which he might have been enabled to form alliances dangerous to their interests. The protection of the pearl banks and pearl fishery, which lie at no great distance from this island, was also another principal object for erecting a fort here. It also contributed considerably to the revenues of government as a station, where certain duties were levied on the vast quantities of calicoes, coarse muslins, cottons, and other articles, brought through this passage to Columbo by the Moors, Malabars, and other inhabitants of the continent.

These circumstances evidently render this place of sufficient importance, to retain a constant garrison there; and the expence of the troops hitherto found sufficient for this service has been greatly overbalanced by the advantages derived from it. In general the garrison stationed here, consists only of a company of Malays or Sepoys, under the command of an European officer. During the season of the pearl fishery, an additional force is sent from Columbo. It was formerly a subaltern's command; but it has been the policy of Governor North to appoint field officers to this and other stations. The chief trouble to the garrison here arises from collecting the taxes. It is not always that this can be done without compulsion; and the exaction has even been sometimes openly resisted. In June 1800, a body of the natives, on the taxes being demanded of them, and the payment about to be enforced, assembled before the fort in a tumultuous manner, and seemed determined not to submit to the exactions. Two companies of the nineteenth, were immediately sent to the assistance of Major Ford, the commandant of the place; but means were found to disperse them before the arrival of this reinforcement. It was these two companies of the nineteenth, which first passed from Manaar to Trincomalee by land. They forded the narrow channel, which, as we have observed, separates Manaar from Ceylon, and thence traversed the country to Trincomalee. Although the season was very bad, they suffered little from fatigue.

These temporary commotions among the natives, though in general repressed with ease, are more frequent than might be expected from the ill success which always attends them. At Nigumbo, and Matura, similar insurrections to those at Manaar, and from the same causes, took place; and they were in the same manner speedily quelled by the arrival of detachments of the nineteenth regiment. Captain Vincent, of that regiment, who commanded at Nigumbo, was attacked by a large body of the natives belonging to our settlements, on his way to that fort from Columbo, accompanied with a small party of Malay soldiers; but he maintained a post, which he had taken, with very great ability, till a body of Europeans arrived to his assistance. The severe exactions of the Dutch, and the little attention they paid to the customs or prejudices of the natives, seems to have excited this spirit of discontent and insurrection among them: but a different mode of treatment; a mild, but at the same time steady enforcement of the laws, will, it is to be hoped, speedily put an end to all such commotions.

As we proceed along the coast of Ceylon from Manaar, we find the country sandy, wild, and barren; equally destitute of accommodation and provisions. The woods are so infested with wild animals, that it is extremely dangerous to travel along the roads here without a proper guard. About six miles onward we meet with the village of Arippo, where the civil and military officers, who attend the pearl fishery, reside during the season when it is carried on. They have here built for their accommodation a *choultry*, or stone barracks, which also serves for the reception of occasional travellers. During the pearl fishery, a detachment, usually of Sepoys, from the garrison of Manaar or Columbo, are stationed here to protect the pearl merchants, and prevent depredations or riots. They are also found necessary to enforce the orders of the gentleman appointed by government to superintend this department. A flag-staff and a field-piece, are attached to the party to make signals to the boats, and to give notice of their going out or return.

Arippo is the only place hereabouts where good water can be procured. This necessary of life, at that part of the coast, is not only bad, but very scarce, and often procured with great difficulty. Where any good springs are found, the Europeans take care to have themselves in the first place supplied; the natives often find it difficult to obtain the smallest quantity.

There is here a chapel for those of the Roman catholick persuasion, who consist chiefly of the Parawas and Malabars, resorting hither during the season of the pearl fishery. They attend the chapel on Sundays and holidays, in great numbers; and it is their constant practice, devoutly to offer up their vows and offerings before they commence diving for the oysters.

In the neighbourhood of Arippo, the woods are very full of deer and wild hogs. Great abundance of these animals are brought by the Cinglese peasants to the officers stationed here, during the season of the fishery.

Six miles further on, and at about twelve miles from Manaar, lies the bay of Condatchy, where all the boats are collected for the pearl fishery. The bay forms nearly a half-moon; the beach which surrounds it is an extensive sandy waste, with only a few miserable huts scattered along the shore, between the bay and the woods which skirt the beach. Such is the appearance which the bay of Condatchy presents at most seasons of the year; but during the fishery, the picture is entirely reversed. At that time the bay is crowded with small vessels, and the beach presents an astonishing multitude of people from every quarter of India. The difference of their appearance, their language, their manners, all afford a most entertaining spectacle. But it is not amusement alone that demands a minute description of the scene; several of the following particulars, which I have with much care and attention brought together, will be found connected with objects of public utility.

CHAPTER III.

The Pearl Fishery—Customs of the various Indian nations who frequent it.

THERE is perhaps no spectacle which the island of Ceylon affords, more striking to an European, than the bay of Condatchy, during the season of the pearl fishery. This desert and barren spot is at that time converted into a scene, which exceeds in novelty and variety, almost any thing I ever witnessed. Several thousands of people of different colours, countries, casts, and occupations, continually passing and re-passing in a busy crowd: the vast numbers of small tents and huts erected on the shore; with the bazar or market place before each; the multitude of boats returning in the afternoon from the pearl banks, some of them laden with riches; the anxious expecting countenances of the boat-owners, while the boats are approaching the shore, and the eagerness and avidity with which they run to them when arrived, in hopes of a rich cargo; the vast numbers of jewellers, brokers, merchants, of all colours and all descriptions, both natives and foreigners, who are occupied in some way or other with the pearls, some separating and assorting them, others weighing and ascertaining their number and value, while others are hawking them about, or drilling and boring them for future use: all these circumstances tend to impress the mind with the value and importance of that object which can of itself create this scene.

The bay of Condatchy is the most central rendezvous for the boats employed in the fishery. The banks, where it is carried on, extend several miles along the coast from Manaar southward, off Arippo, Condatchy, and Pomparipo. The principal bank is opposite to Condatchy, and lies out at sea about twenty miles. The first step, previous to the commencement of the fishery, is to have the different oyster banks surveyed, the state of the oysters ascertained, and a report made on the subject to government. If it has been found that the quantity is sufficient, and that they are arrived at a proper degree of maturity, the particular banks to be fished that year are put up for sale to the highest bidder, and are usually purchased by a black merchant. This, however, is not always the course pursued: Government sometimes judges it more advantageous to fish the banks on its own account, and to dispose of the pearls afterwards to the merchants. When this plan is adopted, boats are hired for the season on account of government, from different quarters; the price varies considerably, according to circumstances; but is usually from five to eight hundred pagodas for each boat There are however no stated prices, and the best bargain possible is made for each boat separately. The Dutch generally followed this last system; the banks were fished on government account, and the pearls disposed of in different parts of India, or sent to Europe. When this plan was pursued, the governor and council of Ceylon claimed a certain per centage on the value of the pearls; or, if the fishing of the banks was disposed of by public sale, they bargained for a stipulated sum to themselves over and above what was paid on account of government. The pretence on which they founded their claims for this perquisite, was their trouble in surveying and valuing the banks.

As neither the season, nor the convenience of the persons attending, would permit the whole of the banks to be fished in one year, they are divided into three or four different portions, which are fished one portion annually in succession. The different portions are completely distinct, and are set up separately to sale, each in the year in which it is to be fished. By this means a sufficient interval is given to the oysters, to attain their proper growth; and as the portion first used has generally recovered its maturity by the time the last portion has been fished, the fishery becomes almost regularly annual, and may thus be considered as yielding a yearly revenue. The oysters are supposed to attain their completest state of maturity in seven years; for, if left too long, I am told that the pearl gets so large and so disagreeable to the fish, that it vomits and throws it out of the shell.

The fishing season commences in February, and ends about the beginning of April. The period allowed to the merchant to fish the banks is six weeks; or two months at the utmost; but there are several interruptions, which prevent the fishing days from exceeding more than about thirty. If it happens to be a very bad season, and many stormy days intervene during the period allotted, the purchaser of the fishery is often allowed a few days more as a favour. One considerable interruption proceeds from the number and diversity of holidays observed by the divers of different sects and nations who are employed. Many of the divers are of a black race, known by the name of Marawas, and inhabiting the opposite coast of Tutucoreen: these people, although of the Malabar cast, are Roman Catholicks, and leave off work on Sundays to attend prayers at the chapel of Arippo. But if many stormy days, or Hindoo and Mahomedan festivals (which are never neglected on any account by the natives) occur to interrupt the regular course of fishing, the farmer is sometimes desirous that the Catholick Marawas should make up the lost time by working on Sundays: but this he cannot compel them to do, without an order from the chief civil officer of government, who is appointed to superintend the fishery.

The boats and donies employed in the fishery do not belong to Ceylon, but are brought from different ports of the continent; particularly Tutucoreen, Caracal, and Negapatam, on the Coromandel coast; and Colang, a small place on the Malabar coast, between Cape Comorin and Anjanga. The divers from Colang are accounted the best, and are only rivalled by the Lubbahs, who remain on the island of Manaar for the purpose of being trained in this art. Previous to the commencement of the fishery, all the boats rendezvous at Condatchy; and it is here they are numbered and contracted for.

During the season, all the boats regularly sail and return together. A signal gun is fired at Arippo, about ten o'clock at night, when the whole fleet sets sail with the land breeze. They reach the banks before day-break; and at sun-rise commence fishing. In this they continue busily occupied till the sea-breeze, which arises about noon, warns them to return to the bay. As soon as they appear within sight, another gun is fired, and the colours hoisted, to inform the anxious owners of their return. When the boats come to land, their cargoes are immediately taken out, as it is necessary to have them completely unloaded before night. Whatever may have been the success of their boats, the owners seldom wear the looks of disappointment; for, although they may have been unsuccessful one day, they look with the most complete assurance of better fortune to the next; as the Brahmins and conjurers, whom they implicitly trust in defiance of all experience, understand too well the liberality of a man in hopes of good fortune, not to promise them all they can desire.

Each of the boats carries twenty men, with a *Tindal* or chief boatman, who acts as pilot. Ten of the men row and assist the divers in re-ascending. The other ten are divers; they go down into the sea by five at a time; when the first five come up the other five go down, and by this method of alternately diving, they give each other time to recruit themselves for a fresh plunge.

In order to accelerate the descent of the divers, large stones are employed: five of these are brought in each boat for the purpose; they are of a reddish granite, common in this country, and of a pyramidal shape, round at top and bottom, with a hole perforated through the smaller end sufficient to admit a rope. Some of the divers use a stone shaped like a half-moon, which they fasten round the belly when they mean to descend, and thus keep their feet free.

These people are accustomed to dive from their very infancy, and fearlessly descend to the bottom in from four to ten fathom water, in search of the oysters. The diver, when he is about to plunge, seizes the rope, to which one of the stones we have described is attached, with the toes of his right foot, while he takes hold of a bag of net-work with those of his left; it being customary among all the Indians to use their toes in working or holding as well as their fingers, and such is the power of habit that they can pick up even the smallest thing from the ground with their toes as nimbly as an European could with his fingers. The diver thus prepared, seizes another rope with his right hand, and holding his nostrils shut with the left, plunges into the water, and by the assistance of the stone speedily reaches the bottom. He then hangs the net round his neck, aud with much dexterity, and all possible dispatch, collects as many oysters as he can while he is able to remain under water, which is usually about two minutes. He then resumes his former position, makes a signal to those above by pulling the rope in his right hand,

and is immediately by this means drawn up and brought into the boat, leaving the stone to be pulled up afterwards by the rope attached to it.

The exertion undergone during this process is so violent, that upon being brought into the boat, the divers discharge water from their mouth, ears, and nostrils, and frequently even blood. But this does not hinder them from going down again in their turn. They will often make from forty to fifty plunges in one day; and at each plunge bring up about a hundred oysters. Some rub their bodies over with oil, and stuff their ears and noses to prevent the water from entering; while others use no precautions whatever. Although the usual time of remaining under water does not much exceed two minutes, yet there are instances known of divers who could remain four and even five minutes, which was the case with a Caffree boy the last year I visited the fishery. The longest instance ever known was that of a diver who came from Anjango in 1797, and who absolutely remained under water full six minutes.

This business of a diver, which appears so extraordinary and full of danger to an European, becomes quite familiar to an Indian, owing to the natural suppleness of his limbs, and his habits from his infancy. His chief terror and risque arise from falling in with the groundshark while at the bottom. This animal is a common and terrible inhabitant of all the seas in these latitudes, and is a source of perpetual uneasiness to the adventurous Indian. Some of the divers, however, are so skilful as to avoid the shark even when they remain under water for a considerable time. But the terrors of this foe are so continually before their eyes, and the uncertainty of escaping him so great, that these superstitious people seek for safety in supernatural means. Before they begin diving, the priest, or conjurer, is always consulted, and whatever he says to them is received with the most implicit confidence. The preparation which he enjoins them consists of certain ceremonies according to the cast and sect to which they belong, and on the exact performance of these they lay the greatest stress. Their belief in the efficacy of these superstitious rites can never be removed, however different the event may be from the predictions of their deluders: Government therefore wisely gives way to their prejudices, and always keeps in pay some conjurers, to attend the divers and remove their fears. For though these people are so skilful and so much masters of their art, yet they will not on any account descend till the conjurer has performed his ceremonies. His advices are religiously observed, and generally have a tendency to preserve the health of the devotee. The diver is usually enjoined to abstain from eating before he goes to plunge and to bathe himself in fresh water immediately after his return from the labours of the day.

The conjurers are known in the Malabar language by the name of *Pillal Karras*, or *binders of sharks*. During the time of the fishery, they stand on the shore from the morning till the boats return in the afternoon, all the while muttering and

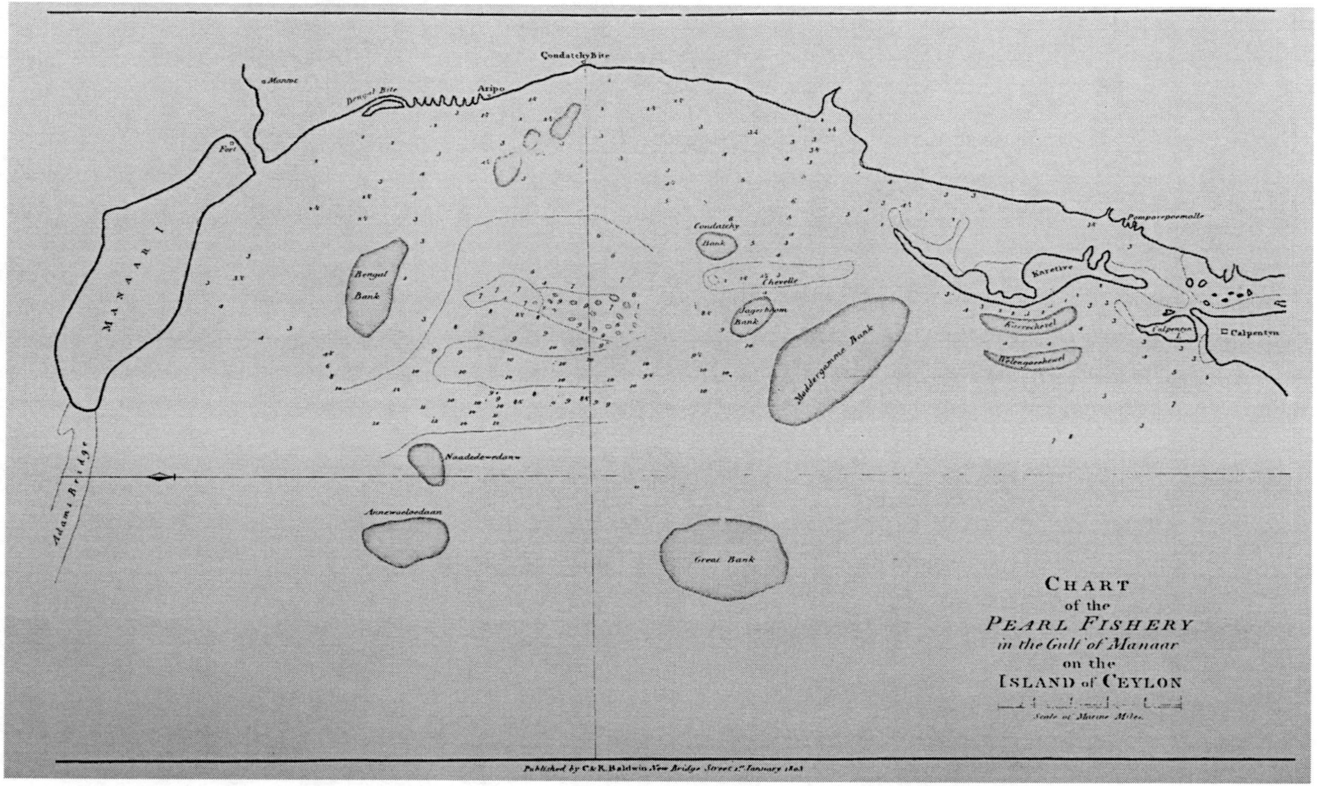
CHART
of the
PEARL FISHERY
in the Gulf of Manaar
on the
ISLAND of CEYLON
Scale of Marine Miles.
Published by C.&R. Baldwin New Bridge Street 1st January 1803
Condatchy Bite
Aripo
Bengal Bite
Manaar I
Fort
Adam's Bridge
Bengal Bank
Naadedeondaan
Annewoeloedaan
Great Bank
Condatchy Bank
Chevelle
Jageshom Bank
Maldergamme Bank
Karetive
Pomparipoemalle
Calpentyn
Calpentyn I.

mumbling prayers, distorting their bodies into various strange attitudes, and performing ceremonies to which no one, not even themselves I believe, can attach any meaning. All this while it is necessary for them to abstain from food or drink, otherwise their prayers would be of no avail. These acts of abstinence, however, they sometimes dispense with, and regale themselves with *toddy*, a species of liquor distilled from the palm-tree, till they are no longer able to stand at their devotions.

Some of the conjurers frequently go in the boats with the divers, who are greatly delighted at the idea of having their protectors along with them; but in my opinion, this fancied protection renders the divers more liable to accidents, as it induces them to venture too much and without proper precautions, in full confidence of the infallible power of their guardians. It must not however be imagined, that these conjurers are altogether the dupes of their own arts, or that they accompany their votaries to the fishery merely from an anxious care of their safety; their principal purpose in going thither is, if possible, to filch a valuable pearl. As this is the case, it is evident that the superintendant of the fishery must look upon their voyages with a jealous eye; such, however, is the devoted attachment of their votaries, that he is obliged to pass it over in silence, or at least to conceal his suspicions of their real intentions. He must also never hint a doubt of their power over the sharks, as this might render the divers scrupulous of committing themselves to the deep or indeed deter them from fishing at all. The conjurers reap here a rich harvest, for besides being paid by the government, they get money and presents of all sorts from the black merchants and those successful in fishing up the oysters.

The address of these fellows in redeeming their credit, when any untoward accident happens to falsify their predictions, deserves to be noticed. Since the island came into our possession, a diver at the fishery one year lost his leg, upon which the head conjurer was called to account for the disaster. His answer gives the most striking picture of the knowledge and capacity of the people he had to deal with. He gravely told them, " that an old witch who owed him a grudge, had just come from Colang on the Malabar coast, and effected a counter-conjuration, which for the time rendered his spells fruitless; that this had come to his knowledge too late to prevent the accident which had happened; but that he would now shew his own superiority over his antagonist by enchanting the sharks and binding up their mouths, so that no more accidents should happen during the season." Fortunately for the conjurer the event answered his prediction, and no further damage was sustained from the sharks during the fishery of that year. Whether this was owing to the prayers and charms of the conjurer, I leave my European readers to decide; but certainly it was firmly believed to be the case by the Indian divers, and he was afterwards held by them in the highest esteem and veneration. His merits however in this transaction might be disputed, for there are many seasons in which no such accidents occur at all. The appearance of a single shark is indeed sufficient to spread dismay among the whole body of divers; for as soon as one of them sees a shark he instantly gives the alarm to his companions, who as quickly communicate it to the other boats; a panic speedily seizes the whole, and they often return to the bay without fishing any more for that day. The sharks which create all this alarm sometimes turn out to be nothing more than a sharp stone on which the divers happen to alight. As false alarms excited in this manner prove very injurious to the progress of the fishery, every means is employed to ascertain whether they are well or ill founded; and if the latter be the case, the authors of them are punished. These false alarms occurred more than once in the course of the last two or three seasons.

The divers are paid differently according to their private agreement with the boat-owners. They are paid either in money, or with a proportion of the oysters caught, which they take the chance of opening on their own account; the latter is the method most commonly adopted. The agreements with the people who hire out the boats are conducted much in the same manner. They contract either to receive a certain sum for the use of their boats, or pay the chief farmer of the banks a certain sum for permission to fish on their own account. Some of those who pursue the latter plan are very successful and become rich; while others are great losers by the speculation. Oyster lotteries are carried on here to a great extent; they consist of purchasing a quantity of the oysters unopened, and running the chance of either finding or not finding pearls in them. The European officers and gentlemen, who attend here upon duty or through curiosity, are particularly fond of these lotteries, and very frequently make purchases of this sort.

The boat-owners and merchants are very apt to lose many of the best pearls while the boats are on their return to the bay from the banks, as the oysters when alive and left for some time undisturbed frequently open their shells of their own accord: a pearl may then be easily discovered, and the oyster prevented by means of a bit of grass or soft wood from again closing its shell, till an opportunity offers of picking out the pearl. Those fellows who are employed to search among the fish also commit many depredations, and even swallow the pearls to conceal them; when this is suspected, the plan followed by the merchants is to lock the fellows up, and give them strong emetics and purgatives, which have frequently the effect of discovering the stolen goods.

As soon as the oysters are taken out of the boats, they are carried by the different people to whom they belong and placed in holes or pits dug in the ground to the depth of about two feet, or in small square places cleared and fenced round for the purpose; each person having his own separate division. Mats are spread below them to prevent the oysters from touching the earth; and here they are left to die and rot. As soon as they have passed through a state of putrefaction, and have become dry, they are easily opened without any danger of injuring the pearls, which might be the case if they were opened fresh, as at that time to do so requires great force. On the shell being opened, the oyster is minutely examined for the pearls: it is usual even to boil the oyster, as the pearl, though commonly found in the shell, is not unfrequently contained in the body of the fish itself.

The stench occasioned by the oysters being left to putrefy is intolerable; and remains for a long while after the fishery is over. It corrupts the atmosphere for several miles round Condatchy, and renders the neighbourhood of that country extremely unpleasant till the monsoons and violent south-west winds set in and purify the air. The nauseous smell however is not able to overcome the hopes of gain: for months after the fishing season, numbers of people are to be seen earnestly searching and poring over the sands and places where the oysters had been laid to putrefy; and some are now and then fortunate enough to find a pearl that amply compensates their trouble in searching after them. In 1797 while Mr. Andrews was collector, a Cooly, or common fellow of the lowest class, got by accident the most valuable pearl seen that season, and sold it to Mr. Andrews for a large sum.

The pearls found at this fishery are of a whiter colour than those got in the gulph of Ormus on the Arabian coast, but in other respects are not accounted so pure or of such an excellent quality; for though the white pearls are more esteemed in Europe, the natives prefer those of a yellowish or golden cast. Off Tutucoreen, which lies on the Coromandel coast, nearly opposite to Condatchy, there is another fishery but the pearls found there are much inferior to those two species I have mentioned, being tainted with a blue or greyish tinge.

In preparing the pearls, particularly in drilling and stringing them, the black people are wonderfully expert. I was very much struck with the instrument they employ in drilling, as well as the dexterity with which they use it. A machine made of wood, and of a shape resembling an obtuse inverted cone, about six inches in length, and four in breadth, is supported upon three feet, each twelve inches long. In the upper flat surface of this machine, holes or pits are formed to receive the larger pearls, the smaller ones being beat in with a little wooden hammer. The drilling instruments are spindles of various sizes according to that of the pearls; they are turned round in a wooden head by means of a bow handle to which they are attached. The pearls being placed in the pits which we have already mentioned, and the point of the spindle adjusted to them, the workman presses on the wooden head of the machine with his left hand, while his right is employed in turning round the bow handle. During the process of drilling, he occasionally moistens the pearl by dipping the little finger of his right hand in a cocoanut filled with water which is placed by him for that purpose; this he does with a dexterity and quickness which scarcely impedes the operation, and can only be acquired by much practice.

They have also a variety of other instruments, both for cutting and drilling the pearls. To clean, round, and polish them to that state in which we see them, a powder made of the pearls themselves is employed. These different operations in preparing the pearls occupy a great number of the black men in various parts of the island. In the black town or pettah of Columbo in particular, many of them may every day be seen at this work, which is well worth the attention of any European who is not already acquainted with it.

Such are the circumstances relative to the pearl fishery, which have fallen under my observation. Owing to its having been formerly inconsiderately exhausted by the avarice of the Dutch, it is not perhaps so productive as it once was. The revenue which Government derives from it is still however considerable, and may by good management be increased. Pearls are considered as the next staple of the island to cinnamon; the concourse of people which it attracts affords a facility for disposing of the other produce; and by proper management, advantage might be taken of the opportunity here offered to introduce our manufactures into various parts of India.

Before we leave the bay of Condatchy, it may be amusing to take a view of the various objects which most attract the attention of a stranger during the pearl fishery. The remarkable display of Indian manners, which are here seen in all their varieties, is, perhaps, the most striking of these. Every cast has its representatives; the arts practised by some, the ceremonies performed by others, and the appearance of all, present the richest repast to the curiosity of an European. In one place he may see jugglers and vagabonds of every description practising their tricks with a degree of suppleness and skill, which appear supernatural to the inhabitant of a cold climate; in another he may observe Fakeers, Brahmins, Priests, Pandarams, and devotees of every sect, either in order to extort charity, or in consequence of some vow, going through the most painful operations with a degree of obstinate resolution, which I could scarcely have believed or even conceived, had I not been an eye-witness. I hope it will not be thought an improper digression from my narrative, if I mention a few of those circumstances which most attracted my notice: they are not particularly connected with a description of Ceylon, but they will certainly afford one source of amusement to the traveller who visits it.

The most painful acts of penance which the Indians undergo, are in order to regain their cast, when they have lost it either by eating things forbidden by the rules of their sect, or by having such connection with people of a different description as is supposed to defile them. In this state they are held in abhorrence by persons of their own sect, debarred from all intercourse with them, and prohibited even to touch them. From such a dreadful state of defilement they can be purified only by paying a large sum of money, or by undergoing the most incredible penances. Among those which I observed, I shall mention a few of the most remarkable. One of them will vow to hold his arm elevated over his head for a certain number of years, without once letting it down; and this he will actually continue to do, till the arm can never afterwards be recovered to its natural position. Another will keep his hand shut till the nails on his fingers absolutely grow into the flesh, and appear quite through at the back of his hand. Many never suffer their hair to be combed, or their beards to be shaved: in this state the hair of their heads, which is of a brown or burnt colour, gets matted, and appears not unlike the mops we use in Europe; or hangs down in long dishevelled strings, similar to that which grows on a species of French lap-dogs. Some will vow never to lie down; while, at the same time, they wear round their necks a large iron instrument not unlike a gird-iron without a handle.

But one of the most extraordinary of these ceremonies which I have witnessed is, swinging for their cast, as it is termed. A very high and strong post, or cocoa-tree, is planted firmly in the ground, crossways; on its top, another beam is placed in such a manner as to turn round on a pivot, and made fast to the upright post by ropes reeved through both, like the yards to the mast of a ship; and from the end of the transverse beam, ropes and pullies are suspended to hoist up the devotee. He then is brought out, attended by a number of people dancing before him; and is led thrice round the swinging post by the Brahmins and his relations, with loud shouts, accompanied by music. In the mean time a sheep is sacrificed, and the blood sprinkled about on the surrounding multitude, who are eager that it shall fall upon them. Barren women, in particular, are anxious to catch the drops, in hopes of being by this means rendered fruitful; and with a view to secure the efficacy of this charm, they contrive to work themselves up, during the ceremony, to the highest pitch of religious delirium, tearing their hair and shrieking in the most dreadful manner. After the sacrifice is performed, the devotee is placed on his belly flat on the ground; and two very large hooks, which have been previously fixed to the ropes suspended from the end of the cross-beam, are inserted deep into the flesh of his back just under the shoulders: other ropes are also placed under his breast and across his thighs, to help to sustain the weight of his body. He is then, by means of the ropes and pullies, hoisted up to the cross tree, immediately under which he continues suspended; and in this position he is drawn round the post two or three times. During this painful ceremony he repeats a certain number of prayers, and continues to throw among the crowd flowers which he had taken up with him for the purpose: these are considered as sacred relicks, which will keep away all disease, and ensure happiness ever after; and the surrounding multitude scramble for them as eagerly as an English mob for money thrown among them.

This ceremony is by no means unfrequent, and I have had occasion to be present at more than one, during my stay in Ceylon. The last I saw performed was at Columbo in 1799, when the cross beam broke, and the man falling to the ground was killed on the spot. A moor of the Moply cast had previously observed to the crowd, who were principally Malabars of the same sect with the devotee, that the timber was not strong enough to bear the man, and would certainly break. This proving actually to be the case, the Malabars affirmed that the Moor had by his prediction bewitched it; and in revenge they attacked him with such fury, that he would certainly have been killed, had not I with a few other European officers and Sepoys, whom curiosity had brought to the spot, interfered and rescued him out of their hands.

The priests who attend at Condatchy on account of these and other ceremonies, as well as many other sects of religious mendicants, are a great nuisance there; for, besides being exceedingly lazy and idle, they are likewise very impudent and troublesome. But they are not the only pests which annoy the multitudes collected at the pearl fishery. There are besides a crowd of jugglers, snake-catchers, dancing boys and girls of all descriptions, as well as many who follow no other occupation but to procure their livelihood by the arts of filching and thieving, at which they are exceedingly dexterous. This practice, however, is the more pardonable in them, as it appears to be an inherent propensity in an Indian. In their dealings with an European, whenever an opportunity presents itself, they never fail to employ their skill in overreaching him. It is only however by pilfering and stealing that he suffers from them, for they hardly ever venture to rob or take his goods from him by open force. So great, indeed, is the awe which the atchievements of the Europeans have inspired into the natives of India, that a black man is scarcely ever known to meet a white man hand to hand, either in private conflict or in battle.

There is no scene at which the native Indians can have a finer opportunity of turning their dexterity to account, than the bay of Condatchy, at the season of the pearl fishery. For this reason, rogues flock thither from all parts of India, and no precaution is sufficient to prevent their depredations. Their practice of picking out the pearls from the oysters and secreting them is, in particular, carried to a great height, and it has been found impossible to put a stop to it. In this general censure of the natives of India, I do not include the native Ceylonese; for, although the pearl fishery be carried on in their island, yet few of them attend it, in comparison of the numbers who flock from other parts of India. Nor are they at all so much addicted to roguery, nor equal in slight of hand, to the Indians of the continent, who seem to have these accomplishments by inheritance, and are very proud of them, it being a common proverb with them, "The greater "rogue the greater man." I speak of this disposition among them from my own experience, as I and my brother officers were repeatedly sufferers by it. Indeed there are few who visit India, who will not soon have occasion to acquire personal knowledge of it.

At Condatchy their depredations are reduced to a system, and no precautions can entirely guard against them. The boat-owners and merchants dealing in the oysters, are obliged to hire people to collect the pearls out of them; and to prevent embezzling, confidential persons are appointed, who constantly attend to watch over and observe them. One instance I recollect of the ingenuity employed by the Indians to evade the care of the superintendants. A band of them having been employed by a boat-owner to open his oysters, they concerted a regular plan for pilfering the most valuable pearls. One was appointed to be the thief, and to contrive to steal away a valuable pearl; while another, on a signal being previously given, was to make a shew of carrying off one of small value, and to run the risk of being punished for this offence, in order to attract the attention of the superintendant, and thus afford an opportunity to the real thief to get his booty clear off. This plan having been arranged, they went on very quietly with their work, till one of them lighted upon a very valuable pearl, and instantly made the signal to the thief who was to aot the feigned part. The latter, according to his cue, immediately began to secrete some pearls of small value, in such a manner as to be observed by the superintendants, who, in consequence, seized upon him, detected the pearls about him, and began to punish him. This occasioned a great bustle, for the fellow made as much noise and resistance as he could; while, in the mean time, the real thief laid hold of the opportunity to secrete and secure the valuable pearl. This roguery was afterwards discovered in consequence of a quarrel among themselves about the division of the booty. It had been agreed that the pearls should be sold, and the price divided amongst them, according to the parts they were to act in procuring it: but the mock thief who had been punished and turned off from his employment on account of his share in the transaction, thought himself also entitled to a greater share in the profits than the rest were willing to allow him; and his claims not being admitted, he discovered the affair to the boat-owner. Upon this, application was instantly made to the officer commanding here, when the whole set were severely punished; and the pearl, being at length traced out, was restored to the proprietor.

CHAPTER IV.

Putallom salt-works—Nigumbo—Fishery there—March of the British troops from Nigumbo—Surrender of Columbo.

THE coast as you pass along from Manaar to Columbo, presents in general nothing but the most desert and barren appearance, except where it is covered by almost impenetrable jungles. A great variety of curious shells are indeed found along the shores, some of them valuable. The oyster shells themselves are a species of mother-of-pearl in the inside, the surface of which is so indented with uneven lines, that when paint or ink is rubbed over it and then gently wiped off, it leaves behind figures of birds, trees, men's heads, and such like appearances, owing to its sinking into the cavities.

The distance from Manaar to Columbo is upwards of one hundred and fifty miles. A few small places occur in the way where detachments are posted for the protection of travellers. Most of the road is extremely bad, and the country very much infested with buffaloes and elephants; in the track which lies between Manaar and Chilou in particular, where the jungle comes down to the very shore, and no other way is to be found for a considerable distance but narrow paths which pass through it, these animals often present themselves in the road to the great annoyance of travellers. Other obstacles also occur in this journey. At Pomparipo a broad lake is to be passed, which becomes impossible during the rainy season. There are besides in the way two or three broad rivers, as the Mosulee and Madragar, which issue from the mountains in the interior.

The first post you come to is Calpenteen, opposite to a small island of the same name which lies a little way out at sea. A company or two of Malays is stationed here, and when I left the island, it was commanded by a Dutch officer who had entered into our service and received this appointment from Governor North. This is one of the best places on the whole island for game.

Putallom, which lies not far distant, is remarkable for its salt-pans. This place before the arrival of Europeans on the island, supplied the natives with salt; and on account of its convenient situation, was pitched upon by the Dutch for manufacturing the salt with which they supplied the king of Candy's dominions, according to the articles of their treaty with him. The salt-pans are formed by an arm of the sea which overflows part of the country between Putallom and Calpenteen. A very large quantity of salt was manufactured here by the Dutch; they looked upon it as of the highest importance to their interests in the island, and the most formidable weapon which it was in their power to employ against the native king, as it was impossible for him to procure any but through their means. Since we have obtained possession of the island, this manufacture has been almost entirely neglected. It is capable however of being rendered very profitable, as it is the only one of the kind on this side of the island, and the most conveniently situated for supplying the king of Candy's dominions. The Dutch enacted severe laws to prevent individuals from manufacturing or trading in this article, the government taking upon itself the management of the works and the care of supplying both its own subjects and the Candians. In order to keep a constant check on the latter, the Dutch were careful not to allow them too great a quantity at once; and whatever remained at Putallom after supplying the demands of each year they destroyed, that it might not be seized upon by surprise.

A little farther southward lies Chilou, a village where the Dutch have erected houses for the entertainment of strangers. It stands on the banks of a broad river; with another at no great distance. The country around this place is particularly wild; and perhaps there is no road in the island more dangerous to travel, from the multitude of wild beasts with which it is infested.

From this place nothing worthy of observation occurs till we arrive at Nigumbo, a very pleasant village, within twenty-four miles of Columbo. The flat and open country to which we are now come, presents a most beautiful prospect to the traveller. The fields are every where fertile, and clothed with a profusion of productions which offer a charming variety to the eye. The pastures are of the greenest and richest kind; and the fields are peculiarly well adapted to rice, from the constant supply of water; as the whole is very easily inundated during the rainy season. The number of rivers which intersect, and shady hedges which surround these rich fields, joined to the beautiful *topes* or groves every where interspersed among them, at once contribute to their fertility, and give them the most luxurious appearance.

Nigumbo is situated on the sea coast in a most picturesque spot, accounted one of the healthiest in the island. Many Dutch families on this account reside here, and have houses and gardens scattered up and down in delightful groves of cocoa-nut and other trees. Nigumbo is the largest village in Ceylon, and for its size contains the greatest number of inhabitants. The Dutch built a fort here for the protection of the cinnamon-cutters, as a considerable quantity of that spice grows in the adjacent district. Store-houses are also erected in the fort, where the cinnamon, after being dried, is lodged, till an opportunity offers to convey it to Columbo. This cinnamon is reckoned equal in quality to any in the island.

The fort is not strong, being only defended by a steep square embankment of sand encompassed with a thick hedge of the milk-tree: the front alone is constructed of stone work, and has a regular gate and draw-bridge at its entrance. At each angle of the square is a bastion with a few old guns planted on them; and in the gateway are guard-houses with an arched cupola for a bell. Within the fort are three long ranges of buildings, which serve for barracks to the troops and for store-houses to the cinnamon. The command was formerly given to a subaltern; but according to the new arrangements made by Governor North, it is given to a field officer, who also acts as president of the *Landraed*, or civil court appointed to hear and determine differences among the natives, and take cognizance of the crimes committed within this district.

These civil courts existed under the government of the Dutch, and are now established by Mr. North at all the military posts and commands round the island. The commanding officer, who is always the president, after investigating any affair brought before him, if he finds it of a trivial nature, has the power to decide the dispute, or punish the offence on the spot, of his own authority. If the affair appears to be intricate or of sufficient magnitude, he remits it to the head court at Columbo, with his own opinion and remarks on the evidence. This institution saves an infinity of trouble that would otherwise arise from the captious and litigious disposition of the natives. It also greatly promotes the distribution of justice, as the president by taking the evidence on the spot has an opportunity of acquiring information which the distance might otherwise prevent from reaching the court at Columbo.

Nigumbo is very advantageously situated for carrying on inland trade, particularly with Columbo and its neighbourhood, as a branch of the Mulivaddy here runs into the sea.

At the mouth of it is a small harbour, where sloops and other small vessels often put in and land their cargoes, which are afterwards conveyed up the Mulivaddy, and then, by canals which communicate with it, to the lake which skirts the town of Columbo. The country through which this communication is carried on is perfectly flat for a great way in every direction, and abounds with considerable lakes and rivers, which give the greatest facility to forming canals. The sides of the rivers and canals are skirted with thick woods and jungle, which afford a most grateful shade to the passengers from the scorching heat of the sun, and also supply the inhabitants with plenty of fuel, as the rivers do with the greatest abundance of fish. With both of these last articles, Ceylon is much better provided than any other part of India which I have visited.

One of the principal articles exported from Nigumbo by the inland communications consists of fish. This trade is considered as the property of government, and is annually farmed out for several thousand rupees. A Moor or Malabar man is usually the farmer, and he alone is allowed to dispose of the fish caught here. He employs all the boats belonging to the place, paying the owners a certain daily hire. The people he engages are compelled by the authority of government to fish every day that the weather will permit, Sundays and particular festivals excepted. These fishermen are obliged to purchase from the farmer any fish they may want for their own use. Whether this system be the best for government, or for the fishermen may be disputed; but it is plainly the worst for the purchaser, as all competition is destroyed.

Although Columbo has a very extensive fishery of its own, yet it is also largely supplied from Nigumbo. The fish as soon as caught are put into boats, conveyed by the rivers and canals during the night, and sold in the bazars next morning.

I was struck with a curious method of catching fish practised by the natives in the lakes and rivers adjoining to Nigumbo. They go into the water up to the middle of the thigh, carrying in their hands a round basket of a conical form, something resembling our wire rat-traps without the bottom. This they suddenly plunge into the water quite down to the mud. They soon find whether they have enclosed a fish by its beating against the sides of the basket: when this is the case, they thrust down their arm through the hole at the top and lay hold of it. They string the fish as they catch them on a piece of rattan or bamboe, which is fastened round their waist; and I have often seen them quite loaded with what they caught in this manner. While the operation of plunging the basket is continued, other persons are employed in splashing the water all around in order to make the fish go towards the basket.

Besides the produce of the fisheries, other sorts of traffic are carried on at Nigumbo to a considerable amount. It is to this place that the adjacent country sends such articles as are destined for exportation; the vessels which are to receive them come to anchor off the harbour, when the goods are carried on board and conveyed to the different parts of India.

The inhabitants contain a number of Moors, Malabars, and Indian Portuguese; and it is remarked, that the women of these casts as well as of the native Cinglese, are prettier here than at Columbo and other more noted places. For its cool, healthy, and pleasant situation, Nigumbo is usually ranked next to Jafnapatam, though some give the preference to Caltura, another delightful village about thirty miles south of Columbo.

The English landed at Nigumbo in February 1796, when they made themselves masters of it without opposition.

From Nigumbo southward the road is extremely pleasant; it is shaded the whole way, and there are a number of resting places provided for travellers. About half way to Columbo is a very large *choultry* or barracks, to which the officers of the garrisons frequently go on shooting parties. It is situated in a most agreeable spot in the midst of a picturesque country; and snipe and other game abound in this quarter.

After the taking of Nigumbo, General Stewart with the fifty-second, seventy-third, and seventy-seventh regiments, three battalions of Sepoys, and a detachment of Bengal artillery, marched to attack Columbo. The road through which he had to pass presented apparently the most formidable obstacles. Those rivers which add so much to the beauty and richness of the country, and those woods which afford so much comfort to the traveller, presented so many bars to the march of an army, and opportunities to annoy them. For twenty miles the road may be considered as one continued defile capable of being easily defended against a much superior force. It was intersected by two broad, deep, and rapid rivers, and several smaller ones, besides ravines whose bridges had been broken down. Each side of the path through which our army marched was covered with thick woods and jungle, from whence the enemy had an oportunity of destroying their adversaries without even being seen themselves. In such a situation General Stewart every moment expected an attack, and was exceedingly surprised, as were all the officers, at being suffered to pass through such a strong and difficult country without the smallest opposition. Nothing can give a more striking idea of the degraded state to which the Dutch military establishments at Ceylon were reduced, than their suffering an enemy to advance unmolested in such circumstances. Neither want of skill or prudence on the part of the officers, nor want of discipline on that of the soldiers could have produced such disgraceful effects. It is only to the total extinction of public spirit, of every sentiment of national honour, that such conduct can be attributed. A thirst of gain and of private emolument appears to have swallowed up every other feeling in the breasts of the Dutchmen; and this is a striking warning to all commercial nations to be careful that those sentiments which engage them to extend their dominions, do not obliterate those by which alone they can be retained and defended.

If their unmolested march seemed unaccountable, the circumstances which followed still more surprised our British soldiers. The first obstacle which opposed itself to General Stewart, was the Mutwal river at the distance of about four miles from Columbo; and here the enemy, who made their appearance for the first time, seemed determined to dispute the passage. Nature had done every thing in her power to render their resistance effectual. The river was here half a mile broad, and ran in such a direction as nearly to cut off and insulate for three or four miles that tract of country which immediately presented itself to our army. A little neck of land on the south-side afforded the only entrance to this tract, which from its strength was called the Grand Pass. A battery erected by the Dutch on the Columbo side, commanded the passages, and General Stewart was of course obliged to halt. The army lay here for two days preparing themselves for a difficult enterprise, when they were astonished to learn that the Dutch had thrown the guns of the battery into the river, evacuated the post, and retreated precipitately into the garrison of Columbo. The British at first doubted the truth of the intelligence, and then supposed it was a stratagem of the enemy to draw them across, and afterwards attack them with advantage. As no opposition, however, now presented itself on the other side of the river, it was resolved to carry over the army, which was speedily effected on rafts of bamboe, and a few boats from our ships lying at anchor off the mouth of the river. Our troops then encamped in a large grove of cocoa-nut trees, with a Malay village in front. The position was very advantageous, as the river, from its winding course, protected our right flank and rear, while the left was skirted by a very thick wood or jungle, which extended nearly to the Black Town of Columbo. Our ships, which lay at no great distance, were ready to furnish the army with every thing necessary. It was of this last circumstance that the Dutch took advantage to excuse their pusillanimous conduct in abandoning such an excellent position. They said they were afraid of troops being landed from the ships between them and the fort of Columbo, and thus cutting off their retreat. But those who are acquainted with the situation of the country will look upon this as a very poor palliation of their cowardice, as even supposing we had attempted to land troops between them and the fort, a secure retreat was opened to them by the thick wood on the left, through which, from our not knowing the ground, it would have been dangerous and improper for us to pursue them.

Whilst our troops lay here, the Dutch sent out from Columbo a large party of Malays under the command of Colonel Raymond, a Frenchman, to attack us, which they did rather unexpectedly in the morning about day-break. Our troops, however, particularly our flank companies under Colonel Barbut, gave them such a warm reception, that they soon retired very precipitately and with great loss; their brave commander was mortally wounded and died a few days after. The loss on our part was not material; and this was the last and only attempt made by the enemy to oppose us.

Our army was now come to Columbo the capital of the Dutch dominions in Ceylon, large, fortified, and capable of a vigorous defence; and here they seemed to have concentrated their resistance. On our appearing before it, however, a capitulation was immediately proposed, and in a few days after, this important place was surrendered into our hands. To examine the causes which led to this unexpected conduct may be of use to our own nation, and the commanders of our garrisons abroad.

Previous to the British troops appearing before Columbo, its garrison had been in some measure weakened by the loss of the Swiss regiment de Meuron, which for a long time had composed part of it. This regiment, upon the term of its agreement with the Dutch having expired a few months before General Stewart was sent against Ceylon, had transferred its services to our government; and other troops had not hitherto been procured from Holland or Batavia to replace it at Columbo. The strength of the garrison was by this means impaired; but the want of numbers was not its principal defect, as upon marching out after the surrender, it was found to consist of two battalions of Dutch troops, the French regiment of Wirtemberg, besides native troops;

forming in all a number fully equal to the force sent against it.

The dissensions among both the civil and military officers of the garrison was a cause which more powerfully hastened its surrender. Those principles which have produced so many convulsions and atrocities in Europe, had also penetrated into this colony. The Governor, M. Van Anglebeck, was a very respectable old officer of moderate principles and a mild disposition. Many of those under him were, however, violent republicans of the jacobin party; they declaimed against the Governor as a man of a weak mind, and wished to place in the government his son, whom they had gained over to their own principles. The violence of this party had gone to an alarming height; they had already begun to denounce their opponents, and several respectable gentlemen would in all probability have fallen victims to their fury, had not the sudden arrival of the English at this critical moment rescued them from impending destruction.

The state of discipline in the garrison had also fallen into the most shameful disorder. Drunkenness and mutiny were carried to the greatest height. The old Governor has frequently declared at the tables of our officers, that he was in constant danger of his life from their mutinous conduct. He had resolved to defend the place to the last, but such was the state of insubordination which prevailed, that he could not by any means induce the Dutch troops, and in particular the officers, to march out against the enemy.

Personal safety, an object scarcely ever attended to by our troops either by sea or land, seemed in them to overpower every sense of duty or honour. A few of them went to accompany the Malay troops on the expedition I have already mentioned; but scarcely had they reached the gates of the Black Town when their courage evaporated, and they left the Malays to their fate. Not above one or two European officers met us in that action besides the brave Colonel Raymond, who was ashamed of being connected with such poltroons, and would have brought their conduct to public censure had not his life fallen a noble sacrifice to his sense of honour.

This state of total insubordination, the violence of the jacobin party, and the fear of an internal massacre, induced the Governor to enter into a private treaty for surrender with the English as soon as they appeared before the place. He let his troops, however, know that such a measure was in agitation; but this produced no effect on their disorders, and he at length signed the capitulation without their knowledge, and I believe without their consent. Our troops were suddenly introduced into the fort, and had nearly entered before the Dutch were aware of it. They were found by us in a state of the most infamous disorder and drunkenness; no discipline, no obedience, no spirit. They now began to vent the most bitter reproaches against the Governor, accusing him as the author of that disgrace which their own conduct had brought upon them; and seemed in a tumultuous crowd determined to display a desperate courage when it was now too late. The Malay troops alone kept up any appearance of discipline. Even they, however, were led away by the contagious example of the rest; and several of them in concert with the jacobin party among the Dutch, attacked the Governor's house, and fired into it with an intent to kill him; crying aloud, that he had betrayed them and sold them to the English. Nor was it without much difficulty that these mutineers were compelled to evacuate the fort, and ground their arms.

It was grateful to the heart of a Briton to behold the steady conduct and excellent discipline of our troops on this occasion, when contrasted with the riotous and shameful conduct of the Dutch soldiers. An officer who was an eye-witness, assured me that the Dutch soldiers went so far as even to strike at our men with their muskets, calling them insulting and opprobrious names, and even spitting upon them as they passed. This behaviour entirely corresponded with their former cowardice, and was equally despised by our countrymen. I have often since conversed on the subject with the Malay officers, who seemed to have embraced entirely the same sentiments with regard to it. They were all highly disgusted with the pusillanimous conduct of the Dutch, particularly in the affair at the Grand Pass, where they left them without any assistance to fight by themselves. Their contempt for their former masters, and their admiration of the valour of our troops, has served to render the Malays our most sincere friends, and they are now formed into a steady and well disciplined regiment in the British service.

These facts with regard to the easy capture of Ceylon tend to throw the severest reflections on the Dutch garrison there, but by no means serve to shew that the enterprise on our part was not attended with the greatest danger. The opposition of even a very small body of men must have occasioned much difficulty and loss to our men, however great General Stewart's military talents, and however brave the troops he commanded. Nature, indeed, seems to have done every thing in her power to secure the approaches to Columbo on this side.

CHAPTER V.

Description of Columbo—The fort—Pettah—Harbour—Inhabitants—Trade—Expence of living.

COLUMBO, the capital of Ceylon, and the seat of Government, is a place of very considerable extent. Although Trincomalee, on account of its situation and harbour, be of more consequence to this nation to retain, yet Columbo in every other respect is greatly superior. The number of its inhabitants is much greater; its fort and black town are much larger; the country where it is situated far more fertile, and the rich district depending upon it much wider, being not less than twenty leagues in length, and ten in breadth. It is situated in the west, or rather towards the south-west part of the island, in about 7° north latitude, and 78° east longitude from London.

The fort is placed on a peninsula projecting into the sea. From this situation it derives many advantages, as it is exposed on all sides to the sea breezes, by which means the air is rendered temperate and healthy, though so very near the equator. The fort is upwards of a mile in circumference, and is in a great measure indebted to nature for its strength; though it is also tolerably well fortified by art. The Dutch were very careless in improving its natural advantages; and neglected many obvious opportunities both without and within of rendering it nearly impregnable. There is no hill or rising ground in the neighbourhood, sufficiently elevated to command it; and but few places near it where boats can land with safety. On the south side the surf runs so high, and the shore is so rocky, that it would be dangerous to approach it. On the west side of the bay where the sea is smoother, and near the wharf or landing place, which at all seasons of the year is safe for boats, the only attempt could be made; but these quarters are so well defended by the batteries which command the harbour, that there is hardly any probability of its succeeding.

On the west side of the fort, and facing the sea, are two very fine batteries, *en barbet,* intended for the security of the harbour. They stand on a part that projects a considerable way from the main body of the fort, from which they are separated by a high wall and ditch flanked with bastions, and having gates that communicate with the interior of the fort. It is here, that the wharf or landing place is formed: it consists of large piles of timber, extended several yards into the sea, and affording a very commodious station for loading and unloading sloops, and large boats, which can be brought close alongside. At this end of the fort several store-houses and barracks, for half a regiment, are erected.

The ramparts of the fort are very strong, having eight principal bastions, including the two already described. They are distinguished by the names of the towns in Holland, the Leyden, Amsterdam, Harlem, &c. There are also a number of lesser ones, with curtains, banquets, and parapets, communicating with each other all around the fort, and fitted for troops to line and defend with musquetry and field-pieces. The want of bomb-proof casements, is the chief disadvantage of the place; the powder magazine is the only building constructed in that manner. Were the fort to be bombarded from ships on the south or west side, as it easily might, this want would be particularly felt.

The whole fort is surrounded by a broad and deep wet ditch, over which draw-bridges are thrown at each of the gates. On the outside are some small magazines, with a powder mill and a saw mill, attached to the fort.

Adjoining to the covert way, and at the foot of the glacis, is a lake in some parts extending three or four miles into the country in a north-east direction. For near a mile on the outside of the fort, the neck of land (which connects it with the country) is not above five or six hundred yards broad; and in the middle of this space lies the lake, leaving only room on each side for a narrow causeway. An approach of this sort, and so completely commanded, would render it very difficult for an enemy to storm. Near the glacis it may be entirely cut off, by opening the sluices and cutting the road across, when the lake would be connected with the sea, and the garrison completely insulated.

In the centre of the lake stands an island, communicating with a sally-port on the east face, by a narrow causeway and draw-bridges. It was called by the Dutch *slave-island*, from its being the place to which they sent their sick slaves. It is a remarkably pleasant spot, full of cocoa-nut trees. A battalion of Malays is stationed here. There is also an excellent house built by the Dutch, which they employed as a mason's lodge, with a very pretty garden attached to it. This island is very convenient, as it lies so contiguous to the fort, and opens the nearest way to the cinnamon gardens, which are close by it.

The fort has three gates; the principal one where the main-guard is stationed, is called the Delft gate, and leads into the pettah or black town. It has two draw-bridges to pass over the ditch, which here forms an angle. At each of the gates are guard houses with a subaltern's guard placed over them.

The plan of Columbo is regular. It is nearly divided into four equal quarters by two principal streets, which cross each other, and extend the whole length of the town. To these, smaller ones run parallel, with connecting lanes between them. At the foot of the ramparts on the inside is a broad street or way, which goes round the whole fort, and communicates with the bastions and soldiers' barracks; and also affords, at the different angles, open spaces for their private parading.

The grand parade is by no means sufficient for the garrison, as it can hardly contain one complete regiment. On one side of it are ranges of public offices for the civil and military departments, with the town or stadt-house in the centre of them, where the Dutch held their High Court of Justice. On our arrival here we found a rack and wheel, with a great variety of other implements of torture, which had been used for inflicting punishment on criminals, particularly slaves; but these modes of punishment, so shocking to human nature, and so abhorrent to the feelings of a Briton, were immediately abolished by our government.

On the other side of the grand parade stand the cinnamon store-houses, or *go-downs,* as they are called here. At the bottom of the parade stands a small building, used as the fort major's office, which is only worthy of notice from a curious circumstance, that gives a very poor idea of the state of civilization among the Dutch at Ceylon. While General Stewart was on his march hither from Nigumbo, during a thunder storm, a very usual occurrence in this part of the world, a weather-cock on the top of this building happened to be struck by lightning; a circumstance which made a very deep impression on the minds of the Dutch, and was considered as an omen of their future ill-success.

At the upper end of the parade, the Dutch government had begun to erect a church, but it has never been finished. The Dutch usually attended divine service at a very handsome and spacious church in the black town, about a mile distant from the fort; and worship is still performed there for the English, either before or after that of the Dutch inhabitants. The march to this church was attended with considerable inconvenience to our troops, in this sultry climate; on which account Governor North was about to roof in the church, within the fort, for their accommodation.

The government house, which faces the harbour, is a very long and capacious building, but more convenient than elegant. Several offices are attached to it, where the business of government is transacted. Behind it is an excellent garden, originally intended for a *tank*, or reservoir, in the event of a siege; for, though every house has a well plentifully supplied with water through the whole year, yet it is of a brackish quality, and unfit to drink. On this account the Europeans belonging both to the civil and military establishment, are supplied with water from springs about a mile from the fort. It is brought by means of bullocks in leathern bags, called here *puckally bags*, a certain number of which is attached to every regiment and garrison in India. Black fellows, called *puckally boys*, are employed to fill the bags, and drive the bullocks to the quarters of the different Europeans. When the troops are on a march, a different mode is practised. A certain number of negroes, appointed for the purpose, carry on their shoulders smaller leathern bags with pipes attached to them, called *beasties*. With these they run along the line, giving water to every soldier who stands in need of it; and as soon as the bags are empty, replenish them at the first spring or river they meet with.

Columbo is built more in the European style, if such an analogy can at all be drawn, than any other garrison in India. The interior of the fort has also more the appearance of a regular town; as none of those huts, peculiar to the natives, are allowed to be erected in it. The Dutch houses are all regularly built, though few of them are above one story high. An Englishman is also surprised to find all the windows here having glass-panes after the European manner; as in our other Indian settlements, Venetian blinds and shutters are chiefly used. This proceeds probably from the particular customs of the Dutch, who love here, as well as in Europe, to keep their houses close shut both in the hot and cold seasons, while we endeavour to have them as open as possible, in order to admit the air freely.

Before each house, and connected with it, is a large open space roofed in and supported on pillars of wood. It is called a viranda, and is intended to afford a shade from the sun, and an opportunity of enjoying any refreshing breeze that springs up from the sea, without being exposed to the scorching beams from above. Here it is customary to see the people walking about, or lolling in a chair with their feet supported against the railing, which is placed along the pillars, to the height of three or four feet. In addition to this refuge from the sultry rays, the houses are agreeably shaded by a double row of thick spreading trees, planted on each side of the several streets. These take off from the dazzling and sultry glare reflected by the walls, which are all plaistered over and white-washed with a very fine bright lime made of burnt shells. The colour is beautifully white, and may contribute to the coolness of the houses, but throws an unsupportable glare in the eyes of the passenger along the streets.

Most of the houses are of the same construction, and consist of the hall in the front, with a chamber at each side, and another room in the back part, equal in length to the other three, and called the *back viranda.* This apartment, owing to the sloping form of the roofs, is much lower than those in the front. Behind the back viranda are one or two ranges of smaller buildings, proportioned to the size of the house to which they are attached, and intended for the accommodation of the servants, for cellars, and sometimes for sleeping rooms.

The houses are covered with indented tiles; very indifferently indeed, as I have had occasion to remember from experience. During the rainy season most of them admit water in such a manner, that it is difficult to find a dry spot to place one's head under. I have frequently been obliged to exert my ingenuity on such occasions; and, after all, could barely make a shift to sleep a whole night in one place without getting drenched. The chief cause of these disasters to the tiles arises from the crows, who are in the habit of picking up bones and other things from the streets and yards, and carrying them to the tops of the houses, where a stout battle usually ensues for the plunder, to the great annoyance of the people below, and the continual destruction of the tiles. The monkies also, a number of whom run wild about the fort, are often very troublesome, and lend their assistance in demolishing the tiles. Both the crows and monkies know how to avail themselves of any entrance, which they find or make into the houses; and it requires no small attention to prevent them from picking up loose articles. While I was at Columbo, I recollect a very mischievous monkey who used to run wild about the fort, and was so very cunning, that it was impossible to catch him. One day he suddenly made his entrance into my apartment, carried off a loaf of bread from my table, and made his escape. I immediately gave the alarm to an officer I observed standing at the next door; upon which he ran in to secure his own breakfast; but, to his great mortification, found that the monkey had been before-hand with him, and was already scrambling up to the roofs of the houses with a loaf in each paw. Next day the same monkey snatched off a very fine parrot before the gentleman's face to which it belonged, tore it to pieces, and then held it out to the gentleman, with many expressions of satisfaction and triumph at the exploit.

In the centre of the principal street is a very handsome and lofty house, which belonged to the Dutch governor, M. Van Anglebeck. At present it is the residence of General Macdowal, who commands our forces on the island. There is also another very handsome and spacious house for the commandant of the garrison, with suitable offices and gardens.

The hospital, which is designed for soldiers and sailors, is roomy and convenient. It is very properly divided into distinct wards, so as to keep the sick of different disorders completely separate, and thus prevent infection from spreading. Close by it is a house for the chief surgeon, where all the hospital stores are prepared and kept. It is with much pleasure I add, that this hospital (an institution so indispensably necessary in those hot climates) is extremely well managed; and that every attention is paid to the health of the troops who are sent here for medical assistance.

The fort of Columbo being of itself very extensive, and its outworks and detached posts numerous, requires a strong garrison. Three or four battalions are usually stationed here. The regular guards placed on the different gates, consist of eighty Europeans, and three times that number of native troops. Besides these, other guards are stationed in the bazars and posts, which are established round the garrison, and also in the cantonments of the native troops. On my arrival in 1796, the garrison consisted of the 73d regiment, half the Madras European regiment, two companies of Bengal artillery, and three battalions of Sepoys. The immediate command of the troops is given to the oldest officer of the battalions on duty here.

The harbour of Columbo, which lies on the west side, is nothing more than an open road, affording good and safe anchorage to ships for only four months of the year, from December to April. During this period the north-west winds, to which this road is much exposed, do not prevail to any violent degree; and ships from different parts of India put in here to trade. But about May, when the monsoon sets in on the Malabar coast, and extends its ravages to the west coast of Ceylon, the roads of Columbo no longer afford any protection. Vessels then find shelter in the more secure ports of Trincomalee and *Point de Galle*, and seldom venture to these roads for the following eight months. Columbo is by this means cut off from any intercourse by sea with the rest of the island, for two thirds of the year. As this is the chief place for the staple trade of Ceylon, the disadvantages arising from these circumstances are very considerable; but such is the fury of the monsoon hurricanes here, that they can only be obviated by improving the communications by land, between Columbo and the more secure harbours on the east coast of the island.

For six months of the stormy season, this side of the island is subject to astonishingly heavy falls of rain, accompanied with dreadful thunder and lightning, and violent winds blowing in shore. In the beginning of May 1799, a thunder storm broke on the fort of Columbo; and several houses, particularly on the south-side, were struck and damaged. About half a mile from the fort a number of goats and oxen were at pasture, under the care of a boy; when he, and two and thirty of the cattle, were struck dead on the spot by one flash of lightning. A woman, in the black town, was also at the same time killed, and a child much hurt. For the space of an hour this storm continued, with the greatest fury I ever remember to have seen. Nor did the electric matter in the air seem at all exhausted by this explosion; as, a few nights after, there was another storm almost equally severe: but although the hospital, and several private houses, were struck by the lightning, providentially no lives were lost.

During this season, the variations of the climate are very great. The heavy rains, which predominate most by night, render the atmosphere at that time extremely chill and damp; while the excessive heat of the sun is by day almost insupportable. This, added to the very sudden transition from a warm clear day to cold and wet weather, makes the climate more unhealthy at this season than during the hot weather. But I have observed these changes affect the negroes much more than Europeans.

The Sepoys, in particular, and other natives of the continent of India, who come hither in the service of the European officers, or for the purposes of trade, are not at all able to endure the colds and damps occasioned by those violent rains, which continue much longer in Ceylon, than on either the Malabar or Coromandel coasts; and from these circumstances, that island is often called the watering-pot of India. During the rainy season, the Indians from the continent are extremely subject to fluxes, dysenteries, and fevers. They are also afflicted by another extraordinary disease, to which they apply as uncommon a cure. This disorder is known by the name of the *Berry berry:* it is occasioned by the low diet and bad water, which the natives are accustomed to use; and in part, perhaps, by the dampness of the climate in the wet season. It swells the body and legs of the patient to an enormous size, and generally carries him off in twenty-four hours. The method employed for the cure, is to rub the patient over with cow-dung, oil, chinam, lime-juice, and other preparations from herbs; and then bury him up to the chin in hot sand. When the legs only are attacked, although the disorder be the same, its name differs: a patient is then said to have got *elephant legs*, from the resemblance their legs bear at that time to those of these animals. They are also called *Cochin legs*, from the disease being very prevalent among the natives of the place of that name on the Malabar coast, owing to the unwholesome brackish water which is drunk there.

The rainy season does not produce consequences so dangerous to Europeans, although fluxes and bowel complaints are then much more frequent among them, than during the dry weather. Our soldiers too, by drinking plentifully of arrack and smoking tobacco, counteract the bad effects of the atmosphere and the water; while the natives on the other hand live so abstemiously, few or none of them eating flesh, or drinking any thing but water, that when once they are seized with these exhausting distempers, their constitutions want strength to resist them, and they usually fall victims.

On the inside of the roads where the larger ships anchor, and separated from them by a sand bank which stretches quite across it, lies a bay sufficiently commodious for the reception of small ships and *donies*, the country name for small sloops and decked boats. This bay forms a half moon on one side of the fort; which, by its projection into the sea, breaks the violence of the storms, and affords shelter from the south-west winds to the vessels moored here. The water on the bar is too shallow to allow ships of a large burden to pass; and several, when driven by the violence of the gales from their anchorage, have been wrecked here. On this account it is not uncommon to fire at vessels approaching too close to it, in order to warn them of their danger, and prevent them from anchoring within a certain distance.

Columbo was particularly unfortunate in the loss of its three first governors after it came into our hands, all in the space of one year. The first was Colonel Petrie, of the seventy-seventh regiment. In December 1796, General Doyle arrived from England with half the nineteenth regiment, to succeed General Stewart in the command, but died on the June following, sincerely regretted. Colonel Bonnevaux of the Company's service, the next senior officer on the island, succeeded him; but had only arrived three or four days at Columbo, from his former command at Point de Galle, when he was killed by his curricle up-setting as he drove out through one of the gates; and was buried within a week after his predecessor. After his death, General de Meuron, who was sent by the government of Madras to investigate into the revenue departments, took upon him the command, which he retained, till the Honourable Frederick North was sent out from England as governor of Ceylon. The conduct of this gentleman to every class of people, since his arrival on the island, is such, as to entitle him to their warmest attachment; and to make them wish, that his residence among them may be prolonged much beyond that of his predecessors.

To every fort in India is attached on the outside of the

walls, a town or village, called in the language of the natives the *pettah,* and by us the *black town,* from its being chiefly inhabited by black merchants and trades-people. The pettah of Columbo deserves particular notice, from its extent and superior structure. It is divided into two parts; that nearest the fort consists of one very broad street, beginning at the esplanade near the walls, and running on till stopped by an old mud wall, and a gate called Kenman's port. In this division of the pettah are several excellent houses, where many Dutch gentlemen and merchants reside. Through Kenman's port there is a narrow passage leading into the other division, which consists of a long straggling town, skirted on one side by the lake I have already described. Besides a principal street, there are several smaller ones running parallel to it. In one of them stands a large well-constructed building, called the Orphan Seminary, or school, where the Dutch used to educate the children of their soldiers and the poorer Europeans, as well as those which they had by native women. These children were here brought up at the public expence, till the boys were old enough to become apprentices to trades; and the females were settled in some comfortable situation, or married to persons of their own rank. This laudable institution is still kept up; and our government, with a liberality highly praise-worthy, contributes to its support.

Close by the esplanade, is the burial-ground of the garrison; the church, as I have already mentioned, stands at the other end of the town.

The shops, bazars, and stalls placed all along the streets, are replenished with various articles of merchandise, peculiarly in use among the natives of India; and the town, during the whole day, swarms with people of all descriptions. In the street, next the sea, is an excellent fish market, well supplied from the sea, the lakes, and rivers in the neighbourhood. Fish, indeed, forms a considerable part of the food of the inhabitants; and procuring and bringing it to market, affords employment to a number of people. The boats or canoes, used in their fisheries, particularly attracted my notice. They are of a curious shape and construction, used only in Ceylon, and extremely well calculated for the purpose they are put to. In length they are about fifteen feet, and not more than two in breadth. This shape is calculated to make them go incredibly fast, especially with the addition of a very large square sail, which one would imagine them incapable of carrying without capsizing. To prevent this, an ingenious, and to an European, a very extraordinary contrivance is employed. A log of wood is extended five or six feet from the end of the boat, by way of out-rigger. It is larger or smaller according to the size of the boat, and is shaped at each end like the prow of a canoe, to cut through the water. This log is fastened to the boat by two long and bent poles; and seems to serve at once for helm and ballast. Strange as this contrivance may appear, it is indispensably necessary; as from their extreme narrowness, the boats would without it be upset by a person simply stepping into them. They have one mast, to which the square sail is attached in such a manner, that the boat is capable of sailing either way; and can be made instantly to move in an opposite direction without turning or tacking, but merely by swinging the sail of the yard round. A paddle, something in the form of a shovel, is used to guide the boat's head.

The body of the canoe is a large tree hollowed out by fire, or scooped out by the carpenters. Along the sides of it, boards are nailed to the height of about two feet, in the form of a gunwale, to prevent the water getting in by raising the boat more above its surface. When it is necessary to carry large burdens inland by the canals and rivers, two or three of these canoes are lashed together without the out-riggers. Split canes, bamboes, or betel-tree, are then laid across them, so as to form a kind of raft; which, though ever so much loaded, will draw but very little water.

Other flat-bottomed boats are also used by the natives. They are of a much greater breadth than those we have described; they are thatched with cocoa-tree leaves, like a house, and are large enough to hold couches. They are very pleasant conveyances, and are much used by our officers when going on shooting excursions. The owners of these boats, and vast numbers of the Cinglese, whose business it is to convey burdens by water from one place to another, live constantly on board of them. Near Columbo, in particular, I have often seen two or three hundred of these boats in regular rows moored along the banks of the rivers, with entire families on board, who made them their habitations. Boats of our European construction, are seldom or never used in Ceylon; and indeed are hardly known to the natives, except at Trincomalee and Columbo.

The street, or rather alley which leads through Kenman's gate to the outer pettah, is exceedingly narrow, and from the nature of the climate and its confined situation, is of course excessively hot. Here the shroffs and money-changers have fixed their stations. The outer pettah is very large, and branches out into a number of streets, which extend some of them two miles. At the further end of one of them stands the church; and behind it a large oblong stone building supported in front with pillars, and intended for the reception of the Candian ambassadors. A number of bazars are here kept by the native men and women: they are abundantly supplied with vegetables, dried fish, and fruit.

In this part of the pettah are vast numbers of carpenters, smiths, and artificers of various sorts, particularly workers in gold and silver. Here are also a great number of black merchants, and canoplies, or black accountants; as also manufacturers and traders in the different kinds of precious stones found in Ceylon.

Columbo taken all together is, for its size, one of the most populous places in India. There is no part of the world where so many different languages are spoken, or which contains such a mixture of nations, manners, and religions. Besides Europeans, and Cinglese, the proper natives of the island, you meet scattered all over the town almost every race of Asiatics: Moors of every class, Malabars, Travancorians, Malays, Hindoos, Gentoos, Chinese, Persians, Arabians, Turks, Maldivians, Javians, and natives of all the Asiatic isles; Persees, or worshippers of fire, who would sooner have their houses burnt and themselves perish in the flames, than employ any means to extinguish it. There are also a number of Africans, Cafrees, Buganese a mixed race of Africans and Asiatics; besides the half-casts, people of colour, and other races which proceed from a mixture of the original ones. Each of these different classes of people has its own manners, customs, and language.

The language spoken most universally both by the Europeans and Asiatics who resort to Columbo, is the Portuguese of India, a base, corrupt dialect, altogether different from that spoken in Portugal. It may indeed be considered as a barbarous compound of a number of Indian languages combined with several European, among which the French is very distinguishable. Though this dialect be considered as the most vulgar of any, yet it is a very useful and even necessary acquisition, as in most of the settlements on the coast, particularly those which have been in the possession of the Dutch, it is common to meet with both Moors and Malabars who speak it. On Ceylon it is particularly useful to be understood; and indeed without it, a person finds it impossible to maintain any conversation with the Dutch ladies, as they seldom address one in any other. This last circumstance a good deal surprised me, as in every other place I always found every thing accounted vulgar the particular abhorrence of the ladies. And yet the Dutch ladies at Columbo hardly ever attempt to speak even in their own families and to their own connexions in Dutch, although it is reckoned the polite language. I am apt to attribute their adherence to the vulgar Portuguese, to their habits of frequent and familiar intercourse with their slaves, who all speak this dialect.

Notwithstanding the difficulty of access to Columbo, and its total want of a secure harbour for large vessels, still the richness of the district where it is situated, and the variety of articles which it affords to commerce, render it a place of very considerable trade. It is much frequented on this account both by Europeans and the natives of the different coasts of India; and the duties on imports and exports bring a revenue of some consequence to Government. It is from this district that large quantities of cinnamon and pepper, the staple spices of the island are yearly transported to Europe in vessels, which touch here on purpose on their voyage from Madras and Bengal. A great quantity of arrack is made in the neighbourhood of Columbo, and the other districts along the west coast. This liquor is sent to our settlements of Bengal, Madras, and Bombay; and in return these send rice and other articles with which Ceylon is not able to supply its own consumption. A large quantity of coya rope, or cordage, is also manufactured here, and supplies of it are sent to our ships on the various stations in those seas. A number of inferior articles, the produce of this quarter of the island, are exported by the Moors and Malabars who reside here for that purpose. These articles are betel-leaf and areka nut, jaggery, a sort of coarse blackish sugar, cocoa-nuts and oil, honey, bees-wax, cardamoms, coral, ivory, fruit, and a variety of other lesser articles. In return they import coarse cotton cloths and calicoes, pieces of printed or painted cloths for women's apparel, coarse muslins, handkerchiefs, palampoes, stockings, china ware, tin, copper, and a variety of toys; also bomeloes, a species of fish peculiar to Bombay, and onions from the same place, where they are remarkably good.

The Dutch exacted a duty of five per cent on all these exports and imports, which is still continued by our Government.

Every year, in general towards February, a Portuguese or Chinese ship arrives from Macao with teas, sugar, candied sweetmeats, hams, silks, velvets, nankeens, umbrellas, straw-hats, all kinds of china-ware and toys. These articles meet with a very speedy sale; and as they are generally paid in hard-money, they occasion a great deal of gold and silver to be carried out of the island.

The current coin here, as well as in the rest of the European dominions on the island, consisted on the arrival of the English, of rix-dollars, a nominal coin, like our pound sterling, valued at a certain quantity of copper money. There were besides several smaller copper coins, called *pice* or *stivers*, half-pice, and dudies. Four pice or two dudies went to a fanam, and seven fanams to a rix-dollar. This proportional value of the coins has however been altered, and new regulations established since the island has come into our possession. There is now current a new coinage of double and single pice and half-pice, made by our East India Company. A pice is about a halfpenny sterling; four pice go to a fanam, and twelve fanams to a rix-dollar, or, as it is usually called by our people, a copper rupee. This latter coin goes for about two shillings sterling; and four of them are equivalent to a star pagoda, a Madras gold coin worth eight shillings sterling. Our troops are generally paid one third in gold, one in silver, and one in copper. This proportion varies however according to the state of the treasury. In issuing the copper money, goverment usually allows forty-five fanams to the pagoda, which is about the same proportion as is charged by the company at Madras. The troops however are rather sufferers by this rate, as the Dutch and English merchants insist upon forty-eight fanams to the pagoda, in their dealings with them. The fluctuation in the value of money in Ceylon is very great, and depends upon the immediate plenty or scarcity of gold and silver there. I have frequently been obliged to give five rupees or ten shillings in copper for a pagoda in gold, and the same proportion between a silver and copper rupee. For three years before my departure, gold had been so scarce, on account of the little influx of it into the island, occasioned by the war and the unsettled state of affairs, that government could not procure a sufficient quantity of it to pay the troops. This we have often felt a great disadvantage when ships occasionally touched at Columbo, particularly the vessel from Macao, as then were the only times at which many necessary articles could be procured. The foreign merchants would not take the copper-money of the island in payment, as it passes no where else; our only resource on such occasions therefore was to carry our copper-money to the shroffs or money-changers, and procure gold and silver from them for it on their own terms.

The expence of living at Columbo is much more considerable than might be expected. Every thing in Ceylon in general is indeed dearer than on the continent of India, from whence most of the articles in use are imported, and the expence of carriage has consequently to be added to their original cost. Horses and servants are particularly expensive. To keep one horse at Columbo will cost as much as to keep two at Madras. Servants' wages are also nearly double, as it is the custom to bring them from Bengal and Madras, and they, as well as their masters, must pay dearer for their clothes and food than in their native countries where these articles are produced. The servants also stipulate for higher wages before they will come to Ceylon, as they are very much prejudiced against it on account of its dearness, and distance from their homes and places of religious worship. There prevails also among the people of the continent a rooted and unaccountable persuasion that Ceylon is the most unhealthy part of India. Europeans are universally convinced of the absurdity of this idea, as they have found by experience, that it has in fact the best climate in that part of the world.

The Dutch, to avoid the expence of keeping coast servants, introduced the practice of rearing slaves of the African casts, and employing Malays who made very excellent cooks and gardeners, and indeed good servants in every respect, although they were kept for a trifle in comparison of the others. It would still greatly reduce the expence if the native Ceylonese could be employed for domestic purposes. The general idea however is, that from their dispositions and habits they are but ill calculated for them; it is particularly complained of that they are very inexpert and ignorant in the management of horses. I cannot, however, see why these objections might not be obviated, if they were early trained to the different offices of a servant. It would be a means of introducing European manners and ideas among the natives, and would likewise retain in the island a portion of wealth that is carried off by strangers.

The other articles of life at Columbo, and indeed in every part of Ceylon, have for some years been proportionably high. They have all advanced very much in price, and vegetables and other provisions that were formerly in the greatest abundance have become equally scarce and dear. This is to be attributed to several causes. Since the British took possession of Ceylon, there has been a great influx of people of all descriptions, both those who only resort hither occasionally for the sake of traffic, and such as come with the intention of making it their permanent residence. This influx of strangers was formerly greatly limited by the narrow and jealous policy of the Dutch; but the liberal policy of our government in encouraging it, although a few temporary inconveniences, such as a rise in the price of provisions, may be the consequence, lays the foundation of a more numerous population, and consequently a future encrease of wealth and prosperity.

One principal cause of the scarcity of vegetables, which form so great an article of food in these warm climates, for the first years after our gaining possession of the island, was the Dutch having failed two successive seasons in procuring their usual annual supply of seeds from the Cape of Good Hope and Holland. The seeds of European plants of all sorts degenerate very much in this climate in a few years, and soon yield but an indifferent produce. They require much care in the rearing, and no less in preserving the seeds from the ravages of the ants and other vermin, which fasten upon every thing of the vegetable kind that comes within their reach. To preserve the quality, it is absolutely necessary to have a fresh impores ion of seeds nearly every year from their natural climates.

Such articles however, as are the native produce of the island, are found in great abundance and at a moderate price.

Beef, fish, and fowl in particular, are both cheap and plentiful. Mutton is excessively dear, as no sheep can be reared in the neighbourhood of Columbo. I have already mentioned that it is only at Jafnapatam they have ever been pastured on Ceylon with success; and the transportation of them from thence or from the continent of India must of course render the price of mutton excessively high at Columbo. I am doubtful, however, if either the climate or pasture of the island be so noxious to them as is generally imagined. I have eat remarkably fine and fat mutton, which had been brought from Bengal and the Coromandel coast, and pastured on Ceylon several months before it was killed. I am led to think that one principal reason why sheep have not been reared here with success, is their falling so easy a prey to jackals, snakes, and other noxious animals. Pigs are reared in great abundance; although neither I nor my brother officers were very partial to them, as soon as we found that cleanliness was reckoned an entirely superfluous article in feeding them. From the same cause we were not very fond of seeing ducks on our tables, although they were rather cheap and in plenty. Geese are rare, and turkeys not to be had, except a few imported occasionally by ships coming from other parts of India.

In consequence of the additional expence to which the military stationed in Ceylon were unavoidably subjected, Government granted them *full batta,* or a double allowance of the East India Company's pay. This however went no farther than the half batta on the continent; where indeed, one might live better in every respect on the lesser allowance. One considerable difference arose from lodging; as on the continent, quarters, or an allowance for finding them, are always given to the officers; whereas in Ceylon, they are obliged to pay for their own houses, generally at the rate of from six to twelve pagodas a month.

CHAPTER VI.

Country, south of Columbo—Galkiest—Puntura—Caltura—Barbareen—Bentot—Point de Galle—Matura—Batacolo.

THE country around Columbo, for several miles, is flat and very rich. It is diversified with fields of rice and pasture, as well as a variety of groves, among which the cocoa-tree is particularly conspicuous. A number of gentle eminences scattered up and down through the plains, afford an opportunity of enjoying this delightful prospect, which is farther embellished with a number of small rivers, lakes, and canals. The shady roads, which every where intersect the country, afford an agreeable shelter to the traveller; while the numerous country-seats and gardens which skirt them, present his eye with a continual change of gratification. Here it is, that the most wealthy Dutch gentlemen have their country residences. The late governor, M. Van Anglebeck, had a very pretty house delightfully situated on the banks of the Mutwal, where the river extends itself into a very broad channel; and with its numerous windings, affords a most enchanting prospect from the road, which runs along its banks for many miles. The house occupied by Governor North, about a mile from the fort, is a very elegant building; and, with the surrounding gardens and grounds, furnishes a delightful residence.

One of the chief beauties in the neighbourhood of Columbo, is the immense number of cinnamon trees, which produce the riches of the island. In the woods they grow wild in abundance; and in the gardens they are now regularly cultivated with the greatest success.

On proceeding southward from Columbo, the large groves of cocoa-trees, which are equally refreshing from their fruit and their shade, still continue to skirt and shelter the road. It is therefore, upon the whole, pleasant to the traveller, although indeed the sand is somewhat fatiguing. The road lies quite by the sea-side for six miles, till we arrive at the small village of Galkiest; where there is a church for the accommodation of both the Dutch and Cinglese; many of the natives having been converted to the christian religion.

From Galkiest to Pantura, a distance of twelve miles, the road is well shaded and pleasantly diversified by a part of the cinnamon gardens, which stretches across this tract. Pantura is a village with a church; and barracks have been erected here for the troops to rest in occasionally, in their route from Columbo to Point de Galle. On our way hither, it is necessary to pass a river of considerable breadth, which runs into the sea close by.

From Pantura to Caltura, a distance of ten miles, the whole country may be considered as one delightful grove; and the road has entirely the appearance of a broad walk through a shady garden. Few spaces of it are so much exposed, as to allow even the hottest sun at noon-day to penetrate it. The grateful refreshment such a road affords to a traveller in this sultry climate, can only be conceived by those who have passed from Columbo to Caltura. The goodness of the roads here is remarkable; and the vigour communicated by the coolness of the shades, is very sensibly felt by an European. I experienced this most satisfactorily, in a walk which I took from Caltura to Columbo in December 1799. It was then nearly the hottest season of the year, and the distance between the two places above twenty-eight miles. I left Caltura at nine in the morning, in company with two sets of palankeen boys, who were to go the same road. In time, however, I left my fellow travellers behind; and after a delay of an hour in crossing the Caltura and Pantura rivers, and resting at Galkiest, I got to Columbo by half past four in the afternoon, having performed the journey in the heat of the day, and in the space of seven hours and a half. I mention this circumstance, to demonstrate how much less enfeebling the climate of Ceylon is to the constitution of an European, than any other part of India. There is no place on the continent which I have visited, where I could have walked above half the distance in the same space of time; and yet the road which I travelled does not lie six degrees from the line. I could mention other instances of exertion, which the climate of Ceylon has permitted Europeans to make, where they were assisted neither by the goodness of the road, nor the shades of the groves. A soldier in the Bengal artillery left Columbo in the morning, and arrived by sun-set at Resouveorti, where we were encamped on our way to Candy, a distance of forty miles; though he was often exposed to the burning heat of the sun, and many parts of the road were very rugged and difficult to travel.

The river at Caltura is one of the largest branches of the Muliwaddy, and is here about a mile broad. It washes two sides of the fort by which it is commanded, and is navigable by boats to the sea. The eminence on which the fort is situated overhangs the river, and commands an extensive and most picturesque prospect.

The fort, from its situation, is capable of being rendered a very strong post: it has however been much neglected, and is at present greatly out of repair. The command of it is given to a subaltern, who is stationed here for the purpose of overawing the native Cinglese, and enforcing obedience to their Moodeliers or magistrates, as well as to keep up and protect the communication between Columbo and Point de Galle. The commanding officer presides in the court of justice, and determines all disputes among the peasants. The sea, the esplanade, and the village on the outside of the fort, as well as the beautiful surrounding country, render Caltura a truly delightful scene. Some tracts of cinnamon are scattered up and down here; and it is not till a short way farther south, that we come to the termination of that fertile district of Columbo, which contains so great a proportion of the wealth of Ceylon.

From the great plenty of game about Caltura, frequent

shooting parties resort to it, and the commander's hospitality is often called forth. Occasional passengers also find good accommodation provided for them, as government has furnished the commanding officer with an excellent house, and also gives him a monthly allowance for keeping open table. The methods employed in hunting the deer and wild hog, are similar to those still employed in the highlands of Scotland by parties hunting the great wild deer in the few extensive forests that yet remain. As the country around Caltura, where the game is found, is covered with extremely close underwood, a number of the native peasants are assembled and sent into the woods and jungles, by the several paths and openings, till they have completely encompassed a large space of ground. They then extend themselves so as to form a wide semi-circle, and in this order approach the place where the sportsmen are stationed at the skirts of the wood; at the same time making a loud noise to rouse the game that may lie concealed in the thickets. The animals finding themselves beset in their haunts, naturally endeavour to make their escape across the valley to some other hill or wood in the neighbourhood; but no sooner have they cleared the openings, than they find themselves assailed by the sportsmen who have carefully secured every passage; and have stationed themselves and their Cinglese marksmen at short distances from each other, all provided with fowling-pieces for the occasion. The dexterity which the natives shew in this species of hunting, and the celerity with which they make their way through underwood and bushes, that appear impenetrable, is very surprising.

Certain native manufactures are carried on to a considerable extent around Caltura. A great quantity of arrack in particular is made from the groves of cocoa-trees, which extend several miles in every direction, and from Columbo to Caltura, and several miles beyond it, form one continued grove. There is also a large plantation of sugar canes here, and a distillery of rum carried on by some Dutchmen, who reside in the village and neighbourhood. It is however very much inferior in quality to the West India rum.

Six miles onward from Caltura lies Barbareen, a small village, with a sort of harbour formed by a projection of land where the river runs into the sea. This is almost the only place where the high surf and rocky shore on this coast permits ship-boats of the European construction to land.

This place was signalized by a shocking catastrophe, which took place here in 1795. A boat from his Majesty's ship Orpheus having been sent in here to procure fresh provisions, the sailors confiding in the peace which then subsisted between the British and Dutch governments, came ashore without any apprehension, and began to look out for water, a few fowls, and vegetables. They were at first received with much apparent civility, and many promises that they should be plentifully supplied with the articles they required. This, however, was only intended to amuse them, while a party of Malays stole unperceived between them and the boat, and fell upon them unexpectedly. Few of our men escaped this shocking treachery, which was of a piece with the jealous and barbarous policy usually practised by the Dutch towards strangers who approached their colonies. The Malays, who were the instruments of their cruelty on this occasion, were afterwards in dread of its being revenged upon them when our troops came before Columbo. Indeed it was a fortunate thing for them that the town was taken by capitulation, as our men were very much exasperated against them both on this account, and their repeated attempts to surprise our camp before Trincomalee and Columbo.

At Barbareen there is a principal manufactory for making cordage and cables from the cocoa-tree. Large quantities are sent from hence to Columbo and Point de Galle, to supply the vessels which trade to these ports.

A few miles farther lies Bentot, only remarkable for producing the best oysters on the island. They are of a different species from the pearl oysters of Mànaar.

Point de Galle, which is considered in point of importance as the third town on the island, lies about sixty miles due south of Columbo, in 6° north latitude. The fort is pretty strong, and has several works attached to it. The garrison generally consists of two or three companies of Europeans, half a company of artillery, and a battalion of native troops. It is commanded by the next senior field officer after the Governors of Columbo and Trincomalee.

The harbour is spacious, particularly the outer road. The

inner harbour is secure during a great part of the year; but it has this disadvantage, that winds from a particular quarter are requisite to carry vessels out. Ships outward bound from Europe, generally come in sight of the first land at Dondre-Head, the southern promontory of Ceylon, and make Point de Galle the first harbour.

The pettah is extensive, and the houses both there and in the fort, are superior to those of Trincomalee. The whole town is populous, and in point of trade ranks next to Columbo. Fisheries to a very considerable extent are carried on here, and indeed form the chief branch of its traffick. A vast number of Malays and natives, are employed in catching, curing, and drying the fish to prepare it for exportation to different parts of the continent of India. Arrack, oil, pepper, cotton, and cardamoms, also form a part of its exports. Cinnamon is also grown here, but not in such quantity as about Columbo: in quality, it is much the same. One of the India ships touches here annually, either before or after she has taken in part of her cargo at Columbo, to carry off what cinnamon is prepared for exportation.

Thirty miles onward from Point de Galle lies Matura, a captain's command. The fort and village are both small; the country round is exceedingly wild, but well supplied with provisions of all sorts; and game, in particular, is here found in great abundance. The house for the commandant is tolerably good, conveniently and agreeably situated near the river which is broad here, and runs into the sea at a small distance. Although this fort is within the district of Columbo, yet it is only subject to the orders of the Governor General; and the same is the case with Caltura, Nigumbo, and Manaar.

The country around Matura abounds with elephants; and it is here they are principally caught for exportation. Every three or four years the elephant is hunted here, by order of government. In 1797 at one of these hunts, a hundred and seventy-six were caught, the greatest number ever remembered to have been taken at one time.

Matura lies nearly at the southmost point of Ceylon, and owing to the nature of the country to the eastward, no other European settlement occurs till we come to Batacolo at the distance of sixty miles. The country which lies between these two places, presents the wildest appearance. Few of the Cinglese have the intrepidity to inhabit those parts, where they are in constant danger of being attacked by the numerous descriptions of wild beasts, by which this quarter is so much infested. Strangers who are unacquainted with the country, and the methods of avoiding its terrible inmates, are very unwilling to travel through a tract where so many accidents occur. Those who are obliged by business to go from Columbo to Batacolo, prefer going by sea; or, if the season be unfavourable they rather take the circuitous route by the west and north-west coast of the island, than proceed by this wild and unfrequented tract; where, besides the danger arising from elephants, buffaloes, and other wild beasts, they run a continual risk of falling in with the savage Bedahs, who inhabit the woods here as well as in the neighbourhood of Jafnapatam.

Owing to these circumstances, Batacolo has little or no connexion with the south and west parts of the island; and is indeed, in every view, a place of small importance. Its harbour only admits of small craft; and the place itself consists of a trifling fort occupied by a subaltern, and a small detachment from the garrison of Trincomalee, with a village where a few Dutch families reside. The surrounding country is very romantic; and the view of the island from the sea off Batacolo, is particularly striking. The shore is uncommonly bold; and many of the immense rocks which rise on it have attracted notice, and acquired names from the grotesque figures they represent. The Friar's Hood, the Elephant, the Pagoda rock, are all well known.

We are now again returned to Trincomalee after having made a tour of the island, and noticed every place that appears worthy of remark in the European dominions. It appears from this survey, that the internal wealth, as well as the population of these possessions, lies on the west and south-west coasts; while that secure station for shipping, which renders Ceylon of so much importance to our other East Indian dominions, lies at the opposite side, and the most barren quarter of the island. The present state of the roads is such, as almost entirely to preclude all intercourse by land between the opposite sides of the island, which are thus prevented from imparting their advantages to each other. In time, however, these defects may in a great measure be remedied; and many beneficial plans have already begun to be executed by the intelligent officers, who at present command in the island. It is probable also, that in time the poorer lands in the north and east parts may be employed to raise the necessaries of life, while the rich plains around Columbo, are entirely devoted to its valuable spices.

The parts of the island which remain to be described are under a different sovereign, and inhabited by people of different appearance and customs from those on the sea coast. Before describing them therefore, it will be proper to give some account of the several races of people who are found on the sea coasts, as the description of the inland country must necessarily be interspersed with observations on the manners of its inhabitants.

CHAPTER VII.

Description of the Ceylonese Dutch—Portuguese—Malays.

THE inhabitants of the sea coasts of Ceylon are composed of a variety of different races. At Columbo in particular, the natives of every country in India appear to have their representatives. The manners and customs of these tribes, however, fall more properly under the description of their several native countries: it is only necessary in this work to describe those which are stationary in Ceylon, and form a a considerable proportion of its population. Besides the native Ceylonese who live under the dominion of the Europeans, and are distinguished by the name of the Cinglese, the coasts are chiefly inhabited by Dutch, Portuguese, and Malays. All these differ so much from each other both in their customs and appearance, that I hope a separate description of each tribe will afford amusement to the public.

The Dutch, and indeed the Europeans of every other nation but our own, who are born and reside in India, differ much in their habits and modes of life from those of Europe. Our own countrymen alone, in whatever climate or situation they are placed, still remain steady to the manners and customs of Great Britain; and though the prejudices of the people among whom they live, and the nature of the climate, may force them to make occasional deviations, yet they never altogether lose sight of their native habits. The chief trait of the original Dutch character which those in Ceylon retain, is their fondness for gin and tobacco: in other respects they adopt the customs and listless habits of the country. A Ceylonese Dutchman usually spends his time as follows. He rises early, about six, and either goes to walk, or sits down by his door in a loose robe and night-cap to smoke a pipe. This with a glass of gin, which is called a *soupkie*, fills up the interval to seven. A dish of coffee is then handed him by his slaves, and his lounging posture and tobacco-pipe are resumed for another while. He then gets up, dresses, and goes to business, or more frequently to pay visits; a mode of spending time of which his countrymen are particularly fond. In these visits the Dutchmen usually take a pipe and glass at every house to which they go. In their salutations they are wonderfully ceremonious, and make a profusion of bows with a stiffness peculiar to themselves. If they have leisure to prolong their visit, they take off part of their dress, and put on a little night-cap, which they bring with them on purpose, and then set themselves to smoke and talk till noon. Their dinner hour is about twelve. On their tables they have very gross and heavy food, and are particularly fond of having a great quantity of butter and oil mixed with their fish and other victuals. At some of the Dutch houses however, and in particular, at Mynheer Conrade's, at Columbo, I found the dishes extremely well dressed, and the fish in particular appeared exceedingly palatable to an Englishman. After dinner they resume their favourite regale of smoking in an undress, and then go to sleep for an hour. As soon as they are again dressed, they either go abroad to pay visits, or receive company at home; and this with another pipe fills up the interval till supper is announced at nine, when the same heavy sort of food is again served up.

This mode of living cannot fail to make them lazy and indolent, which indeed they generally are to a proverb. As they make no effort to encrease their knowledge, and even appear to have no curiosity, nor enjoyment in any thing beyond the common insipid routine I have described, they are of course ignorant and stupid, without capacity and without desire of excelling by exertion. Their children are treated with the same neglect as other objects, and are usually committed to the care of the slaves. Their selfish and contracted minds become equally callous to the feelings of humanity, and their poor slaves are treated with cruelty upon the slightest provocation, and often from mere caprice: this treatment they alledge is highly necessary to keep them in proper subjection; an argument employed only by those who feel that they deserve to have their injustice retaliated upon themselves, and who hope to escape punishment by stiffling the feelings of humanity.

The conversation of women, which has tended so much to humanize the world, forms very little of a Ceylonese Dutchman's entertainment. Although the ladies make part of the company, yet they experience none of that attention and politeness to which the fair sex are accustomed in Europe. After the first salutations are over, the men seem to forget that the ladies are at all present; and will sit a whole evening talking politics over their pipes, without once addressing the women or taking the least notice of them. Indeed they avoid as much as possible this dead weight on their social enjoyments, and therefore usually get into another room by themselves; or if they have not an opportunity to do so, they club together at one end of the room, and leave the other to the ladies.

When such is the treatment which they experience from the men, it is not to be expected that the women can be very polished or skilled in the arts of pleasing. In the forenoons their dress is particularly slovenly. I have seen many of a morning with only a petticoat and a loose gown or jacket upon them, their hair rolled up in a knot on the crown of their heads, without either shoes or stockings on their feet; and yet these very women at their evening parties appeared dressed out in abundance of finery. Their minds are still less cultivated than their bodies; and they are nearly as ignorant on their wedding-day as in their infancy. Those charms of polite conversation, and that knowledge of useful subjects which render the society of our fair countrywomen at once so delightful and improving, are utterly unknown among the ladies of Ceylon. Their education indeed is such, that accomplishments of any description are not to be expected among them. From their infancy they are entirely given up to the management of the female slaves, from whom they imbibe manners, habits, and superstitious notions, of which they can never afterwards divest themselves. Under this tuition they continue till they get married; and even in this new state, from the description I have already given of the men, it will not be expected that they should make any considerable improvements. As they find such a cold reception among the men, they are glad to return to the attentions and obeisance paid them in the society of their slaves, to which they have been most accustomed. Their morals being derived from the same source, are equally destitute of dignity or virtue as their manners are of politeness. They usually converse in that barbarous Portuguese, which is reckoned extremely vulgar and only fit for slaves. They seldom or ever speak before an Englishman in any other dialect, but look upon Dutch as rather calculated for men, and too harsh for the mouth of a lady.

Although the men would not apear very amiable in the eyes of our British ladies, yet their Dutch wives look upon them with the greatest veneration and affection. Conscious of their own defects, and always kept at a great distance by their husbands, they look upon their caresses as a high honour, and are therefore extremely jealous of their favours. And yet their own manners after marriage are the worst calculated possible to conciliate the attachment of their husbands; indeed, in men of any delicacy, they could only produce aversion and disgust. The Dutch ladies, while young and unmarried, dress well and are tolerable in their persons, and many among them pretty and even handsome; but afterwards they contract such lazy and indolent habits that they become coarse, corpulent, and dirty in their persons· and their dress during the day is slovenly and negligent to excess.

In this climate, and with these habits of life, it would be in vain to look for the bloom of health and the European red and white in the cheeks of the women; their complexions are for the most part of a pale deadly white, although there are some exceptions to this observation, and a few female countenances to be found that might be accounted handsome even in the opinion of an European. Those women, who have a mixture of the native blood are easily distinguished by a tinge in the colour of the skin, and their strong thick black hair; marks which are not to be removed in the course of many generations. The women of this mixed race, of whom there are a great number in all the Dutch settlements, sooner begin to look old than those who are wholly of European extraction. The Dutch ladies have a custom of cracking their joints, and rubbing them over with oil, which renders them uncommonly supple.

Dancing is the principal amusement of the younger women; while the chief pleasure of the married and elderly ladies consists in paying formal and ceremonious visits to each other. To these visits they go attended by a number of slave girls, dressed out for the occasion. These girls walk after them carrying their betel-boxes, or are employed in bearing umbrellas over the heads of their mistresses, who seldom wear any head-dress, but have their hair combed closely back and shining with oil. Their chief finery consists in these female attendants, and their splendour is estimated by the number of them which they can afford to keep. These slaves are the comeliest girls that can be procured, and their mistresses in general behave very kindly to them. With that caprice however, which always attends power in the hands of the ignorant and narrow-minded, the Dutch ladies frequently behave in a very cruel and unjust manner to their female attendants, upon very trifling occasions, and in particular on the slightest suspicion of jealousy.

The unmarried ladies usually pay considerable attention to their dress; and since the conquest of the island by our forces, have greatly improved their appearance by adopting the English fashions. On my first arrival in the island, they dressed in the Dutch manner with long waists and stiff high stays, which to me appeared very grotesque and awkward. The dress worn by many of them, which is a mixture of the European and native fashions, is light and pretty. It consists of a piece of fine cotton cloth wrapped round the body, and fastened under the arms, which forms the under dress. Above it is worn a jacket of fine muslin or calico, and a petticoat of the same. Over the whole is thrown the *kabey*, or muslin robe with sleeves fitted close to the arms, and reaching down to the wrist, with five or six buttons of gold, silver, or precious stones. A long or short *kabey* is used according to fancy.

Some wear their hair loose, and others in a wreath round the back of their heads. These wreaths are fastened with gold pins, known by the name of *conde*, very large, like skewers, of a peculiar shape, and bent at the end like the handle of a table-spoon: they serve to fasten a plate of gold or tortoise-shell in the shape of a half-moon, which compresses the hair and keeps it firm on the back part of the head. To this head-dress they frequently add by way of ornament a wreath of the Arabian jessamine, a small white flower of a most exquisite scent, which is also worn in garlands round their necks. The women of the half cast are obliged to keep their hair constantly moist with cocoa-nut oil, for if this precaution were omitted for one week, it would, owing to its thickness and the heat of the climate, begin to fall off. The odour of the cocoa-nut oil, however, joined to the perfumes of the jessamine wreaths, quite overpower the senses of an European, and render the approach of these women disgusting.

Neither the persons nor the apartments of the women are in general very cleanly. Many of the elderly ladies, and most of the lower orders chew the betel-leaf, and areka-nut, with a mixture of *chinam*, or lime made of burnt shells, to render it hotter and more pungent to the taste. In every house there are a number of brass vases employed as spitting pots for the women who chew these substances, and for the men when they smoke. The women are in general very neat and exact in the arrangement of their sitting-rooms and where they receive company; these are kept remarkably clean, and the tiled floors are highly polished. But I cannot say so much for their inner apartments and the other parts of their houses, which are quite the reverse. I do not mean to insinuate that I have particularly examined their sanctoriums, which indeed few Europeans are tempted to do, but all the houses in India are so open and exposed, that thus much may be observed by a passing glance of the eye. Their furniture is remarkably heavy and clumsy, and of a shape which was perhaps in fashion some centuries ago. Their carriages and other pleasure vehicles in particular present the most grotesque and ludicrous appearance imaginable, and often afford a subject of much diversion and laughter to our countrymen, who have been accustomed to more recent modes.

A race known by the name of *Portuguese,* forms another part of the inhabitants of Ceylon. From their name, it might be supposed that they were the descendants of that European nation whose appellation they bear; but this in fact is by no means the case. The name is indeed derived from the spurious descendants of that people by native women, who were scattered in great numbers over this island and all their other settlements in India. But both the manners and colour of these original Indian Portuguese, are now equally lost among that race which now bears their name. The present Portuguese of Ceylon are a mixture of the spurious descendants of the several European possessors of that island by native women, joined to a number of Moors and Malabars. A colour more approaching to black than white, with a particular mode of dress, half Indian, and half European, is all that is necessary to procure the appellation of a Portuguese.

These people are found in all the European settlements in India, particularly those belonging to the Dutch, who often form intermarriages with them. It is in particular very common in Ceylon to see a respectable and wealthy Dutchman married to a Portuguese woman of this description; a connection which our countrymen look upon with the greatest abhorrence, and would not enter into on any account. The Dutchmen alledge that the cause of these intermarriages being so prevalent, is, that scarcely any woman leaves Holland to come to India except those who are already married.

The manners of the Portuguese differ from those of the Moors, Malabars, and other Mahometans. They affect rather to adopt those of the Europeans; and wear hats instead of the turbans, and breeches in place of the pieces of cloth, which other Indians wear wrapped round their waists, and drawn together between their legs like loose trowsers. At present it is customary for any black fellow who can procure a hat, and shoes, with a vest and breeches, and who has acquired some little smattering of the catholic religion, to aspire to the title of a Portuguese, a distinction of which he is extremely proud.

Although the black Portuguese universally profess the Christian religion, and are commonly Roman Catholics, yet they retain many Pagan customs, and their religion may be considered as a compound of both. They affect to derive their religion as well as their descent from the European Portuguese, though the name be almost the only thing they retain of either. The Dutch have allowed priests and other missionaries to go among them; and there are many of them who profess the Protestant religion and go to the churches of the Dutch. In general they are somewhat fairer than the Moors and Malabars; but those who are so to any considerable degree, may be looked upon as the offspring of the Dutch in later times; for the blood of the European Portuguese has been so intermixed as to leave scarce a trace behind. Complexions of all sorts are indeed found among this mongrel race, from a jetty black to a sickly yellow, or tawny hue. Their hair, which is black or dark brown, is worn long, and usually tied, contrary to the custom of the Mahometans. Some of their women are pretty, and much admired for their figures. The men are about the middle size, slender, lank, and ill-made, so as easily to be distinguished. Their whole expence runs upon dress; they are fond to excess of shew and finery, and never stir out without putting on their best clothes. They are lazy, treacherous, effeminate, and passionate to excess; and retain so much of the character of their boasted progenitors, as to be distinguished for a ridiculous pride. Like the Portuguese of Europe, they have always a long string of sounding names, beginning with Don Juan, Don Fernando, &c.

They have no regular cast, and are usually esteemed the worst race of people in India. Originally a spurious and outcast brood, they retain only the blemishes which tarnished the characters of their ancestors; and they combine all the vices of the Europeans and Indians, without any of their virtues.

It was from these black Portuguese, that the troops known by the name of *Topasses* were taken. They were called *Topasses* from wearing hats, instead of turbans; the word *topee*, or *chaupee*, which appears to be a corruption of the French *chapeau*, being the term used in their language for a hat. They were never accounted good soldiers, being neither so hardy nor so brave, as the Sepoys; and were seldom employed in the English service. The French, however, very generally had corps of them at Pondicherry, and their other settlements.

The *Malays* are another race, who form a considerable proportion of the inhabitants of Ceylon. This race, which is known to Europeans chiefly by the accounts of its barbarous ferocity, is widely scattered over the Eastern parts of India. Their original empire lies in the peninsula of Malacca; and from thence they have extended themselves over Java, Sumatra, the Moluccas, the Phillippines, and a vast number of other islands in the Archipelago of India. It is difficult to determine the date of their first introduction into Ceylon; but it has for many years been customary for the Dutch to bring them to this, and their other settlements in Asia and Africa, for the purpose of carrying on various branches of trade and manufactures, and also to employ them as soldiers and servants.

The religion, laws, manners, and customs of the Malays, as well as their dress, colour and persons, differ very much from those of all the other inhabitants of Asia. The Malays of the various islands and settlements also differ among themselves, according to the habits and appearance of the nations among whom they are dispersed. Yet still they are all easily distinguished to be of the Malay race. For, although they intermarry with the Moors and other casts, particularly in Ceylon, and by this means acquire a much darker colour than is natural to a Malay; still their characteristic features are so strikingly predominant, that they cannot be mistaken. Those who are born and brought up in the European colonies, naturally contract more of the habits of civilized society; they never indeed get entirely rid of their natural ferocity, but they become much less cruel and vindictive, than that part of their race who reside in the peninsula of Malacca and their other native possessions.

The men are of a middling stature, remarkably well proportioned, and of a strong and muscular make. Their legs and arms are particularly well-shaped, and very slender at the wrists and ancles; an ill made leg is scarcely ever to be seen among them. They are of a light brown or yellow colour, which approaches nearer to a copper hue in their old age, or when they are much exposed to the sun. Their forehead is broad and flat; their eyes small, black and very deep sunk; their nose flattish, broad towards the nostrils, with a sort of curve at the extremity approaching the lip. Their hair is long, coarse and black, and always moistened with a quantity of cocoa-nut oil. By some it is worn flowing loose over their shoulders, while others twist it up into a knot which they fasten on the back of the head with tortoise-shell combs. Some of the poorer sort bind it up with a coloured handkerchief.

The Malays of a higher rank wear a wide Moorish coat or gown, which they call *Badjour*, not unlike our dressing-gowns. It is composed of rich flowered silk, or fine cotton of various colours, according to the fancy of the wearer. Their under dress consists of a vest of silk or calico, called *Hadjou*, and worn close to their bodies, with loose wide drawers of the same stuff. On their head, they wear a dress of a curious shape, neither turban nor cap, but something of both, and often elegantly ornamented. The slipper or sandal in use among them, is the same with that worn by the Moors. The dress of the poorer sort consists of a piece of cotton wrapped round their waists, with one end drawn through between their legs, and tucked up at the lower part of the back. It is fitted close to their bodies, and the arms are left completely bare. Some wear a kind of vest or jacket without sleeves; and most of the slaves in the service of Europeans, instead of the piece of cloth, have breeches of some coarse stuff given them by their masters. None of the Malays suffer their beards to grow, but pluck out the hairs as soon as they appear, it being against their religion to allow them to remain.

The dress of the poorer classes of the women consists simply of a large piece of coarse calico, or cotton called a *Sarow*. It is folded and wound round the body above the bosom, which it partly covers, and reaches down to the ancle or the middle of the leg; the upper end of the cloth is tucked up, and fastened immediately under their arm pits. Their hair is twisted up behind like that of the men, and fastened with a fillet, or *condés*, those large pins or skewers I have already described.

The women of a superior station dress with much care and splendour, and sometimes a good deal of taste. They wear the *sarow* I have just mentioned, but of a finer stuff, and folded lower down on the waist. They have also a kind of boddice or close waistcoat, with sleeves reaching below the waist; it seems intended to cover the bosom, which, at the same time, it compresses and prevents from having its full and natural appearance. Over it they wear either a coloured silk, fine muslin, or calico garment of a wider shape and longer; with a girdle of the same, finely embroidered, drawn three or four times loosely round the waist. Over the whole is thrown the *badjou*, or loose robe, nearly resembling that worn by the men. Some instead of the *badjou*, use the *salendang*, a piece of silk or muslin about five feet long, thrown loosely around the neck and shoulders, so as to fall down before, and be brought across the waist backwards. Their hair is dressed with the conde-pins, and shines with cocoa-nut oil: on the crown and back part of the head are stuck three or four tortoise-shell combs with plates of gold. About their necks and arms they wear chains of gold or filigree and are all provided with ear-rings. Those of the higher order are remarkable for the expence of their dress. The Malays make most beautiful filigree work in gold, for ornaments to their persons.

The greater number of Malays have remarkably ugly faces; and their features strongly indicate their ferocious, treacherous, and revengeful dispositions. Yet some have comely countenances, and many of the women may even be accounted beautiful, especially such as are not much exposed to the sun, and have not had their noses compressed. It is a common practice with the mothers, soon after the birth of their children, to break by compression the gristle of the upper part of their noses, as the flat nose among this people is looked upon as a symbol of beauty. I have seen many very handsome young Malay women of a bright yellow or gold colour, and some even approaching to white. Yet Europeans will do well to avoid their allurements; for such connections are attended with much danger, and often end fatally. The men are extremely jealous, and particularly of the decided preference which the women give to Europeans. They never pardon infidelity in a wife; and although they allow an European to have connection with one unmarried woman, yet he runs little less risk from the object of his affections, than from a jealous husband. The passions of the women are equally violent with those of the men, and they are equally capable of taking the most terrible revenge. If their European paramour offers them the slightest neglect, or if he is suspected of having formed another attachment, they will not hesitate to revenge themselves either by stabbing him, or the equally fatal method of administering poison; a practice to which they are very prone.

The habits of the Malays in their infancy, are calculated to render them hardy. They go naked till about twelve years of age; and are shortly after married. As they are of the Mahometan religion, the higher casts marry as many wives as they can maintain; while their poverty restricts the lower classes to one wife.

Their usual food consists of fowl, fish, rice, and vegetables. The better sort also eat beef and mutton, when killed by one of their own race, and prepared in their own manner. When the Governor of any of our forts in Ceylon is to give an entertainment to the officers of the Malay corps, he sends for some of their own people to kill and dress the beef and mutton intended for table. They adhere very strictly to the Mahometan prejudices against swine, which they hold in such abhorrence that they will not so much as touch their flesh. I have seen servants of some of the Malay casts, even young boys, refuse to carry away a plate which had ham or bacon on it.

Their common drink is water, or the juice of the *palmyra;* although some of them make no scruple to drink arrack when they can procure it. All day long they chew the betel or penang, and smoke *bang* From this last herb a species of opium is prepared, which they chew in great quantities, as Europeans use strong drinks, to exhilarate their spirits. Too much of it, however, entirely deadens their senses, and reduces them to a state of complete stupefaction. I have frequently seen these people, after having chewed too large a portion of this noxious drug, lying speechless on the ground with their eyes fixed in a ghastly stare. Yet, such is the effect of habit, that they get completely infatuated with fondness for this drug, and absolutely cannot do without it.

The amusements of the Malays are suited to their dispositions, and are either bold, vigorous or ferocious. Both the men and women are intemperately fond of bathing, and often go into the bath several times in one day. They have a game which very nearly resembles our football; only the ball they use is made of twisted ratan. But the amusements of which they are particularly fond, are gaming and cock-fighting. Their passion for these is frequently carried to such excess, as to be attended with the most dreadful consequences. The poorer sort in particular, (like what is told of the ancient Germans), after having been stript of every thing else, will sell themselves and their families to procure the means of gratifying their passion for play; and after having lost their last stake, they often sacrifice themselves and their lucky antagonist to their despair.

The Malays have a great variety of musical instruments,

which are usually employed in a band or concert at their religious ceremonies, their marriages, and feasts. On these occasions that barbarous and grotesque pomp, in which uncivilized nations so much delight, is displayed in great profusion. A vast number of flags, streamers, figures of their gods, of men and beasts, which seem to delight in proportion to the hideousness of their appearance, are carried along in great pomp. The *Gong gong* is one of their principal instruments. It consists of a large hollow plate of a compound metal, so contrived in substance and shape as to return a very loud noise when struck. The *Tom tom*, is a drum of a peculiar fashion; and other instruments are formed of bamboes bound together with iron wire, something in the shape of a dulcimer. By means of this variety of instruments, which are made of all sizes from the most unwieldy bulk to the smallest, an effect not unpleasing is produced, from the contrariety of sounds.

The Malays universally profess the Mahometan religion, although, as to some inferior points and duties, the several classes differ among themselves. They have temples and mosques dedicated to their saints and their dead; and at these they punctually attend with great devotion.

A skill in medicinal herbs is almost universal among this race; and they have a variety of prescriptions for curing diseases by their application. This knowledge is owing to their peculiar fondness for gardening, and rearing all sorts of plants, an employment in which they are engaged from their infancy;

and it is from among them that the European gentlemen are anxious to procure their gardeners.

They are uncommonly ingenious in all sorts of cane-work, and in ratanning couches and chairs; and are accounted capital builders of *bungaloes*, or houses of the cocoa-tree.

In other respects, such as the manner of eating their victuals, and their modes of salutation, they very much resemble the natives of the Malabar and Coromandel coasts. They are, however, sufficiently distinguished from them, and indeed from all the other natives of India, by the difference of their institutions, and the peculiar ferocity of their dispositions.

The government, under which the Malays live in their own country, in some degree resembles the ancient feudal institutions of Europe; and war is consequently the business of the nation. The manners and disposition which naturally proceed from these institutions are found among them. They are all bold, warlike, and prepared for the most desperate enterprizes; they hear the commands of their superiors with the most profound reverence, and yield implicit obedience to their most rigorous orders. But the fierce temper arising from these military institutions, which in Europe has been softened by the Christian religion, has rather been exasperated by the religion which the Malays have embraced. None of that romantic spirit of chivalry, which produced the courtesy of civilized society amidst the ferocity of perpetual bloodshed, is to be found among the Malay followers of a prophet, who was as fierce and warlike as themselves. Accustomed to depend upon their courage, and avenge their own cause, there is more independence of spirit, and more appearance of a lofty intrepidity found among them, than among any other of the servile tribes of the east. Brave, ferocious, and desperate to the last dogree, on any occasion that requires blood to be shed; cruel and revengeful in their wrath, beyond what human nature can almost be thought capable of, they are looked upon with horror by the effeminate and timid Indians. I have often had occasion to observe these sentiments in the natives of Ceylon, who start affrighted on accidentally meeting a Malay soldier.

The arms which the Malays carry, are well suited to their savage and bloody disposition; and as on receiving any real or imaginary injury, they make no hesitation to sacrifice their own life in taking away that of the object they have marked out for vengeanee, they often do incredible mischief with the weapons which they wear about them. These consist of a kind of dagger, called a *Kreese* or *Crisse;* the blade of which is of the best tempered steel, and often made of a serpentine form, so as to inflict a most dreadful wound. The handle is of ivory or wood, carved into the figure of a man's body and arms, with a head representing something between that of a man and a bird. This they call their *Swammy* or god; and to this figure they make their *salam*, or obeisance, before they draw the kreese to execute any bloody purpose on which they have determined. After they have by this ceremony confirmed their vow, they draw their kreese, and never again sheath it till they have drenched it in blood. So resolute is this ferocious determination, that if their adversary is placed beyond the reach of their vengeance, sooner than infringe it, they will plunge the dagger into the body of a pig, a dog, a chicken, or any live animal they chance to meet. The scabbard is made of wood, frequently ornamented with gold or silver wire: and the whole appearance of the weapon, as well as the mode of wearing it on the right side, greatly resembles that found in the ancient dress of the Celtic nations. This terrible instrument is rendered still more so by its being always poisoned; generally by the juice of some poisonous herbs, and among those who can any wise procure it, with poison from the Upa tree.

In the use of their fatal weapon they are particularly dextrous, and like other barbarians make no scruple to employ treachery or surprise in destroying their enemies. They generally watch their opportunity, and stab their victim in the back or shoulder before he is aware. These daggers, the instruments of their ferocious cruelty, are looked upon by them with a degree of veneration. They descend, as a most sacred relic, from father to son, and from generation to generation: no money is accounted sufficient to purchase them, and no violence can compel their owners to give them up. When a Malay is pressed in battle, he will sooner be slain, or kill himself, than surrender his kreese to the enemy.

Before entering upon any desperate enterprise, it is customary with the Malays to take opium, or, as they term it, to *bang* themselves. This plant, the bang, which is used among the natives of India as an instrument of intoxication, is found over all that continent as well as in Ceylon. It is a small shrub, with a leaf in shape and texture resembling that of the tobacco, but not larger than the leaf of the sage. From this plant a species of opium is extracted, and being made into balls, is taken internally, and operates in the same manner as a dram of spirits among the European nations. The leaf of the bang is also dried and smoked like tobacco, with a still stronger intoxicating effect than the opium. After employing this method of rendering themselves insensible to danger, they are prepared for the most sanguinary atchievements, and rush blindfold into every atrocity. The horrid barbarities, however, which they commit on such occasions, are not so much to be attributed to their intoxication as to the natural savage cruelty of their dispositions. It is true, indeed, that before any bloody enterprise is undertaken, they first throw themselves into a state of temporary madness by means of bang; but the resolution to commit the crime preceded this state; they first in cold blood resolve to perpetrate their atrocities, and then use means to throw themselves into a phrenzy, that no sentiment either of humanity or fear may turn them aside from their bloody purpose. Some, who are anxious to clear human nature from such stains, without considering that they arise from situation and circumstances, attribute the unparalleled barbarity of the Malays to the quantity of opium which they take from their infancy, in consequence of which they are in an almost perpetual state of delirium. This delirium, however, is not of longer continuance than till the intoxicating quality of the drug has spent its force. In the intervals they are completely master of themselves; it is then they plan their enterprises; and the quantity of bang which they take is proportioned to their determination to perpetrate the crime they are about to commit. In fact, their institutions and their religion are sufficient to account for their character, without seeking for any other cause, and without accusing nature of having produced monsters.

The manner in which the Malays undertake to accomplish their revenge gives the most striking example of their ferocious dispositions. When a Malay has suffered any injury or grievance, real or imaginary, and ever so slight, the most dreadful thirst of revenge appears to take possession of his whole soul. He makes a vow to destroy the object of his vengeance, together with every other person who comes in his way, till he meet death from some hand or other. To prepare himself for this dreadful exploit, he takes a large quantity of bang, then draws his poisoned kreese, and rushing headlong into the street, stabs indiscriminately every one that comes in his way; at the same time crying aloud, *amok, amok*, or kill, kill, from whence this horrid mode of revenge is termed by Europeans *running a muck*. The fury of the devoted wretch is indescribable, and the mischief he often does is very great before a lucky shot brings him down. The natives fly before him in the utmost consternation, and hardly any person but an European dares venture to attack him. It is indeed a service of incredible danger to hunt down the mad savage, as he defends himself desperately to the last, and even though mortally wounded often contrives to destroy his antagonist by a stab of his poisoned kreese. The Dutch government at Ceylon found it necessary to repress this ferocious practice by the severest punishments. A reward of one or two hundred rix-dollars was offered for the destruction or capture of those who ran a muck; and such of them as were taken alive were put to death with the most excruciating torments.

The frequency of mucks in the Dutch settlements, seems attributable to the manner in which that nation behaved to their Malay dependants. The slaves and servants of the Dutch were chiefly composed of that race; and it is among this class that the instances of savage fury which we have described usually occurred. The cruel, capricious, and insulting behaviour of their masters exasperated their natural ferocity; and the impossibility of obtaining legal redress from their tyrants stimulated them to seek vengeance in the destruction of their masters, themselves, and the human species. At Batavia, and the Dutch settlements to the eastward, where their conduct is most despotic and cruel, mucks are greatly more frequent than in Ceylon, or at the Cape of

Good Hope. Since the arrival of the English at Ceylon, the barbarous practice has almost been unknown; and a few private murders committed on the Sepoys and black people in the Pettah, were the only crimes of this nature attributed to Malays during my stay at Columbo. No other cause can be assigned for this difference in the conduct of these people, but the superior mildness of the English government. So dreadful indeed is the frantic mode of revenge adopted by the Malays, that as long as their feelings continue to be exasperated by bad usage, it is necessary to impress their minds with fear by the severest punishments. But it is consistent with the nature of man to suppose that mild treatment, and the example of human manners, would by degrees soften their minds and restrain their passions within the bounds of civilized society, without these dreadful punishments which are too shocking ever to reform. The Malays, indeed, in their present state are, from their ideas of morality, almost incapable of being admitted into social life. They have no idea of revenge being a crime, and they triumph in shedding blood on such an occasion. Nothing indeed seems to prevent them from putting the most atrocious purpose into execution, when they have once resolved upon it. The introduction of Christianity among them, is the only means by which this unprincipled ferocity can be radically reformed; and it would certainly in a political view be of infinite service to us, that those Malays in our settlements should embrace this religion. It would be the firmest link which could unite them with this country. At present it is very uncomfortable for Europeans to be as much afraid of their servants and attendants as of a mad dog.

The Dutch Government at Ceylon had always a regiment of Malays in their service. That corps for a considerable time past seemed to form the strength of their garrisons, and were the only troops which either kept up discipline, or displayed any sort of bravery in the field. I have already mentioned that it was from them alone our troops met with any opposition, either at Columbo or Trincomalee. They seemed, indeed, to have imbibed such a rooted aversion for the English, that there was at first little appearance of their ever becoming our friends. This hatred had been inspired by the ungenerous policy of the Dutch, who endeavoured to secure their colonies by cherishing among the natives an implacable detestation of the other European nations, and in particular by representing the English as a nation of cruel and inhuman tyrants, who carried destruction and oppression wherever they came. These base and unjustifiable arts were not however always confined to mere misrepresentation; but the massacre of foreigners was at times had recourse to as a measure of precaution. The infamous affair at Amboyna has through the whole world circulated the eternal disgrace of the Dutch name. There is another instance of their abominable policy which is less known in Europe, but has excited general indignation in the Eastern world. In the year 1798, Captain Packenham of the Resistance happening to be with his ship at Timar, one of the Spice Islands which we have lately conquered, he was invited, along with his officers, by the Dutch Governor to an entertainment. Some circumstances prevented the Captain from accepting the invitation: his officers however went, and found with astonishment and horror, that the Dutch had made hospitality a pretext to obtain an opportunity of assassinating them. They were set upon without the least warning, and the first lieutenant and one or two more infamously murdered with some Sepoys who attempted to defend their officers. The surgeon, however, who was a very strong man, with the assistance of a couple of Sepoys fought his way to the beach, and made good his retreat to the ship. Upon the surgeon's representing this barbarous conduct of the Dutch, Captain Packenham instantly gave orders to fire upon the town, and it was in consequence soon reduced to ashes. The Dutch inhabitants, and all those who were concerned in the massacre, fled precipitately into the interior of the island. Several of the perpetrators of the crime were afterwards taken, and suffered for their treachery.

In the same year, an unfortunate affair took place at Amboyna, where the Malays murdered Lieutenant M'Crae of the Company's service, who happened to be quartered there; and several more of the English officers would have shared his fate, had they not been rescued by the troops. I will not take upon me to say how far the Dutch were implicated in the crime; but from their usual policy, and their conduct on other occasions, it was strongly suspected that they had instigated the Malays to perpetrate this savage act.

By such arts as I have described, the Dutch succeeded in inspiring the Malays with the most rooted aversion to our countrymen, and there was no piece of atrocity which they were not ready to commit on our troops. Several of the Malays have since told me, that on our taking possession of Ceylon, their minds had been exasperated to such a degree by misrepresentation, and an assurance of the Dutch that the English would give them no quarter, as to determine them to do us all the mischief in their power. The cowardly and base conduct of the Dutch, however, both in yielding without resistance to our troops, and in abandoning the Malays who fought their battles to their fate, has completely alienated the Malays from their former masters. They now look upon the Dutch with contempt, and call to mind their former tyrannical behaviour; while the brave and open conduct of the English has gone far to do away their former prejudices against us. After the capture of Columbo, the Malays for the first time during our long intercourse with India entered into our service. The regiment stationed there in the service of the Dutch was brought over to the British, and the command given to Captain Whitlie, one of the East India Company's officers. By his assiduous exertions and judicious conduct in the management of them during a considerable time, this corps was brought to a very excellent state of discipline, and rendered much attached to our government. They have since behaved universally with great respect and obedience to their European officers, and from being always well used by us have contracted a sincere regard to our service.

Soon after the arrival of Governor North on the island, he new-modelled this corps, and put it on a larger and more respectable establishment. Another European officer besides Captain Whitlie was assigned to it; the companies were officered by their own native captains and subalterns; and the Governor at the particular request of the corps took upon himself the station of their Colonel. Another change has since been introduced into the establishment of this regiment: the command has been given to Colonel Champagne, officers for it have been sent from Europe, and it has obtained a place among our other regiments of the line.

The Malay troops are armed and clothed much in the same manner as the European, with the exception of shoes, the wearing of which is contrary to the rules of their religion; instead of them they use a particular species of sandal. Along with their other arms they always wear their kreeses or poisoned daggers by their sides: in the heat of an engagement they often throw down their musket and bayonet, and rushing upon the enemy with these kreeses carry terror and destruction wherever they come. From having done duty in the same garrison with them for three years and a half, and having during that period lived in habits of intimacy with their native officers, I had an opportunity of minutely observing the character of the Malays as soldiers. From their natural intrepidity and hardiness, they are well calculated to become very useful and serviceable troops if properly officered and commanded. It requires however much management, much attention to their tempers, skill in regulating their economy, firmness in maintaining discipline, and at the same time great caution in punishing misbehaviour, to make our service reap in its full extent the advantage that might be derived from them. To their native officers, who were at that time chiefly from among their own princes and great men, they always paid the most implicit obedience, and seemed to hold them in the highest veneration. On being punished by sentence of a court-martial they never murmur, and their darling passion of revenge seems to be entirely laid aside. The contrast of this behaviour with their usual furious resentments on the most trivial occasions, struck me so forcibly, that I was induced to enquire the cause of some of their officers. I was told, that it was an ordinance of their religion, and a rule among their customs which was never infringed upon, to pay implicit obedience to all their officers, European as well as Malay, and to execute military orders with the strictest punctuality; and they were also enjoined never to murmur at any conduct of their superiors, or hesitate to execute orders as long as they received pay and continued in the service of any power. In addition to this, they are always tried for any offences by a court composed wholly of their own native officers, who are acquainted with their language and customs, and thus afford a security of every justice being rendered to the accused. The patience with which the Malays submit to the sentence of their court-martial, and their refraining from revenge when they are assured that justice is intended them, is another striking argument in support of what I have already advanced, that mild and generous treatment will in the end have the effect of subduing their natural ferocity.

CHAPTER VIII.

The Ceylonese—Their origin—Manners—Language—State of Society.

I Have now described those various races who for the purposes of conquest or commerce have settled in the sea-coasts of Ceylon. The far greater proportion of the inhabitants consists of the native Ceylonese who have submitted to the dominion of Europeans. When the Portuguese first arrived on the island, the whole of it, with the exception of the woods inhabited by the wild Bedas, was possessed by one race. The natives who inhabited the sea-coasts however were soon compelled either to fly for independence to their mountains, or to submit to their invaders. A great proportion of them chose the latter alternative, and preferred the comforts of the plains to the poverty and independence of barren fastnesses. It was indeed imposible for them all to retire to the mountains, as the interior parts barely supply the wants of their thinly-scattered inhabitants. It is known from their frequent insurrections that they at first bore the yoke of the Portuguese with reluctance: time however has rendered it familiar, and they are now reduced to a degree of abject obedience; in which they must continue to serve, unless some extraodinary chain of circumstances should concur to rouse their natural feelings.

The Ceylonese under the dominion of Europeans retain their original appellation of *Cinglese,* while those who live in those parts which acknowledge only the authority of their native princes, are distinguished by the name of *Candian,* from the country they inhabit. The constant intercourse of the Cinglese with Europeans, and the aversion which the Candians have uniformly entertained to their several invaders, have introduced considerable shades of difference into the manners of these two branches of the same people. In most points however they still continue to resemble each other; and a description of the one cannot fail to include most of the circumstances which characterize the other. I shall therefore give an account of these circumstances which apply to both under the general name of Ceylonese, and then point out those characteristics which distinguish the one from the other.

Whether the Cinglese were the original inhabitants of the island, or from what other country they came, and at what time they effected a settlement there, are points of which neither they themselves nor any one else has been able to give a distinct account. There is an ancient tradition among them that after the expulsion of Adam from this island, which they universally look upon to have been Paradise, it was first peopled by a band of Chinese adventurers who accidentally arrived on its coasts. This tradition is however extremely improbable, as they have nothing in common with the Chinese, either in their language, manners, or dress.

Those who suppose that Ceylon once formed part of the continent of India, and was disunited from it only by some unusual shock of nature, find no difficulty in peopling it with the same race who inhabited it before it became a separate island. Indeed the distance is so small between Ceylon and the continent, that it requires no stretch of imagination to suppose that it was peopled either from the Coromandel or Malabar coasts; and this is in fact the received opinion among most people. Some circumstances however seem to indicate that they have come from a greater distance; their complexion, features, language and manners are so similar to those of the Maldivians, that I should for my part be apt to conclude that both were of the same stock. The Maldive islands are only two or three days sail from Ceylon; and from the dissimilarity of the habits found among them to those of the Indians on the continent, it might be argued that the natives of these islands have not directly originated from those of Hindostan.

The Ceylonese are of a middling stature, about five feet eight, and fairer in complexion than the Moors and Malabars of the continent. They are however at the same time neither so well made nor so strong. I know no race they resemble so much in appearance as the Maldivians. The Candians are both fairer, better made, and less effeminate than the Cinglese in our service.

The women are not so tall in proportion as the men; they are much fairer, and approach to a yellow or mulatto colour. They continually anoint their bodies with cocoa-nut oil; and in particular always keep their hair moist with it. Both sexes are remarkably clean and neat both in their persons and houses. In dressing their victuals they are scrupulously nice. They are cautious not even to touch the vessel out of which they drink with their lips; but (what would seem a very awkward method to an European) they hold the vessel at some distance over their heads, and literally pour the drink down their throats. It is perhaps from the fear of not doing it with sufficient dexterity that they never use their left hand in preparing their food, or in eating it. While at meals, they seldom converse with each other: they even seem to look upon the whole business of eating as something rather required by necessity, than very consistent with decency: while drinking they never turn their faces towards each other.

In their diet they are exceedingly abstemious; fruits and rice constitute the chief part of their food. In some places where fish abounds, they make it a portion of their meals but scarcely any where is flesh in common use.

The Ceylonese are courteous and polite in their demeanour, even to a degree far exceeding their civilization. In several qualities they are greatly superior to all other Indians who have fallen within the sphere of my observation. I have already exempted them from the censure of stealing and lying, which seem to be almost inherent in the nature of an Indian. They are mild and by no means captious or passionate in their intercourse with each other; though when once their anger is roused, it is proportionably furious and lasting Their hatred is indeed mortal, and they will frequently destroy themselves to obtain the destruction of the detested object. One instance will serve to shew the extent to which this passion is carried. If a Ceylonese cannot obtain money due to him by another, he goes to his debtor, and threatens to kill himself if he is not instantly paid. This threat, which is sometimes put in execution, reduces the debtor, if it be in his power, to immediate compliance with the demand; as by their law if any man causes the loss of another man's life, his own is the forfeit. "An eye for an eye, and a tooth for a tooth," is a proverbial expression continually in their mouths. This is on other occasions a very common mode of revenge among them; and a Ceylonese has often been known to contrive to kill himself in the company of his enemy, that the latter might suffer for it.

This dreadful spirit of revenge, so inconsistent with the usual mild and humane sentiments of the Ceylonese, and much more congenial to the bloody temper of a Malay, still continues to be fostered by the sacred customs of the Candians. Among the Cinglese however it has been greatly mitigated by their intercourse with Europeans. The desperate mode of obtaining revenge which I have just described has been given up from having been disappointed of its object; as in all those parts under our dominion the European modes of investigating and punishing crimes are enforced. A case of this nature occurred at Caltura in 1799. A Cinglese peasant happening to have a suit or controversy with another, watched an opportunity of going to bathe in company with him, and drowned himself with the view of having his adversary put to death. The latter was upon this taken up and sent to Columbo to take his trial for making away with the deceased, upon the principle of having been the last seen in his company. There was, however, nothing more than presumptive proof against the culprit, and he was of course acquitted. This decision, however, did not by any means tally with the sentiments of the Cinglese, who are as much inclined to continue their ancient barbarous practice as their brethren the Candians, although they are deprived of the power.

There is no nation among whom the distinction of ranks is kept up with such scrupulous exactness as among the Ceylonese; even in the dimensions and appearance of their houses they seem restricted, and a house of a certain size commonly announces its proprietor to have been born in a certain rank. This strong trait of barbarism is of course more glaring among the inhabitants of the interior, than those who have been civilized by an intercouse with Europeans. The Candians are not allowed to whiten their houses, nor to cover them with tiles, that being a royal privilege, and reserved solely for the great king. Even among the Cinglese there is still something more than the difference of riches which affects their domestic economy.

It is difficult to say whether it be the remains of a tyrannical prohibition, or a superstition arising from the danger of electricity in this climate, that the Ceylonese never employ nails in the construction of their houses. Their small, low huts, which are too frailly united to admit of above one story, are fastened entirely with withes made of ratan, or coya rope. They are constructed of slender pieces of wood or bamboe, daubed over with clay, and covered with rice-straw or leaves of the cocoa-tree. Round the walls of their houses are small banks or benches of clay, designed to sit or sleep on. The benches as well as the floors of their houses are all laid over with cow-dung, to keep away vermin, and to preserve their surface smooth, and not so easily rendered dirty by rain as if it were of clay.

In such a state of society, and where luxury seems almost unknown, sumptuous furniture is not to be expected even in the best houses. That of the cottages is in the last stage of simplicity, and consists merely of the indispensable instruments for preparing their victuals. A few earthen pots to cook their rice, and one or two brass basons out of which to eat it; a wooden pestle and mortar for grinding it, with a flat stone on which to pound pepper, turmeric, and chillies for their curries; a *homeny*, or kind of grater, which is an iron instrument like the rowel of a spur fixed on a piece of wood like a boot-jack, and used to rasp their cocoa-nuts; these and a few other necessary utensils form the whole of their household furniture. They use neither tables, chairs, nor spoons; but like other Indians, place themselves on the ground, and eat their food with their hands. The houses of the Candians, are neater and better constructed than those of the Cinglese; for although the latter are accustomed to better models, yet the abject state to which their minds have been reduced by the successive tyranny of the Portuguese and Dutch, has made them rather go back than advance in improvement, since they ceased to form part of a barbarous empire.

Their villages and towns, instead of presenting that compact appearance to which we are accustomed, look more like a number of distinct houses scattered up and down in the midst of a thick wood or forest. There is not the smallest regularity observed, but every one places his hut in the centre of a cocoa-tree tope, in the most convenient spot he can find. In those mountainous parts where sustenance itself can scarcely be procured, and where the natives live in constant danger of attack from wild beasts, of being annoyed by reptiles, or suddenly overtaken by inundations, it is usual for them to build their huts on the summits of rocks, or the tops of high trees. Some of them fix a number of high posts in the ground, and place upon them a sort of hurdle which serves them for a nocturnal habitation. To preserve themselves from the intense rays of the sun, they universally have the large leaf of the talipot-tree carried over their heads.

The Ceylonese are exceedingly polite and ceremonious, and

never fail on meeting to present each other with the betel-leaf, their constant mark of respect and friendship. All ranks universally chew the betel-leaf; it is the dessert to all their entertainments, and the unfailing supplement to all their conversations. The betel-leaf in shape resembles ivy, but in colour and thickness it approaches more nearly to the leaf of the laurel. Along with the betel-leaf they mix tobacco, areka-nut, and the lime of burnt shells, to render it more pungent, as is the custom with other Indians. When chewed this mixture becomes as red as blood, and stains their mouth, lips, and teeth, of a black colour which can never be effaced. This effect, which to an European would deform the countenance, with them is considered as beautifying it, for they look upon white teeth as only fit for dogs, and a disgrace to the human species. The hot mixture, however, speedily destroys their teeth, and often renders them toothless at an early age. They also frequently stain their nails and fingers with the juice of the betel-leaf; but this seems to be attended with no bad consequence, as their hands are delicate and well formed in an uncommon degree.

There is a wonderful degree of gravity observed in conversation even among relations and intimate friends. It is not unusual to see a party of Ceylonese sit for a long time together as grave and mute as an assembly of Quakers when the spirit does not move them; and during all this while, they continue chewing betel-leaf as if for a wager, and apparently enjoying it as much as an Englishman would a bottle of old port.

In their salutations they are particularly punctilious: the form which they use is that common to all Indians, of bringing the palms of the hands to the forehead, and then making a *salam*, or low bow. It is here that the distinctions of rank are peculiarly observable: a person of a lower class on meeting his superior, almost throws himself prostrate before him, and repeats his name and quality fifty different ways; while the superior, stalking past with the most unbending gravity of features, scarcely deigns the slightest nod in return.

The natives of Ceylon are more continent with respect to women, than the other Asiatic nations; and their women are treated with much more attention. A Ceylonese woman almost never experiences the treatment of a slave, but is looked upon by her husband, more after the European manner, as a wife and a companion. These traits may seem very inconsistent with that licentious commerce among the sexes, which is so contrary to Asiatic customs and ideas, and which has prevailed from time immemorial in this island. Mr. Knox has drawn a picture of their total disregard to chastity, or any bounds to sexual intercourse, which is extremely abhorrent to the ideas not only of an Asiatic, but even to the inhabitants of the most dissolute Metropolis in Europe: and from my own observations among the Cinglese, and all the accounts which I could obtain of the Candians, I am convinced that he has in very few instances exaggerated their licentiousness.

A Cinglese husband is not in the smallest degree jealous of his wife, and is rather ambitious to display her to the public eye. Nor is he particularly offended at her infidelity to him, unless she be caught in the fact; in which case he thinks himself entitled to exercise the rights of an Asiatic husband. The infringement of chastity scarcely subjects a woman either married or unmarried to the slightest reproach, unless indeed they happen to have connexion with one of a lower cast; an act which is looked upon as the very excess of infamy. Among the Candians, in particular, this only distinction of moral turpitude, which is so worthy of a barbarous nation, is carried to the highest pitch. Even a man will scarcely venture to marry a woman of an inferior rank, nor would the King allow of it without exacting a large fine; but a woman is never known to form a connexion below her own sphere, as it would disgrace her in the eyes of the world for ever. With people of their own rank, on the contrary, the most unbounded commerce is carried on in private; and it is by no means uncommon, nor attended with any disgrace, for the nearest relations to have connexion with each other.

Among the Cinglese, the distinction of rank has indeed begun to be less strictly attended to; but without any better boundary being established in its place. A mother makes no scruple of disposing of her daughter's favours for a small sum to any one that desires them. They are particularly fond of forming such connexions with Europeans; and, instead of accounting it any reproach, a mother in quarrelling with any of her neighbours, will silence them at once on the score of her superior dignity, by telling them that her daughter has had the honour to lie with an European. Even women of the highest rank do not think themselves degraded by having connexion with Europeans, and are not ashamed to be seen by them in public. This forms a remarkable contrast with the Mahometan women of the continent, who would think themselves disgraced and polluted if any of their features were even by accident discovered to a stranger.

In some respects the accounts given of the matrimonial connexions of the Ceylonese are incorrect. It has in particular been said that each husband has only one wife, although a woman is permitted to cohabit promiscuously with several husbands. This however is not always the case: many of the men indeed have but one wife, while others have as many as they can maintain. There is no positive regulation on the subject, and it is probable that the ease with which promiscuous intercourse is carried on, and the ease with which marriages are dissolved, is, together with their poverty, the true cause why polygamy is not more general among them. In their particular circumstances indeed. where the houses consist often of but one apartment, and even the necessaries of life are so scanty, it is not to be supposed that a man will voluntarily undertake the burden of maintaining two wives, when he can at pleasure put away the wife he begins to get tired of, and take in her place the new object of his affections.

The marriage ceremony, which among nations with stricter ideas of chastity is looked upon with a degree of mystery and veneration, is a matter of very small importance among the Ceylonese, and seems to be at all attended to only with a view to entitle the parties to share in each others goods, and to give their relations an opportunity of observing that they have married into their own cast. The marriages are often contracted by the parents while the parties are as yet in a state of childhood, merely with a view to match them according to their rank, and are often dissolved by consent almost as soon as consummated. It is also customary for those who intend to marry, previously to cohabit and make trial of each others temper;. and if they find they cannot agree, they break off without the interference of the priest, or any further ceremony, and no disgrace attaches on the occasion to either party, but the woman is quite as much esteemed by her next lover as if he had found her in a state of virginity.

After the parties have agreed to marry, the first step is, that the man present his bride with the wedding-clothes, which indeed are not of the most costly kind: they consist of a piece of cloth, six or seven yards in length, for the use of the bride, and another piece of cloth to be placed on the bed. It gives us a striking idea of the total want of industry among the Ceylonese, and their extreme state of poverty, that even these simple marriage presents are frequently beyond the ability of the man to purchase, and that he is often obliged to borrow them for the occasion from some of his neighbours.

The wedding presents are presented by the bridegroom in person, and the following night he is entitled to lie with the bride. Upon this occasion is appointed the day for bringing her home, and celebrating the wedding with festivities. On that day he and his relations repair to the bride's house, carrying along with them what they are able to contribute to the marriage-feast. The bride and bridegroom, in the presence of this assembly, eat out of one dish to denote that they are of the same rank. Their thumbs are then tied together; and the ceremony concludes by the nearest relations, or the priest, when he is present, cutting them asunder. This, however, is accounted a less binding ceremony, and indeed scarcely intended for continuance. When it is desired to make the marriage as firm and indissoluble as the nature of their manners will allow, the parties are joined together with a long piece of cloth, which is folded several times round both their bodies; and water is then poured upon them by the priest, who always officiates at this ceremony although rarely at the former. After the marriage ceremony, whether the stricter or the less binding one, is performed, the parties pass the night at the bride's house; and in the morning the husband brings her home, accompanied by her friends, who carry with them provisions for another feast. In bringing home the bride a strange ancient custom is observed; the bride is always obliged to march before her husband, and never to be out of his sight by the way. The traditionary reason for this practice is, that a man on this occasion once happening to walk foremost, his wife was carried off from him before he was aware; a circumstance not at all unlikely to happen more than once among a people who think so lightly of the marriage ties. The wedding-day is always looked upon as a time of particular festivity; and those who are able to afford it, never fail to have the feasts accompanied with music and dancing; the merriment is often protracted, and certain nuptial songs continue to be carolled the whole night long.

The portion given with the daughter is in proportion to the ability of the parents; and if the young couple are not in circumstances to maintain themselves, they still continue to reside with their parents. If the young people find after marriage that their dispositions do not agree, they separate without ceremony; only the woman carries with her the portion she brought, in order to make her as good a match for her next husband. Both men and women often marry and divorce several times in this manner, before they have found a partner, with whom they can reconcile themselves to spend the remainder of their days.

Owing to the early intercourse of the women with the

other sex, for they are in general even regularly married at twelve, they soon lose the appearance of youth, and get old and haggart in their looks immediately after they pass twenty. The climate indeed conduces much to this early decay; and they expose themselves so much to the sun, that were it not for the quantities of cocoa-nut oil with which they anoint themselves profusely, their skins would soon crack and break out in blotches.

The Cinglese women are much more pleasant in their manners, and I may add, more elegant in their persons than those of the other Indian nations. Their extreme cleanliness is a trait which renders them particularly agreeable to an Englishman, although he finds it something difficult to reconcile himself to the strong exhalations of the cocoa-nut oil.

The Ceylonese, like other inhabitants of warm climates, are particularly fond of bathing, and often plunge into the water several times a day. In this gratification, however they are often interrupted by alligators of whom they entertain the greatest terror; and are obliged to have recourse to precautions against this dreadful enemy, by inclosing with a strong paling a little spot on the side of a pond or river, sufficiently large to allow them room to wash and refresh themselves.

Gravity, that constant characteristic of the savage state, still continues among the Ceylonese in a much greater degree than might be expected from their stage of civilization. This is probably owing to the gloomy superstitious fears which they imbibe from their infancy, and which continue to embitter their existence ever after. Sports and diversions are almost entirely unknown among them. None of them attempt those tricks and feats of activity for which the natives of Hindostan are so famous; for all the jugglers, dancers, and conjurors, who are at any time found in Ceylon, are universally from the continent. The dispirited and oppressed state under which the Cinglese have so long groaned, may indeed be supposed to have among them extinguished the practice of their original amusements; but during the whole time of my stay on the island, and after the minutest enquiries, I never could learn of any diversions in use among the Candians. It is indeed to be supposed that in their more flourishing state, they had like other nations, some recreations for their leisure hours; and Mr. Knox records one or two which in his time still continued in use at new-years and particular festivals: but their perpetual contests with the Portuguese and Dutch, joined to the tyranny of their own internal government, have probably succeeded, along with the gloom of their superstition, in destroying those glimmerings of humane and social enjoyment, which were just beginning to break through the dark ferocity of barbarism.

During the wet season, the Ceylonese are subject to a variety of diseases. Every man is here his own physician, and the mode of cure practised is of course very simple. A plaister of herbs or of cow dung is universally applied to the part affected; and I have seen the same remedy applied to a man in a high fever, when his whole body was daubed over with this ointment. Leprosy appears to be very prevalent among them, and the streets of Columbo swarm with Cinglese beggars labouring under this distressing disease. I have seen some of these objects with their skins party-coloured, half black and half white; for this disease leaves white blotches and spots in all those places of the skin where it breaks out, and it is not uncommon to see one limb completely white while the other retains its natural black colour.

The disease which particularly excites their apprehension is the small-pox. It is looked upon as the immediate instrument of God's vengeance, and therefore they do not venture to use any charms or incantations for their recovery, as they are accustomed to do in all other diseases. If any one dies of it, he is looked upon as accursed, and even his body is denied the rites of burial. It is carried out to some unfrequented place, and there left with a few bushes or branches of trees thrown over it. It is to be hoped that an intercourse with our countrymen will in time do away these gloomy notions of fatality, and that the effect of remedies on the Europeans will induce the natives also to adopt them. It would be an object worthy the attention of Government to cause to be introduced among them, the inoculation for the cow-pox, which has lately been discovered for the deliverance of mankind from a most fatal pestilence. The Governor might insist that all the children within our jurisdiction should undergo this operation.

The language of the Ceylonese may appear the best clue by which to trace out their origin; but it only serves to involve our conjectures in greater obscurity. Their language appears almost completely peculiar to this island. It is spoken by none of the Malabars or other nations on the continent of India; nor can any of them be instructed in it without considerable difficulty. If I might be allowed to offer an opinion on a subject that requires the profound investigation of the learned, I should say that it appears to me most nearly allied to the Maldivian. I had an opportunity of observing the similarity both in this and in other respects between these people and the Ceylonese, while I was stationed at Columbo; it being a custom with the King of the Maldive Islands to send an ambassador yearly with presents to our Governor at Ceylon, in order to maintain a friendly understanding with us. The Maldivians of his retinue both in shape, complexion, and habit, approached much nearer to the Ceylonese than to any of the Malabar race; and their language appeared to me to follow the same rule.

There are in fact two dialects of the Ceylonese language differing very considerably from each other, and having each a separate Grammar. The poetic or court language is also styled the *Candian Sanscrit,* or more properly the *Paulee,* or *Mangada.* This dialect, which is retained in those parts of the interior, where the language may be supposed to be preserved in its greatest purity, contains a considerable mixture of Arabic, and is accounted the most elegant as well as the most smooth and sonorous. The learned will judge of the inference to be drawn from the Arabic forming so considerable a portion of the Ceylonese language in those parts where it is spoken in its original purity. The current opinion among the natives is, that Arabic is their original language, and that some mixture of the Sanscrit was introduced by a colony who came over by Adam s bridge from the continent of India. Among the Cinglese on the coasts, the vulgar dialect, distinguished by the name of the *Cinglese,* is spoken: it has been greatly corrupted by the introduction of foreign words, and that melody and force which is attributed to the language of the interior, is here no longer discernible. If I may judge from the impression made upon me during my residence on the island, the Cinglese spoken on the coasts is much inferior to any of the other Indian languages which I have heard.

The hyperbolical strain of compliment and adulation which is common to all the Asiatic nations, is found no where in greater perfection than in the island of Ceylon. There is here a degree of punctilious minuteness with which the phraseology employed is exactly adjusted to the rank of the person addressed, that altogether astonishes an European. There is no impropriety which a man can be guilty of more unpardonable in their eyes, than addressing a superior in language that is only fit for an equal or an inferior.

There is something very peculiar in the pronunciation of the Ceylonese. They seem to steal out the first part of the sentence in such a manner as scarcely to catch the attention, and then dwell with a loud and long accent on the concluding syllables. They are particularly fond of closing with an emphatic *ye* or *ah*, which forms the last syllable of a great number of their words.

They divide their time nearly as we do, only their year commences on the twenty-eighth of March. The manner in which they make allowance for Leap-year, and the odd portions of time which are not reduceable to the regular calculation, is by beginning their year a day sooner or later, or in other words by adding a day to the former year. The first month of the year they name *Wasachmahayé*, the second *Pomahayé*, and so on; every one ending in the favourite syllable *ayé*. Their months are, like ours, divided into weeks of seven days. The first day of the week which corresponds with our Sunday, they call *Fridahé*, then, *Sandudahé*, *Onghorudahe*, *Bodadahé*, *Braspotindahé*, *Secouradahé*, *Henouradahé*. Wednesday and Saturday are the days on which they perform their religious ceremonies. The day, which is reckoned from sun-rise to sun-set, is divided into fifteen hours, and the night into as many, which forms a pretty regular division of time, as the length of the day and night varies very little in this latitude.

In their state of society, the exact measurement of time is

not of particular consequence, and therefore we find them very little solicitous about dealing out scrupulously an article of which they do not understand the value. It does not appear that before the arrival of Europeans on the island, the Ceylonese had contrived even the rudest species of dial. On any particular occasion, they employed a vessel with a hole in the bottom, that let out the water with which it was filled in one hour according to their division. This rude instrument was sufficient for all their purposes; and was even seldom employed unless at court ceremonials.

The learning of the Ceylonese consists chiefly in some pretended skill in astrology. It appears indeed, that they were formerly possessed of some literature, as well as of some refinement in the arts. At Adam's peak, their principal place of worship, and in the ruins of some of their temples, certain inscriptions have been discovered which they are now unable to decypher. The Dutch repeatedly sent some of the most ingenious Malabars, as well as persons from the various continental tribes, to examine these inscriptions; but although they were accompanied by the natives, and assisted by all their traditions, no interpretation could be effected. In the neighbourhood of Sittivacca I had an opportunity to see several of these inscriptions among the ruins of a pagoda.

To read and write are no ordinary accomplishments among the natives of Ceylon. These arts are among the Candians chiefly confined to the learned men of the sect called *Gonies*, who are retained by the king to execute all the writings of state, and those which respect religious affairs. The Arabic is the character which they employ on these occasions.

For writing, as they do not understand the art of making paper, they employ the leaf of the talipot tree. From these leaves, which are of an immense size, they cut out slips, from a foot to a foot and a half long, and about a couple of inches broad. These slips are smoothed, and all excrescences pared off with a knife, and are then, without any other preparation, ready to be used. A fine pointed steel pencil, like a bodkin, and set in a wooden or ivory handle, ornamented according to the taste of the owner, is employed to write or rather engrave their letters or characters on these talipot slips which are very thick and tough. In order to render the characters more visible and distinct, they rub them over with oil mixed with charcoal reduced to powder, and this has the effect also of rendering them so permanent, that they can never be effaced. When one slip is not sufficient to contain all that they intend to write on any particular subject, they string several together by a piece of twine passed through them, and attach them to a board in the same way as we file news-papers.

Palm leaves are sometimes employed for the same purpose, but those of the talipot both from their breadth and thickness are preferred. Few of the natives, and those only of the higher order who have much connexion and long accounts to keep with the Europeans, employ any other materials in writing than those which I have just described.

There is also a sort of paper, made of the bark of a tree, sometimes used.

I have seen several of those talipot books or files, called by the natives *olioes*, richly ornamented and bound in thin lacquered boards of ivory, or even silver and gold. They are particularly dexterous and accurate in their mode of writing. In those letters or dispatches which were sent by the king to the Dutch government, the monarch seemed particularly anxious to display his magnificence in the richness and splendour with which they were executed. The writing was enclosed in leaves of beaten gold in the shape of a cocoa-tree leaf. This was rolled up in a cover richly ornamented and almost hid in a profusion of pearls and other precious stones. The whole was enclosed in a box of silver or ivory, which was sealed with the Emperor's great seal The same splendour has been observed in the letters sent to our Governor since we have had possession of the island.

The progress of the Ceylonese in the other arts of life is proportionate to their literature. Their agriculture is still in the rudest state; and perhaps there is no other part of India where the lands are cultivated with more negligence. The Ceylonese are naturally, like other tribes who inhabit a mountainous country, and have been accustomed to the habits of pastoral life, indolent in the extreme. Their soil, where it can be watered, yields them a sufficient quantity of rice to maintain their existence, and this seems almost as much as they desire. The example of the Europeans in the cultivation of the cinnamon has not yet awaked a spirit of emulation among the natives, nor has any improvement of their rude agricultural instruments been as yet introduced. Their plough consists merely of a crooked piece of wood, shaped in such a manner that the one end serves for a handle, while the other which is shod with iron to prevent the wood from wearing, ploughs, or rather tears up the ground. This very rude instrument however, serves their purpose, as it is not required to make regular furrows, but merely to loosen the earth so as to allow the water with which they inundate it to drench it completely. After a first ploughing with this instrument the fields are flooded; and after they have lain some time under water, it is let off, and they are ploughed anew. The water besides nourishing the rice serves the purpose of rotting the weeds. The only good trait in their husbandry is the care with which they guard against weeds: this indeed costs them little labour where they have an opportunity of flooding the grounds. The other tools they employ in agriculture are a board for smoothing their fields, which they drag over them edgewise with their oxen; and a piece of board fastened to the end of a long pole, which serves them in place of rakes.

When the season for ploughing arrives, each village makes it a common concern, and every one attends with his plough and his oxen till the whole of the fields belonging to that society be finished. The same method is followed in reaping the corn; and both the seed time and harvest become in this manner the seasons of general industry and good fellowship. Each person of the society affords provisions to the whole during the time they are cultivating his fields. The women are not employed in either of these laborious operations; their business is to gather the corn after the reapers, and assist in saving it.

Oxen are employed both in ploughing and in treading out the corn. This method of separating the rice from the straw, is in reality much more expeditious than our method of threshing out corn; and as it is also attended with much less labour, a consideration always of the highest importance to a Ceylonese, it is probable that the practice will be continued. For unhusking their rice, the mode they employ is to beat it in a mortar, or more frequently on a hard floor; or if the rice be of a brittle sort, and likely to break in pieces, they boil it previous to beating it out. Water is the only manure which they think requisite.

It is evident from this sketch of their agriculture, that the lands of Ceylon do not produce a crop at all equal to what by proper cultivation they might be made to bear The introduction of a more improved method would, in all probability, soon render the island capable not only of supporting its present inhabitants, but also of affording resources sufficient for a much encreased population.

The extreme indolence into which the Ceylonese are at present sunk, makes them employ every expedient to escape labour, and the small quantity of food which is necessary for the support of their existence, enables them throughout the greater part of the year literally to live without doing any thing. Small as is the labour required for the cultivation of their rice fields, many of them let their grounds to their neighbours, who are not altogether so lazy, for a certain proportion of grain, generally about one-third of its produce. There are a number of deductions which prevent them from receiving a larger proportion: a considerable quantity is carried off by the priests for the service of their temples, or is offered up for protection and thanksgiving, both on account of the blessings they have received, and in the hope of farther assistance.

CHAPTER IX.

Religion of the Ceylonese.

THE religion of the Ceylonese is one of the most prominent features in a description of them, and mixes with every circumstance of their lives and manners. There is no people who labour more under the influence of superstitious fears. Omens regulate their whole conduct, and even decide upon their destiny from their birth. When a child is born, the first step is to call the astrologer, and enquire of him whether it is destined to be fortunate or unfortunate. If the astrologer declares that it was born to misfortune, they frequently anticipate its future evils by destroying it. On going out in a morning, they anxiously observe the first object which occurs to them, and according to their opinion of its good or bad luck, they prognosticate whether the business they go about shall be prosperous or unsuccessful. A white man or a woman with child are looked upon as omens particularly fortunate; but to meet with a beggar or a deformed person, they account a grievous mischance, and will not proceed for that day on their intended business if they can avoid it. I have in my morning rides seen a string of Cinglese, cautiously treading in one another's footsteps and anxiously expecting, from the omen that should occur to the foremost, their good or bad success for that day. I, as an European, was always a glad sight to them.

The excess of trembling superstition which unhinges the minds of the Ceylonese is in a great measure to be attributed to the climate in which they live. One might imagine from the frequency of thunder storms in Ceylon that the natives would become gradually accustomed to it. But the noise of the thunder is too terrible, and the unseen effects of the lightning too dreadful, for the minds of any but these who know something of the causes of those natural phænomena, ever to get completely rid of their apprehensions of them. The poor Ceylonese looks upon these storms as a judgment from heaven, and as directed by the souls of bad men who are sent to torment and punish him for his sins. The frequency of thunder storms with them, they consider as a proof that their island is abandoned to the dominion of devils; and recollect with melancholy regret that this fated spot was once inhabited by Adam, and the seat of Paradise. The fiends which they conceive to be hovering around them are without number. Every disease or trouble that assails them is produced by the immediate agency of the demons sent to punish them: while on the other hand every blessing or success comes directly from the hands of the beneficent and supreme God. To screen themselves from the power of the inferior deities, who are all represented as wicked spirits, and whose power is by no means irresistible, they wear amulets of various descriptions; and employ a variety of charms and spells to ward off the influence of witchcraft and enchantments by which they think themselves beset on all sides.

Such is the hold which these chimeras have from their infancy taken of the distempered brain of the Ceylonese, that they find it impossible by any extension of their knowledge or experience of their folly, ever to escape from their grasp. Many even of those who have been converted to Christianity, still labour under their original terrors; and look with regret and envy on the fortitude of the Europeans that is able to resist these delusions; for delusions they own and believe them to be even while they groan under their influence. Those however who live in Columbo and the other towns of the island where they have an opportunity of profiting by the example of Europeans, have been able to bring their minds to a comparative state of tranquillity. Some of them even go so far as to set their inferior deities at open defiance. It is not indeed uncommon with the Cinglese, upon not having their desires complied with, or upon meeting with a series of bad luck in spite of their repeated prayers, to quarrel with their divinities, revile them, and even trample their images under foot. It is probable that by degrees intercourse with Europeans will entirely do away these superstitious fears, as the Cinglese of the towns have already made considerable progress in subduing their gloomy apprehensions.

Not so the poor wretched peasants who inhabit the more mountainous parts of the country, and live at a distance from our settlements. These unhappy people have never for a moment their minds free from the terror of those demons who seem perpetually to hover around them. Their imaginations are so disturbed by such ideas, that it is not uncommon to see many driven to madness from this cause. Several Cinglese lunaticks have fallen under my own observation; and upon enquiring into the circumstances which had deprived them of their reason, I universally found that their wretched state was to be traced solely to the excess of their superstitious fears.

The spirits of the wicked subordinate demons are the chief object of fear among the Ceylonese; and impress their minds with much more awe than the more powerful divinities who disperse blessings among them. They indeed think that their country is in a particular manner delivered over to the dominion of evil spirits; nor is this idea confined to themselves alone; the Malabars and other Indians are also possessed with it, probably from the uncommon frequency of thunder storms there; and the same cause has made this idea current even among the Dutch inhabitants.

There is a curious proof of superstitious opinions in the narrative of our countryman, Mr. Knox, who himself believed that he had heard in Ceylon the devil crying aloud in the night-time with a voice something resembling the barking of a dog.

The progress of civilization and the removal of superstitious fears among the Ceylonese are greatly opposed by the interested arts of their priests; and they well know how to make the devils forage for them. To prevent fruit being stolen, the people hang up certain grotesque figures around the orchard and dedicate it to the devils, after which none of the native Ceylonese will dare even to touch the fruit on any account. Even the owner will not venture to use it, till it be first liberated from the dedication. For this purpose, they carry some of it to the pagoda, where the priests, after first receiving a certain proportion for themselves, remove the incantations with which it was dedicated. If any part of the fruit, after its dedication has been stolen by some of their less scrupulous neighbours, they break out into the most extravagant execrations against the devils who have been base enough to betray the pledge entrusted to their charge.

The superstitious fears and ceremonies of the Ceylonese form the chief part of their devotion towards supernatural beings. With regard to what may be properly termed their religion, neither the Europeans nor indeed they themselves seem to have formed any clear idea. Some have asserted that it is the same with that of the Hindoos with only a slight variation of forms and names. Nothing however is easier than to trace resemblances between religions where we give free scope to the imagination, and allow ourselves the liberty of altering terms at pleasure. The religion of the Ceylonese appears to me to be founded on a different system of idolatry from that practised among the Hindoos. A variety of ideas indeed seem to be borrowed from the latter; and with these a large mixture of Mahometanism is very perceptible. In one point they agree with both, as well as with Christians, in acknowledging one Supreme Being who made and governs all things. They differ however as widely from the Mahometans and rigid Hindoos in another respect; for although they are unable to conquer their original superstitions, they entertain the highest reverence for the Christian religion; and some of the Cinglese have been converted without being hardly censured by others for their apostacy. It gives us a striking proof of the wonderful confusion of their ideas with regard to religion, when we find that the same people who adore one Supreme Being more powerful than all others, should at the same time offer up their devotions to devils, animals, and the very productions of the earth.

Besides the one Supreme Being, who is worshipped as the Creator and Ruler of heaven and earth, the Ceylonese have a number of inferior deities besides tormenting demons. The inferior deities who watch over them for good are supposed to be the souls of good men; while the demons are looked upon as the spirits of the wicked; and both are supposed to act by the permission of the Supreme Being.

The next in dignity to him is their God Buddou, the Saviour of souls. This idea of a Saviour seems in some degree to pervade every religion in the world, although tainted by a variety of different superstitions which are joined to it; and what is remarkable, the expectations formed from the interference of this Saviour are in almost every religion nearly the same. Buddou, according to the most general tradition, was originally the spirit of a good man, who was again sent to revisit the earth; and after having performed a prodigious number of virtuous actions, and been transformed into a hundred and ninety-nine different shapes, reascended into heaven, and is still employed in procuring the pardon of his worshippers. The introduction of the worship of Buddou into Ceylon is fixed at about forty years after the Christain era, at which time, some say, a violent quarrel took place between the Brahmins and the followers of Buddou who then formed one of the religious sects on the continent. The Brahmins prevailed, and the Buddites were compelled to take refuge in Ceylon. What religion subsisted there before, or if the same religion then prevailed, is a fruitless and unavailing inquiry. The Buddites are said to have been originally a sect of monks, or rather hermits, who led a wandering solitary life, remarkable for chastity, renouncing all the pursuits of the world, and all care of property, and contented with the support of piety amidst the extremest poverty.

It is alleged that Buddou is worshipped in Pegu and

several other parts of the continent, under a different name, the deity of the moon.

The priests of Buddou are in Ceylon accounted superior to all others. They are called *Tirinanxes*, and are held in high estimation at the court of Candy, where indeed they have the chief management of affairs. The king has no authority over them, but endeavours to gain their good-will by respecting their immunities, and loading them with distinctions. They have on many occasions shewn their gratitude for these attentions, and have materially assisted him both in repressing disturbances in his own dominions. and by exciting the people to support him in his wars against the Dutch. The followers of Buddou believe in the immortality of the soul and its transmigration into various bodies before it reaches Nimban or the region of Eternity.

In such high veneration are the Tirinanxes held that their persons are accounted sacred; and the king of Candy, absolute as he is, has no power to take away their lives or anywise punish them even for conspiring against his own life. They chuse their own superiors; and their chief priest or archbishop is invested with the power of settling all religious disputes. The body of the Tirinanxes are elected by the king from among the nobles, and they are consequently men possessed of power and influence even independent of their sacred character. The honours and respect with which they are every where attended shew the strong hold which they have on the minds of the people. All ranks bow down before them; when they sit down, they find their seats covered with a white cloth; and when they walk forth, the broad end of the Talipot leaf is borne before them: All these are privileges of the highest kind, and shared with them only by the monarch. The Tirinanxes are also exempted from all taxes. They are placed under certain restrictions, and are totally debarred from wine or women. They have however an opportunity of escaping from these restraints; and are allowed to lay aside their order when it suits their inclination.

Their dress consists of a large loose piece of yellow cloth thrown over their left shoulder, and fastened round the waist by a girdle of the same. The right shoulder, the arms, the head, and the feet, are completely bare. In one hand they carry a painted cane, and in the other an umbrella of the broad end of the Talipot leaf.

The temples of Buddou are superior to those of all the other deities; for they never dedicate temples to the Supreme Being, nor represent him by any image. In the temples of Buddou are figures of men habited, like his priests, and placed in various postures: some of them are seen setting cross-legged on the ground with long bushy heads of hair like their women, while others recline at full length on the ground. At Ruanelli in the interior, I saw a monstruous figure upwards of twenty feet in length, placed in the cavern of an immense rock which lay at the bottom of a hill: I shall describe it more particularly in my account of the embassy to Candy.

In the interior of Ceylon, the ruins of the pagodas and temples which fell in my way were all of hewn stone, and of much superior workmanship to these in the lower parts of the country. Several of them were in a perfect state of preservation; and on a comparison with those erected in later times, they afford the strongest proof either that the Ceylonese had formerly attained a much higher state of civilization, or that the island had anciently been inhabited by a different race from its present possessors. Most of these ancient monuments however have suffered severely from the ravages of the Portugueze, whose policy it was to destroy all monuments of art or former splendour among the unhappy natives. But the religious buildings of the Ceylonese were not only defaced and ruined by their barbarous invaders; even the materials which composed them, the hewn stones and massy pillars, were transported to the sea-coasts to erect fortifications, and rivet those chains which were imposed on their former worshippers.

The temples dedicated to the inferior gods are poor, mean, and contemptible; and usually constructed of clay and wood. In general they are mere huts one story high, without windows, and covered with cocoa-tree leaves. At the doors of these homely edifices, a pole or flag is commonly placed, and by it a priest is seen sitting during the whole course of the day. There is no figure too ridiculous to find a place within: besides Swammies of all constructions, there are representations of wild beasts, birds, pieces of consecrated armour, and some very indecent figures of men and women.

The priests of the inferior deities, though dressed in the same manner with the Tirinanxes, are easily distinguishable by the smaller degree of respect which is paid them. They are continually met in their wandering excursions over the island, and, like all these of the same class in India, are a set of lazy, impudent vagabonds, who, without any exertion or industry, are enabled to live well by the extortions which they practise on the people. Even those who supply their demands are conscious of their vices; but superstitious fears have taken too deep a hold on the minds of the votaries to permit them to withdraw themselves from the yoke.

The superstition of the Ceylonese serves instead of regular endowments for the support of their religious establishments. The Candians indeed allow certain portions of land and particular taxes to maintain their priests and religious houses, particularly those of Buddou. The inferior priests however are left to support their temples and themselves by their own dexterity, and in this task they are very successful. As all sorts of diseases are accounted immediate indications of the divine wrath, the priest and the temple are the constant remedies. Hence all the religious resorts are daily crowded with diseased votaries, who expect, by the prayers which they offer up, to appease the incensed gods. Nor do they ever neglect to enforce their prayers by a gift, which they devoutly deposit on the altar. The priest presents it up with all due ceremony to the god; and after its purpose is thus served, very prudently converts it to his own use. It is a rule with their priests never to quit the temple till replaced by some of their own order; and by this means the offerings of the devotees are punctually received, while another party of the priests are making a tour of the country in search of casual contributions.

The time of sickness is of course the season when the priests expect their principal harvest. Besides other offerings, it is usual for a Ceylonese when he is apprehensive of danger from his illness, to devote a cock to the devil or evil spirit who he imagines torments him. The animal is then left at home to fatten till the Jaddese or priest finds it convenient to dedicate him at the Covel or temple. When any particular festival or sacrifice is intended, it is usual to see the priest going from village to village to collect the dedicated cocks for the occasion; and he often procures several dozens at a time.

The days appointed for attendance on the places of religious worship, are the Wednesday and Saturday of every week: the sick however flock daily to them. There are several particular festivals held in honour of their gods, and with a view to conciliate their favour. In the month of June or July at the new moon called *perahar,* a solemn and general concourse takes place to the various religious resorts on the islands. Every one that regards the festival betakes himself to some pagoda or other; there is however nothing compulsory in these acts of worship, and with the usual indifference of the Ceylonese to religious matters where their fears are not interested, many keep away from mere caprice. At Candy, this festival is celebrated with great pomp, and is attended by the king in person accompanied with all the splendour of his court. It is on this occasion that he makes his princely offering to the deities, and joins his people in their acts of devotion.

In November, when the moon is at full, there is another festival, which is celebrated in the night-time. It is customary on this occasion for the people to make contributions of oil for lighting up their temples during the continuance of the festival.

The festivals in honour of Buddou are not held in the temples where he is usually worshipped, but at a high hill and a consecrated tree. The mountain called Hammalleel, or Adam's Peak, is one of the highest in Ceylon, and lies at the distance of about fifty miles to the north east of Columbo. It is from the summit of this mountain, as tradition reports, that Adam took his last view of Paradise before he quitted it never to return. The spot on which his foot stood at the moment is still supposed to be found in an impression on the summit of the mountain resembling the print of a man's foot, but more than double the ordinary size. After taking this farewell view, the father of mankind is said to have gone over to the continent of India, which was at that time joined to the island; but no sooner had he passed Adam's bridge, than the sea closed behind him and cut off all hopes of return. This tradition, from whatever source it was originally derived, seems to be interwoven with their earliest notions of religion, and it is difficult to conceive that it could have been engrafted on them without forming an original part. I have frequently had the curiosity to enquire of black men of different casts concerning this tradition of Adam. All of them with every appearance of belief assured me that it was really true, and in support of it produced a variety of testimonies, old sayings and prophecies which have for ages been current among them. The origin of these traditions I do not pretend to trace, but their connection with scriptural history is very evident; and they afford a new instance how universally the opinions with respect to the origin of man coincide with the history of that event as recorded in the bible.

A large chain, said also to be the workmanship of Adam, is fixed in a rock near the summit of the mountain. It has the appearance of having been placed there at a very distant period; but who really placed it there, or for what purpose, it is impossible for any European to trace amidst the confused and unintelligible superstitions which the natives have mingled with their obscure traditions.

The ascent of the mountain is exceedingly steep and difficult, and in some parts near the summit the devotees are obliged to be assisted in climbing by ropes and chains fixed by hooks to the rocks. The night time is usually pitched upon to ascend, in order to avoid such fatiguing exertions during the excessive heat of the day. On the summit are a number of large flat rocks plentifully supplied with water. It is on one of them that the print of Adam's foot is shewn.

This mountain, which is looked upon as the original residence of Adam, is held in great veneration not only by the natives of Ceylon, but also by a variety of persons of different casts and persuasions throughout India. Most of these have particular places of worship on it to which they make pilgrimages at certain seasons of the year. The Roman Catholic priests have also taken advantage of the current superstitions to forward the propagation of their own tenets; and a chapel which they have erected on the mountain is yearly frequented by vast numbers of black Christians of the Portugueze and Malabar race.

It is to Adam's Peak that the Ceylonese repair to worship at the great Festival of Buddou. The Cinglese of the coasts in particular resort to it in vast multitudes. A large proportion of the Candians likewise attend; but whether from a fear of mixing with foreigners, or from ideas of superior sanctity, they seem more inclined to hold their great festival under the shade of the *Bogaha* tree, which stands at Annarodgburro, an ancient city, in the northern part of the king of Candy's dominions; and none but his own subjects are permitted to approach this sanctuary. The Bogaha tree, says tradition, suddenly flew over from some distant country, and planted itself in the spot where it now stands. It was intended as a shelter for the god Buddou; and under its branches he was wont to repose while he sojourned on earth. Near this hallowed spot ninety kings are interred, who all merited admission to the regions of bliss by the temples and images they constructed for Buddou. They are now sent as good spirits to preside over the safety of his followers, and protect them from being brought into subjection to Europeans; a calamity against which they continually pray. Around the tree are a number of huts, erected for the use of the devotees who repair hither; and as every sort of uncleanness and dust must be removed from the sacred spot, people are retained for the purpose of continually sweeping the approaches before the worshippers, and to attend the priests during the performance of the ceremonies.

As the preference was given by Buddou to the shade of the Bogaha tree above all others, it is universally held sacred among the Ceylonese. Wherever it is found throughout the island, persons are appointed to watch over it and preserve it from dirt or injury. The Bogaha tree is held in the same estimation among the followers of Buddou, as the Banyan tree among the Brahmins.

Notwithstanding the many religious ceremonies and superstitions which prevail among the Ceylonese, they are far from being such devotees and zealots as any of the sects on the continent. Indeed, they seem to be more actuated by apprehension than by any real sentiment of zeal; and they seldom think themselves called upon to take much concern in religious matters till they fall into sickness, or verge towards the close of life. The injustice of the Portuguese in forcing religious tenets upon them, must have shocked them the more as they have not the smallest idea of intolerant zeal. So far are they from being displeased at Europeans, or people of other persuasions entering their temples and observing their ceremonies, that they are rather gratified by such marks of attention, and account the presence of visitors as an honour done themselves. On being questioned about their superstitions, they do not hesitate to confess the absurdity of their apprehensions, but still they look upon themselves as unable to escape from them; and dread even to attempt vindicating their freedom, from a fear that they may be instantly delivered over to the vengeance of those malignant spirits who infest their country. The Christian priests and missionaries, though often successful in propagating their doctrines, have never yet been able totally to eradicate superstitions which have been imbibed from the cradle.

I was very much surprised to observe the Ceylonese wear

beads, and mutter prayers as they count them and go along the road, in the same manner as I have seen done in Roman Catholic countries. I at first imagined that these were converts to that religion, but upon enquiry, I found that they were all staunch adherents to the worship of Buddou. Their high respect for the customs of the Europeans led them early to adopt this usage from the Portuguese; but the prayers which they mutter over their beads, have no reference whatever to those used by the Roman Catholics, but are directed entirely to their own superstitions, and intended as preventives against the influence of the evil spirits which surround them.

The immortality of the soul and the resurrection of the body, are tenets firmly believed among all the Ceylonese. They believe that the souls of the just are immediately after death admitted into the rank of gods, and that their ancient prophets and good kings are long since employed in exercising the powers of this station: while on the other hand, the souls of the wicked, particularly of unjust tyrants and impious priests, are supposed to have passed into wild beasts and reptiles.

The Ceylonese are rigid predestinarians, and believe that people are born to their particular destinies, whether good or bad, without any possibility of avoiding or altering them. Spells and charms are indeed supposed in some measure to lighten the effects of appointed calamities; and considerable reliance is placed on giving alms. On this account the Ceylonese are very liberal in the distribution of charity. They consider giving presents to their priests and alms to their beggars as essential acts of goodness. The Cinglese in our service in particular, who have the natural ferocity of their minds more completely subdued, often give remarkable proofs of their extended good nature in these respects. It is customary for them even to lay by a certain proportion of their food to distribute among the poor; and although distressed strangers are among the Indians accounted objects of very little compassion, yet a Cinglese will not shut his hand to the Malabar or Moor who asks him for relief. Their tenderness is at times extended even to the brute creation; and it is customary for them to bind themselves during the continuance of certain festivals or seasons of devotion, to refrain from killing any living creature, but subsist entirely on herbs and fruits.

I have already observed, that the Ceylonese are much more conscientious in their dealings than the natives of the continent. This remark applies particularly to the Cinglese, who, besides being naturally abstemious, frugal, and free from covetousness, are not tempted by want to purloin the property of their neighbours. The Candians, though endued with much more pride and spirit, are by no means so conscientious or honest. Those indeed among them, who are guilty of stealing or lying, are exposed to public reproach, while just and honourable actions never fail to meet with applause; but when they expect to escape detection, they are seldom deterred from trespassing by scruples of conscience. The rapacity of their governors, and their frequent inroads into the European settlements seem to have depraved their originally good dispositions.

Their burials are not attended with any particular religious solemnity. Mr. Knox states, that in his time it was customary to burn the dead, particularly the bodies of persons of distinction. If this practice still subsists in any part of Ceylon, it has entirely escaped my researches, and must be both rare and confined to the remotest parts of the interior. The analogy of several of the casts on the Coromandel and Malabar coasts, among whom the practice of burning the dead is general, may be alledged as a proof of its once having been customary among the Ceylonese. At present, as far as I have been able to discover, the funeral ceremony is very simple, and nearly resembles what takes place among ourselves. The body is wrapped in a mat or piece of cloth, and carried to some unfrequented spot where it is deposited.

Such are the circumstances I have been able to collect, which apply to the native Ceylonese in general. There are some particular shades of difference which arise between the Candians and Cinglese, both from the nature of the country they inhabit, and from the more frequent intercourse of the latter with foreigners. These chiefly relate to their political situation, and their forms of administering justice, which among the Cinglese are of course considerably assimilated to those of the people which holds them in subjection. It will consequently be necessary to mention such circumstances separately. I shall therefore at present describe the few additional particulars concerning the Cinglese which have fallen under my observation: and reserve any further account of the Candians till I come to describe their country.

CHAPTER X.

Circumstances which distinguish the Cinglese from the Candians.

THE Cinglese, who inhabit the low lands and parts contiguous to the coasts, live entirely under the dominion of whatever European nation has been able to acquire possession of that part of the island. The nature of the country they inhabit indeed leaves them hardly any alternative but unconditional submission, unless they could either meet the Europeans in open battle, or consent to quit their plentiful fields for the barren mountains of the interior.

The subjection under which they have for a considerable time lived, while it has effaced the manly features of barbarous independence, has at the same time tended to humanize and soften their dispositions. The Cinglese are a quiet, inoffensive people; exceedingly grave, temperate, and frugal. Their bodies partake of the indolence of their minds, and it is with reluctance they are roused to any active exertion. When, however, they are obliged to apply themselves to any work, such as agriculture, they are capable of undergoing a great deal of labour. They are not indeed so strong as the Moor or Malabar race, and never make good palankeen bearers, or coolies to carry burthens.

The milder virtues form the most prominent features of the Cinglese character. They are gentle, charitable, and friendly, and have scarcely any of the false, treacherous, and designing arts which are often found among the Candians. With much less smoothness and courteousness of face and manner than the latter, they have much sincerer hearts. On examining the countenances and carriage of these two classes of Ceylonese, it is easy to perceive the difference arising from the respective circumstances in which they are placed. The countenance of the Candian is erect, his look haughty, his mien lofty, and his whole carriage marked by the pride of independence. The humble yielding deportment of the Cinglese, on the other hand, with the patient or rather abject endurance which is painted in their faces, plainly denotes the dependent and helpless state to which they are reduced.

The looks of the Cinglese even denote a degree of effeminacy and cowardice, which excites the contempt of the Candians; although the latter, with all their boasted spirit, can never venture to attack an European but by the same method as the Cinglese, and are equally cautious in waiting the convenient moment of assaulting him from the bushes, or jungle, in which they have concealed themselves.

I have already mentioned some efforts which the Cinglese made to resist the orders of our government; but the vigorous measures instantly taken on the occasion, soon convinced them that the power of the English was still more irresistible than that of their former masters. The cause of their rebellion was the imposition of certain taxes by Mr. Andrews, the head servant of the Company, and the Collector of the revenues. A body of the Cinglese took up arms and retired into the woods at the distance of a few miles from Columbo: several of the corles and districts at the same time declared openly in favour of the rebellion. A detachment of Sepoys was sent against them: several severe combats ensued; and it was not till after a considerable loss of men on both sides that the insurgents were completely subdued. Such is the nature of the country, full of thick woods, narrow passes, and rivers, that our troops often wanted a proper opportunity to act, and were frequently attacked before the rebels were perceived, or even suspected to be near them.

It may not be improper here to observe, that although in this and another commotion which happened two years after, our troops were ultimately successful, yet much inconvenience and danger might eventually be incurred from a general revolt among the Cinglese. The preventives against it are, however, no less obvious than certain. A mild and equitable government with a strict administration of justice, cannot fail to conciliate the minds of these people, who have already been trained to submission and an unbounded reverence for Europeans. As a sure precaution, however, against all contingencies, every effort should be made to clear the woods and improve the roads, so as to enable troops with ease and without risque to watch over the security of our plantations. It was suspected that these unusual commotions among the Cinglese might be connected with a more extensive plan concerted among the natives for the assertion of their independence; and a strict enquiry was instituted by our government, to find out whether the king of Candy had any share in exciting the rebellion. It could not however be ascertained that he had any connexion with it, or had given them the slightest encouragement.

The warlike habits of the Candians make them naturally look with contempt on the Cinglese, who are almost entirely unacquainted with the management of arms, having no occasion to use them except in procuring game for the tables of the Europeans.

The dress of the poorer sorts of the Cinglese in a particular manner bespeaks their indolence and wretchedness. It consists merely of a piece of coarse cloth wrapped round their loins, and covering their thighs, or frequently only the parts which decency requires to be concealed. Their hair is either tied up in a bunch on the crown of the head, or cropped quite close, which is the usual custom among the lower orders of the peasants. The women wear their hair tied up in the same way, or fastened with tortoise-shell combs. Their dress consists of a piece of cloth wrapped round the waist, and reaching down to their ancles; among the very poorest class it does not reach below the knee. They wear also a short jacket which usually covers the bosom and shoulders, leaving the middle of the back bare; the bosom is also frequently exposed. This class of women are employed to do all manner of servile work, and to bring the fruits and vegetables to market.

But although the poorer Cinglese use no more clothing than a very small attention to decency obliges them, the superior ranks are far from being regardless of dress. The men of the better sort usually wear a piece of calico wrapped round their waists, and either allowed to hang loose down to their ancles, or drawn together between the legs in the form of wide trowsers.

The body is covered by a jacket with sleeves, which unites the appearance of a shirt and waistcoat, and is buttoned at the neck and wrists. The buttons are the articles on which the magnificence of this piece of dress is supposed particularly to depend, and no expence is spared to have them as splendid as possible. A great number of buttons are used, and they are either of silver, gold, or precious stones. Enormous ear-rings are another piece of finery in which the Ceylonese cope with their neighbours the Malabars. In order to prepare the ear for these unwieldy rings, which often hang down to the shoulders, pieces of wood are employed to keep open and widen the orifice which is made for the purpose in their infancy. As the climate hardly requires any covering, the shoulders and body are often left completely bare. On their heads they wear caps of various shapes, and others of them coloured handkerchiefs, according as fancy dictates, or the rules of their cast prescribe.

The dress of the higher ranks of women is similar to that worn by the black Portuguese ladies, which I have already described. The young Cinglese women of rank dress by no means inelegantly, and neither their appearance nor manner are disagreeable. They are frequently met at the parties of the Dutch, who are much more partial to their company than the English. From the naturally distant and haughty temper of our countrymen, and their unacquaintance with the native language, they never dream of associating with the Cinglese, or receiving them into their parties.

The Cinglese are ingenious and expert artificers, and display particular dexterity in gold, silver, and carpenters' work. In this last branch, they have already made great proficiency since the arrival of the English. Their implements are very few, and simple in the construction; the mode of using them is readily acquired, and the toes are occasionally employed as well as the hands. They have none of that ponderous machinery which is employed to facilitate the vast manufactures of the Europeans; their implements are easily transported, and as easily set to work. When a smith is called for, he carries along with him his bellows, anvil, hammer, files, and all his other apparatus, and sets himself to work on the spot in a few minutes. The number of persons who are employed in all sorts of handicraft work, renders furniture, and other articles of that description, both good and cheap.

The Cinglese supply our garrisons plentifully with beef, fowls, eggs, and other articles of the same sort, at a very moderate rate, as they seldom make use of them for their own consumption: beef in particular they never taste, as the cow is an object of their worship. A few of them, particularly those most conversant with Europeans, venture to drink arrack; and all ranks use toddy, as well for medicine as for the sake of the liquor itself. The vessels which they employ to hold the juice of the palmyra and cocoa-tree, is a rind of the betel-tree, which forms a coating over the leaves; in colour and texture it resembles bleached sheep-skin, and is fully as strong, and much better adapted for retaining liquor. Fowls are brought to market in great abundance: a good fowl sells at from four-pence to eight-pence; eggs at two-pence a dozen; and a good dish of fish may be bought at from one-penny to two-pence, according to the state of the market.

As the Cinglese live under the protection of the British Government, they are also subjected to our laws and forms of administering justice, except in a very few points, in which their ancient customs, as they do not materially interfere with our modes, are permitted to be retained. The same laws of inheritance remain in force among all the Ceylonese: the lands descend to the eldest son, if the father makes no will; but a certain proportion of the property must always go to the maintenance of the widow and the younger children.

The Cinglese under our dominion are governed by their native magistrates, only the supreme controlling power always resides in the servants of our government. All our possessions on the island are divided into corles and districts, the subordinate superintendence of which is given to the Moodeliers, or native magistrates, who are always chosen from among the class of the nobles styled Hondrews and Mahondrews. These magistrates superintend both the country parts and the villages, and exercise a power similar to our country and city magistrates in Great Britain. It is the business of the Moodeliers to assist in collecting the revenues, settling the proportion of the taxes and contributions, assembling the peasants for government service, procuring provisions and other supplies to the different garrisons when required, providing coolies for conveying stores or baggage from one station to another; in short, it is their business to observe the conduct of the natives, and prevent either public or individual interest from sustaining any loss.

The Moodeliers have under them an inferior class of petty officers, who are also chosen from among the Hondrews. Their business is to assist the Moodeliers, and carry their orders into execution. In those parts where it is not thought requisite to quarter a body of troops, there is a police corps of the natives appointed to enforce the commands of government in each district: they are composed of *Conganies*, or sergeants, *Aratjies*, or corporals, and *Lascarines*, or common soldiers, and perform the same offices as our sheriff's men, or constables. They are armed with short swords and spears: a large body of them attend the Governor in his tours round the island, and on other occasions, either for state or expediency.

The Moodeliers as well as the inferior class of police officers, are under the immediate orders of the commanding officer of the military post to which their district or corle is attached, with the exception of a few corles on the borders of the Candian territory, where it has not been found expedient to hold any military station. It is through these commanding officers that all reports, intelligence and complaints are carried to the Governor. The Moodeliers at the same time make a report of what passes in their respective districts to the Maha or Ma Ma Moodelier, the chief of the whole order, who resides in the Black Town of Columbo; and he on his part lays these reports before the Governor. There are particular Moodeliers appointed to superintend the barking of the cinnamon, who interfere in nothing else, and are responsible to the European officer who is intrusted with the management of that department.

The nobles or Mahondrews, from among whom the Moodeliers are chosen, form a particular cast completely distinct from the others, and both their appearance, dress, and manners denote superiority to the rest of the natives.

The Mahondrews are fairer than the other Cinglese, probably owing to their being less exposed to the sun. When they go abroad, their rank and wealth entitles them to be carried in coolies or palankeens; or if they prefer going on foot, their attendants hold the leaf of the talipot over their heads. When they appear in public, or wait on Europeans, a numerous body either of their own servants or of the peasants of their district are employed to carry their umbrellas and betel boxes. The latter are made very handsome as if to denote the quality of the owner: they are usually of ivory, tortoise-shell, silver, or calamander wood inlayed. In their own hands they carry a small silver box, resembling a watch, to hold their chinam.

In their manners the Mahondrews are extremely affable, and much more polite and engaging than the natives of the Continent of India. They are very partial to Europeans, and treat them both with candour and confidence; nor do they look upon them with that suspicious eye, nor behave with that fawning and hypocritical servility which is so observable in the conduct of the Dubashes, and other Moors and Malabars towards Europeans. For these reasons the Dutch found it their interest to use them well on all occasions, and to grant them large indulgences and privileges. Our Government continues the same policy; and, by treating them with confidence and gentleness, has secured their sincere esteem and attachment.

The Mahondrews discover on all occasions a great desire to copy the manners of the Europeans, and in their address and conversation this predilection is particularly discernible. Most of them speak the Dutch and Portuguese languages fluently, and many of them already begin to converse in English with considerable facility.

They dress very richly, and by no means inelegantly according to the fashions of that country. Their dress is peculiar to themselves, and seems to combine the ancient European with the Asiatic. It consists of a long wide coat of fine cloth and a dark blue or crimson colour, with the buttons reaching down all the way to the bottom, and the cuffs wide like those of a former century. The button-holes are embroidered with gold or silver, and the buttons the same or covered with lace. The vests are of white flowered calico, single-breasted, and with pockets after our old fashion. They button at the collar like a shirt, and, as we have already observed in the description of the dress worn by the better orders of the Cinglese, they serve both purposes of a shirt and waistcoat; the buttons are always of gold or precious stones. In place of breeches, they wear a piece of white or coloured calico, wrapped round the waist and drawn together between the legs like loose trowsers. Across their shoulders they wear a broad belt of gold or silver lace or embroidery work, to which is attached a short curved sword or dagger, with a handle and scabbard variously ornamented according to the fancy of the wearer. On their feet they have a kind of sandal, but commonly go bare legged. They wear their hair fastened up in a bunch with several tortoise-shell combs: sometimes they chuse to go bare-headed; at other times they have on a cap or hat of the same materials as those worn by us, and only differing in shape; the brim with them is turned up before and behind, and is entirely removed at the sides which are generally embroidered. The Maha Moodelier occasionally appears in a coat of crimson cloth or velvet, and his dress in other respects corresponds to the numerous retinue which always attends him.

The Mahondrews are fond of magnificence, and seem anxious to make a figure in the eyes of Europeans. It is at their wedding-feasts that they seem particularly anxious to exhibit their splendour, and the Europeans are often invited to these parties. I have frequently been present at such feasts, which were indeed prepared without any regard to expence. A ball and supper given by the Maha Moodelier to celebrate his daughter's marriage with a noble of the same class particularly attracted my notice by the grand and expensive style in which it was conducted. The Governor and most of the officers of the garrison were present, as well as a great number of Dutch ladies and gentlemen; and as the company was too large for any room to contain, a house was built and covered in for the purpose. In the course of the evening the Governor presented the Moodelier with a gold chain, as a testimony of the high sense entertained of his faithful and upright conduct in our service.

The Moodeliers are of infinite use in preserving the obedience of the natives, and it is extremely fortunate that they are upon so good a footing with our countrymen. The whole cast of Mahondrews, like the nobility of other conquered countries, have transferred their pride from real power to the preservation of a fictitious pre-eminence; and a species of scrupulous honour; and therefore it is easy, by paying a proper deference to those objects which they most value, to procure their sincere attachment and assistance.

The natural dispositions of the Cinglese are, as I have already observed, mild and humane; and their morals, except in the promiscuous intercourse of the sexes, far from being depraved. It is to be lamented however that their minds labour so dreadfully under the influence of superstitious fears, and that their morality is not founded on more rational principles. It is to be hoped that more attention will be paid to their cultivation and improvement by our countrymen than their former masters, the Dutch and the Portugueze; who, by their own avaricious and short-sighted policy, precluded themselves from receiving that support from the natives which might still have maintained them masters of Ceylon. Many of the Cinglese have indeed been converted to the Christian faith; and part profess to be Roman Catholics, while others attend the Calvinist and Lutheran worship: but scarcely one of them understands the fundamental principles of Christianity. It seemed sufficient to their former European masters, if they could be brought to practice the outward forms of the Christian worship; and their apparent conversion was therefore more frequently to be regarded as a badge of tame submission than a real improvement in religious and moral principles. A zealous effort on the part of our government to introduce our learning and religion among the natives is the surest means of improving and consolidating our empire in the island. The higher orders of the Cinglese already afford an example of what that people may soon become by an intercourse with civilized society: many of them display minds capable of receiving the most polished and systematic education.

CHAPTER XI.

The king of Candy's dominions—Its divisions—Candy—Digliggy Neur—Nilemby Neur—Anaerodgburro—Climate—Soil—Circumstances which distinguish the Candians from the Cinglese.

I Have now described the sea-coast of Ceylon and it's inhabitants. It is in these parts that we are principally to look for the riches and advantages to be derived from the island. The possession of the interior might tend to the security of our dominion; and an improved mode of cultivation might make it capable of maintaining a much greater number of inhabitants; but these purposes may be as effectually attained by a friendly intercourse with the natives, as by a direct submission to our authority. Our Government will doubtless avoid the error of the former European masters of Ceylon, who wasted unprofitably in vain attempts to subdue the natives that time and those resources which might have rendered this island one of the most valuable colonies in the world.

In a detached island, such as Ceylon, if any where, we might expect to find very little diversity in the nature of the country and the races by which it were inhabited; and yet we are here presented with three different dominions governed by different laws, presenting the greatest variety of soil, climate, and cultivation, and possessed by three distinct races which seem to have no original connexion with each other. In these parts which I have already described, the whole tone of manners is European; and even the Cinglese who inhabit there seem to have lost their most prominent native characteristics. The state of agriculture, of architecture and manufactures along the coasts is so much derived from Europeans, that little of it can be attributed to the native cultivation of Ceylon. In the king of Candy's dominions, which occupy the greater part of the interior, the invasion of Europeans has, on the contrary, rather retarded than changed the progressive state of civilization and the arts. Several features of the native character have indeed undergone some alteration from this cause; and both from opposition and intercourse, the European manners, modes of warfare, and arts, have in some degree become known to the Candians.

Another part of the interior however is possessed by a race, who seem to have scarcely any thing in common either with the Candians or Europeans. The Bedahs in their woods and mountains still retain their primitive state of society, very little improved by intercourse with their neighbours which they anxiously avoid.

The possession and manners of these two races, the Candians and Bedahs, come now to be considered. If the information which we have been able to obtain hitherto on those subjects be still limited and insufficient to satisfy curiosity, it is however so far extended, as to enable us to judge how far they can be rendered of advantage to the colony. Many fabulous stories are told of the interior and its inhabitants, which might have indeed amused the reader, but which at the same time might have misled him. I have only advanced such facts as I either knew to be true from my personal knowledge, or which I found to be consistent with the opinion of the best informed. Several additional particulars relative to the country and manners of the Candians will be found in the journal of an Embassy to the court of Candy subjoined to this volume.

The interior of the island, owing to the jealousy of the Dutch, has been little explored by Europeans; and any traveller who might have obtained the permission of the Dutch to visit it, could not have executed his purpose from the jealousy of the natives. Since the Candians have been driven by their invaders into the mountains of the interior, it has been their policy carefully to prevent any European from seeing those objects which might tempt the avarice of his countrymen, or from observing the approaches by which an army could penetrate their mountains. If an European by any accident was carried into their territories, they took every precaution to prevent him from escaping; and the guards stationed every where at the approaches, joined to the wide and pathless woods which divide the interior from the coast, rendered such an attempt almost completely desperate. When an ambassador was sent from any European government to the King of Candy, he was watched with all that strictness and jealousy which the suspicious temper of uncivilized nations dictates; and from an account subjoined to this volume of an embassy which I attended to the court of that monarch, it will be seen how careful the natives were to prevent strangers from making any observations. Mr. Boyd, who about twenty years ago went on a similar embassy, was watched with the same particular circumspection; and has therefore been able to add little to our stock of knowledge concerning the interior.

The dominions of the native prince are completely cut off on all sides from those of the Europeans by almost impenetrable woods and mountains. The passes which lead through these to the coasts are extremely steep and difficult, and scarcely known even by the natives themselves. As soon as we advance from ten to twenty miles from the coasts a country presents itself greatly differing from the sea-coast both in soil, climate, and appearance. After ascending the mountains and passing the woods, we find ourselves in the midst of a country not advanced many stages beyond the first state of improvement, and which we are astonished to find in the neighbourhood of the highly cultivated fields which surround Columbo. As we advance towards the centre of the island, the country gradually rises, and the woods and mountains which separate the several parts of the country become more steep and impervious.

It is in the midst of these fastnesses that the native

Prince still, preserves those remains of territory and power which have been left him by successive invaders. His dominions are now much reduced in size; for besides the whole of the sea-coasts which were of any value, the Dutch, in their various attacks during the last century, have contrived to get into their power every tract from which they could derive either emolument or security. Those provinces which still remain to him are Nourecalava and Hotcourly towards the north and north-west; while Matuly, comprehending the districts of Bintana, Velas, and Panoa, with a few others, occupies those parts more to the eastward. To the south-east lies Ouvah, a province of some note, and giving the king one of his titles. The western parts are chiefly included in the provinces of Cotemal and Hotteracorley. These different provinces are subdivided into corles or districts, and entirely belong to the native prince. It is needless to recount the names of those divisions which stretch towards the sea-coast, and are now chiefly in our possession.

In the highest and most centrical part of the native king's dominions lie the corles or counties of Oudanour and Tatanour, in which are situated the two principal cities. These counties take the pre-eminence of all the rest, and are both better cultivated, and more populous than any of the other districts, and are distinguished by the general name of Condé Udda; *condé* or *candé* in the native language signifying a mountain, and *udda* the greatest or highest.

This province of Conde Udda is even more inacessible than the others, and forms as it were a separate kingdom of itself. On every side it is surrounded by lofty mountains covered with wood, and the paths by which it is entered seem little more than the tracts of wild beasts. Guards are stationed all around to prevent both entrance and escape; for defence they might seem entirely superfluous, did we not recollect that the perseverance of the Dutch overcame all these obstacles, and forced a way into the very centre of this natural fortification.

In the district of Tattanour lies Candy the royal residence and the capital of the native prince's dominions. It is situated at the distance of eighty miles from Columbo, and twice as far from Trincomalee, in the midst of lofty and steep hills covered with thick jungle. The narrow and difficult passes by which it is approached are intersected with thick hedges of thorn; and hedges of the same sort are drawn round the hills in the vicinity of Candy like lines of circumvallation. Through them the only passage is by gates of the same thorny materials, so contrived as to be drawn up and let down by ropes. When the Candians are obliged to retreat within these barriers, they cut the ropes, and then it is impossible to force a passage except by burning down the gates, which from their green state, and the constant annoyance of the enemy sheltered behind them, would prove an enterprise of time and difficulty. These hedge-rows form the chief fortifications of Candy. The Mali-vagonga also nearly surrounds the hill on which it stands: the river is here broad, rocky, and rapid; a very strict guard is kept on it, and every one who passes or repasses is closely watched and examined.

The city itself is a poor miserable-looking place, surrouded by a mud wall of no strength whatever. It has been several times burnt by Europeans, and was once deserted by the king, who retired to a more inaccessible part of his dominions. It is upon occasion of the embassy of General Macdowal, an account of which is subjoined to this volume, that any information concerning the present state of Candy has been obtained; and even then it could be little more than guessed at, as the embassador and his suite were admitted only by torch-light, and always retired before break of day. From what could then be observed, the city consists of a long straggling street built on the declivity of a hill; the houses mean and low, but with their foundations raised in such a manner above the level of the street that they appear quite lofty to passengers. The reason of this extraodinary taste is to enable the king to hold his assemblies of the people and to have his elephant and buffalo fights in the street, without interfering with the houses. When the king passes along the street, none of

H H 2

the inhabitants are allowed to appear before their houses, or the paths on a level with them, as that would be attended with the heinous indecorum of placing a subject higher than the prince descended of the sun.

At the upper end of this street, stands the palace, a poor mansion for the abode of a king. It is surrounded with high stone walls, and consists of two squares, one within the other. In the inner of these are the royal apartments, and it is there that the court is held and audiences given. The exterior of the palace and the rest of the city could be but very partially observed by those who attended General Macdowal, owing to the pressure of the crowd, and the dazzling glare of the torches. By every account indeed which I have heard, Candy contains nothing worthy of notice, and from the want of either wealth or industry among the inhabitants it is not indeed to be expected that any thing could be met with in this straggling village to attract the attention of the traveller.

The next city in point of importance to Candy is Digliggy Neur, which lies to the eastward of the capital about ten or twelve miles, and in the direction of our fort of Batacolo. The district around Digliggy Neur is still more wild, barren, and impenetrable than that which surrounds Candy. It is on this very account that it has been chosen at times as a royal residence: at one period when the king was driven out of Candy, and his capital burnt, he found here a retreat to which no European army has even been able to penetrate. A few villages are scattered among the surrounding hills; and in those places where the woods leave some clear space, the soil though barren produces rice.

About six or seven miles south of Candy lies the town of Nilemby Neur, which has also at times afforded a retreat to the king: he has here a palace and store-houses. The remains of several other towns are found in various parts of the country. On the road from Candy to Trincomalee stood the town of Aletty Neur, where the king kept stores of grain and other provisions. This however as well as many other towns was burnt to the ground by the Portugueze; and nothing is now left but the remains of some temples and pagodas to testify that such places ever were in existence.

The ruins of some towns, which appear to have been both larger and better built than those hitherto described, prove that the kingdom of the Candians was once in a more flourishing condition, and gradually tending by the natural course of things to civilization and opulence, when the invasion of Europeans deprived them of all those means by which they could have access to foreign nations, and an opportunity of importing either arts or manners into their own. In the nothern part of the kingdom lies the province of Noure Calava, where the ruins of the once famous and splendid city of Anurodgburro are still discovered. It stands almost at the northern extremity of the Candian dominions, and borders on the province of Jafnapatam. In former ages this was the residence of the kings of Ceylon; and has long been the place of their burial. Owing to its being at a distance from Candy, and the terrors of a barbarous court, it is much frequented by priests and other Cinglese, who come here to pay devotion to their saints. It was here that the stately temples and pagodas of the Ceylonese worship formerly stood, as appears by the massy pillars and hewn stones which still remain. The Portuguese, however, made themselves masters of the town, and found in it more objects for their ravages than they had hitherto met with in the other parts of the island. They pulled down without remorse the religious edifices with which it was adorned, and transported the choicest of the materials to fortify Columbo and the other towns which they erected on the sea-coasts. This act of sacrilege tended more than any other thing to alienate the minds of the natives; and the Ceylonese still record it with horror.

The whole of the king's country, with the exception of the plains around Anurodgburro, present a constant interchange of steep mountains and low vallies. The excessive thickness of the woods, which cover by far the greatest portion of the country, causes heavy fogs and unwholesome damps to prevail. Every evening the fogs fall with the close of day, and are not again dissipated till the sun has acquired great power. The vallies are in general marshy, full of springs, and excellently adapted for the cultivation of rice and rearing of cattle. These advantages, however, are greatly counteracted by the unhealthiness of the climate in these parts after the rainy season. The principal difference between the climate of the interior and that of the coasts, is occasioned by the stagnation of the atmosphere in the former. The depth of the vallies and the thickness of the woods conspire to prevent the free circulation of air; and hence the night is constantly attended with excessive cold damps, which are succeeded by days equally noxious from their hot and sultry vapours. An European on coming into the interior is very liable to catch the hill or jungle fever. It is a disease resembling our ague and intermittent fever, and never leaves the person attacked, if he does not immediately change his residence to the sea-coast, where the climate is more cool and refreshing by day, while it is free from the cold and damps of the night.

The country of Candy can never receive any improvement from internal navigation. Several large rivers indeed intersect it; but these during the rainy season are rendered so rapid and impetuous by the torrents which fall into them from the surrounding hills, that no boat can venture upon them; while in the opposite season they are almost completely dried up. The Malivagonga, which is the largest of these rivers, rises at the foot of Adam's Peak, a high mountain to the south-west of Candy, and taking a north-east direction, nearly surrounds the capital, and at length falls into the sea at Trincomalee. The Mulivaddy, the next principal river takes its rise at a small distance from the other, and runs towards the west coast. There are a variety of other rivers, which rise from the hills in various parts of the country: although these be not navigable, yet if properly attended to, they might be employed to the greatest advantage in fertilizing the country.

The rainy seasons vary in different parts of the interior. The south-west quarter is subject to the influence of the western monsoons, while the north-east is but slightly touched by those from the opposite quarter. The high range of mountains which runs across the country of Candy, seems to divide the island into two different climates: it has been a continued drought on one side of them for years, while it has rained on the other without intermission. The eastern parts are by no means so subject to the influence of the monsoons as those to the west, and are consequently much less deluged with rains. The seasons in the mountains of the interior are regulated by different laws, and do not exactly correspond to either of the monsoons. Among them it rains incessantly during the months of March and April, at which period it is dry in the lowlands.

As I have already given a description of the Ceylonese in general, and pointed out the particular characteristics of the Cinglese, a few peculiar circumstances are all that require to be noticed of the manners of the Candians. The excessive jealousy which the latter entertain of Europeans and their connexions, has indeed hitherto rendered every attempt to obtain accurate information concerning them almost completely abortive. It might be naturally imagined that this information could have been obtained by means of the Cinglese in the European dominions; but the intercourse between the two branches of the nation is more completely cut off than that between any of the most savage and hostile tribes in North America. Even during the intervals of peace no communication is opened, nor is there any attempt on either side to carry on a secret traffic or correspondence with the other. The policy of the Dutch therefore succeeded so far as to render the Candians completely isolated, and to make them look with apprehension and hostile jealousy on the approach of a stranger.

As I have already observed, the state of constant hostility in which the Candians have so long continued with the Europeans, and the independence which their mountains enable them to maintain, have rendered the lines of their character more bold and prominent, while the subjection and tranquillity of the lowlanders have greatly softened the more rugged traits of their natural disposition. Although the Candians are governed with the most complete despotism, yet as their prejudices and customs are shared and respected by their monarchs, they are proud of being free from a foreign yoke, and slaves only to a master of their own race. They look upon the Cinglese in our service as a mean, despicable race, who barter their natural rights for peace and protection. The Candians in their appearance retain an air of haughtiness and gravity; they are at the same time more courteous and polite, as well as more crafty and treacherous than their countrymen of the lowlands. They are also accounted more athletic, and superior both in shape and countenance. As they are accustomed from their infancy to bear arms and watch at the different posts where any danger is apprehended, they early acquire a military air which is of itself sufficient to distinguish them from the Cinglese. Their houses are also neater and better constructed, though of the same materials and furnished quite alike.

The dress of the higher orders of the Candians consists of several folds of cotton cloth, or calico drawn close round their waists; while another piece of the same, after being wrapped round the body, has the one end tucked up at the back, while the other is drawn together between the legs, or hangs straight down to the ancles. Their arms, shoulders, and chest, are bare. On their heads they wear a sort of cap, or turban, of a shape peculiar to themselves: it has no resemblance to that worn by the natives of the continent or the Cinglese; it is broad and flat at top and narrow towards the lower part, and is stiffened with *conjee*, a species of starch made of rice. Over their shoulders, or round their waists, they wear a belt, to which a dagger or short hanger is suspended. A purse, like that in the dress of the Scots Highlanders, is worn before them, and is employed to hold betel-leaf, areka-nuts, and tobacco. They have, however, commonly a boy to attend them with a box of ivory or tortoise-shell replenished with these materials. An umbrella of the talipot leaf is their constant and necessary attendant when they walk abroad in the day time. They all wear rings on their fingers; few of them in their ears, as this is one of those indifferent articles in which the king shews his supreme authority by entering his royal prohibition. The chief distinction in the dress of the higher orders among the Candians and the Cinglese, is in the form of the cap, and the immense quantity of cloth worn round the waist by the former.

The appearance of the lower orders among both is in every respect the same, only that the difference in the shape of the cap is still observable. Of the Candian men in general it may be said that they are better drest than the Cinglese, as well as fairer in the complexion.

It may seem strange, that after having lived upwards of three years on the island, and after having traversed the interior even to the capital, I should still be able to describe the Candian women only from the report of others. Such, however, was the watchful suspicion of that people, that during the whole progress of the embassy, not one female was permitted to fall in our way. This is one of the strongest proofs of the apprehension which the conduct of the Dutch has excited among the Candians, as they are by no means particulary jealous of their women, and certainly kept them out of sight merely from a fear of intelligence being communicated to the Europeans. From the enquiries which I have repeatedly made, I never could learn that there is any material difference either in the manners, appearance, or dress of the Candian and Cinglese women.

The Candians are divided into different casts, which take precedence of each other according to the most scrupulous regulations. The first class comprises the nobles: these account it their chief glory to keep their high blood uncontaminated, and for this reason never intermarry with those of an inferior rank. If a woman of this cast were found to have degraded herself by connexion of any kind with a man of a lower cast, her life would be the forfeit. By this regulation they boast that their blood is preserved pure to the latest posterity. This cast, as among the Cinglese, is known by the name of Hondrews; and the dress among both is the same. The Cinglese Hondrews, however, under our government, have begun to relax a little in the strictness of their ideas of blood; and connexions are sometimes formed among them with inferiors without being attended by lasting infamy.

The next rank to the nobles includes artists, such as painters, and what is accounted the better sort of artificers, such as smiths, carpenters, and goldsmiths. The dress of this cast is nearly the same with that of the Hondrews; but they are not permitted to eat with the nobles, or at all to mix in their society.

Those who are employed in what are esteemed the lower occupations of barbers, potters, washers, weavers, &c. form a third cast, with which the common soldiers rank.

The fourth cast includes the peasantry, and labourers of all descriptions, who either cultivate the lands for themselves, or are hired out to work for others. The preference given to artificers above both the husbandmen and the soldiers, is a very uncommon fact in the arrangement of the casts, and peculiar to Ceylon. The circumstance bespeaks a degree of civilization, and a love for the arts, which certainly do not correspond with the present state of these islanders, although by no means inconsistent with the architectural remains of better days, which in some parts have escaped the ravages of time and the foe.

All these four casts, according to the Indian customs, continue unmingled: the son pursues the profession of his father from generation to generation, and love as well as ambition is confined to the cast in which a man happens to be born. But besides these casts, there is here as in other parts of India, a wretched race of outcasts, the martyrs from age to age of this barbarous and unnatural institution. Those who by any crime, or neglect of superstitious rites, have, according to the decree of the priests, forfeited their cast, are not only condemned to infamy themselves, but their children and childrens' children to all generations are supposed to share in the guilt and contamination. No one of another cast will intermarry with them; they are allowed to exercise no trade or profession, nor to approach any of the human race but the partners of their misery; nay if they even by accident touch any thing, it is reckoned polluted and accursed. As they are not allowed to work, they are obliged to beg continually for sustenance, and thus from generation to generation become a dead weight on society. As these wretched people are by the iron sceptre of superstition already degraded to a state which cannot be exceeded in vileness and infamy, and cannot by any good conduct ever retrieve their condition; so they have no restraint to prevent them from being guilty of the most detestable crimes. It would certainly be an object worthy the attention of any government to attempt converting this lost body of men to some useful purpose; and it is plain that the dispelling their superstitious notions by the introduction of another system of religion, must be the first step towards effecting this salutary improvement.

These people of no cast are obliged to pay the lowest of the other Candians as much respect and reverence as eastern servility ordains the latter to pay to the king. As tradition among barbarous nations never wants a legend to account for the origin of every institution, the cruelty exercised towards the outcasts is justified by the recital of a crime said to have been anciently committed by them. It is told that this race of people once formed a particular cast, who were employed as the king's hunters; that upon some provocation they supplied his table with human flesh in place of venison; and that upon the discovery of this atrocious act, the king doomed them to be outcasts from society for ever.

This ridiculous fable, I mention merely to shew the extent to which the natives of the island imagine the king entitled to carry his authority.

The nature of the government and the military and civil establishments form a very considerable part of what is most remarkable among the Candians; and is, perhaps, the most important topic of enquiry to Europeans. I shall therefore endeavour to present my readers with a full account of this subject.

CHAPTER XII.

The Civil and Military Establishments of the kingdom of Candy.

THE Government of Candy is an absolute despotism, and any resistance to the will of the king without power to maintain it, is sure to be attended with immediate destruction. In spite of these circumstances, however, the natives look upon certain fundamental laws and regulations, existing among them from time immemorial, as the real depositaries of supreme power; and they maintain that if the king ventures to encroach upon these, he is amenable to the justice of his country as well as the meanest subject. Some instances of kings who have been deposed and put to death, are cited in support of this idea; although it is evident that as long as the whole force of the state is vested in the king, and as long as there is no counterbalancing power opposed to him, it is a successful rebellion alone that can bring him to justice. The whole doctrine, in fact, serves only to give a handle to any minister or officer, who finds himself sufficiently powerful and ambitious to depose his master. An instance of this kind occurred in the fate of the late king of Candy. His Adigar, or prime minister, having formed a large party, and conceiving that he could govern more absolutely a creature of his own making, than the monarch who had exalted himself, deposed and put to death his master, and then procured a stranger to be elected in his room.

What may seem as inconsistent with the despotic powers of the king of Candy, the monarchy is completely elective by the fundamental laws of the country, and where a deposition takes place, these laws are usually acted upon. It is in the power of the people to put aside the next branch of the royal family, and to elect the more distant, or even a stranger. The present king, who was elected through the influence of the Adigar, I have already mentioned, is a native of the island of Ramiseram, on the Malabar coast, opposite Manaar. His only claim to the succession, except the power of the minister, was his descent from a female branch of the royal family. When the last king has no immediate descendents, and where the hereditary right lies between equi-distant males and females, the preference by the Candian laws, is given to the female branch. In the present instance, however, there were two other of the native princes who advanced claims of nearer alliance to the crown. They came during my residence at Columbo to lay their pretensions before Governor North, and to implore his interference and protection. It is evident, however, that as long as we can preserve terms of amity with the ruling prince, it is by no means our interest to enquire into the merits of any claims which may be advanced to his crown.

The people do not consider themselves in their election

bound to bestow the monarchy on a branch of the royal family; but think they are completely at liberty to elect either a native or a foreigner, though nowise connected with the royal blood. The throne, however, has in general, been for many ages possessed by the ancient Candian royal family, which is now very nearly extinct.

There appears to be no fixed regulation for conducting the election; and what is called the choice of the people may very justly be supposed to mean merely the consent of the ruling party at the time. There have been a number of absurd stories told by some voyagers with regard to the method pursued by the Candians in the election of a king. I had an opportunity of enquiring particularly into the foundation of these tales from some of the principal and best informed Candians whom I met at Sittivacca and Ruanelli. It has been said that when the Candians were about to elect a king, the whole people of the kingdom were assembled for that purpose, and the candidates, together with an elephant, produced before them. The elephant was then made the arbiter of the throne, and the first of the candidates before whom he stopt, and made obeisance, of his own accord and without being anywise instructed to it, was looked upon as the most proper person to enjoy the sovereign dignity, and was accordingly elected without farther contest. This story has long been current on the island, and is still believed by many residing there; and yet upon enquiring into the fact among the best informed Candians, they assured me that no such ceremonial had ever taken place.

The king of Candy yields to no eastern prince in the number and extravagance of his titles. I once had an opportunity of seeing a long piece of parchment on which they were inscribed; but although I had procured a copy of them, I am convinced that few of my readers, even the greatest proficients in heraldry, would have taken the trouble to read it. For several of his titles, the king seems to have been indebted to the Portuguese and Dutch, who were extremely liberal in repaying him with these for any corner of his dominions which they found it convenient to appropriate to their own use. His Candian Majesty is usually designed Emperor of Ceylon, King of Candy and Jafnapatam, Prince descended from the Golden Sun, whose kingdom and city of Candy is higher than any other, and before whom all others must fall prostrate; Prince of Ouva, Duke over the seven provinces and corles on the east, Marquis of Duranuro and the four corles, Lord of Columbo and Galle, Lord of the sea-ports of Nigumbo, Caltura, and Matura, to whom the island of Manaar and Calpenteen belong; Lord of the fishery of pearls, to whom all precious stones belong; he before whom elephants bow: these with a long string of others of the same sort are always added to his Majesty's address. Many of them were evidently invented by his European neighbours to amuse him with an imaginary sovereignty while they had the actual possession.

These lofty titles are attended with correspondent reverence on the part of his own subjects. No one dares approach him without prostrating himself three several times before the throne, each time repeating a long string of his Majesty's titles with the utmost fervour. No one even of the highest rank is allowed to cough, or spit in his presence. Every one is silent before him, nor does any one even in a whisper venture to address another. The solemn gravity of his nobles when admitted into the royal presence, altogether corresponds with the greatness of the occasion. The chief Adigar or Prime Minister is the only person who is permitted to stand in the royal presence; and even he is obliged to be some steps lower than his Majesty, as no one dares be on a level with him who is descended from the Sun, as all the kings of Ceylon are supposed to be. The business of state is transacted between the king and the Adigar in low whispers, so as not to be overheard by any one present; and any message from his Majesty to the others is conveyed in the same manner by the Adigar.

This extreme caution to prevent the smallest appearance of equalization with royalty, is not confined alone to the court, and to those who approach his person. Restraining edicts for the same purpose are attached to indifferent things throughout the kingdom. No one, for instance, is allowed to whiten the walls of his house or to cover the roof with tiles, as these are privileges reserved exclusively to the monarch. In writing a letter and folding it up, no one is allowed to adopt the method peculiar to his majesty.

This very excess of respect, which seems calculated to raise him so high above all his subjects, has the effect of greatly diminishing his personal power. As the Adigar is the only organ of his will, and almost the only one who has any access to his person, that minister has evidently the power of issuing what mandates he pleases, and preventing any complaints from reaching the throne. The present Adigar is a man of great connexions and intrigue, and in addition to the usual power attached to his office, he has also the merit of having raised the reigning sovereign to the throne. From these circumstances, the Minister engrosses the whole government of the kingdom, while the prince has little more left him than the name of royalty.

The kingdom of Candy has entailed upon it all the evils of an absolute monarchy: the lower orders are oppressed by the great Chiefs; and these in their turn are fleeced by the sovereign. Mr. Knox gives a terrible picture of the tyranny exercised by the prince who reigned during his captivity: but whether from the fear of a revolt which he experienced, or from a change of circumstances, the kings of Candy since his time have conducted themselves with much more mildness towards their subjects. The fear of the Europeans, who are always ready to be called in to the assistance of the rebellious, has no doubt contributed greatly to prevent the excesses of arbitrary government. The present king is by far the mildest prince that has ever hitherto reigned over the Candians. He appears to be much attached to us, although the Adigar is said to look upon us with a jealous eye.

The king of Candy affects to be the greatest prince in the whole world, and endeavours, by the state he maintains to make good his pretensions. He is the only prince in India, or, as the Candians tell you, in the whole world, who wears a crown.

When the king appears in public, he is always attended with what in the eyes of a Candian appears magnificence, although to an European it may seem scarcely deserving that name. He seldom makes use of a horse or elephant, but is generally carried in a palankeen. A number of his guards and persons of the first rank always accompany him; while a profusion of flags and streamers of white calico or cloth, are carried before the procession. In these are painted or wove of a red colour figures of the sun, of elephants, tygers, dragons, and many other hideous creatures. The richest of them, however, though sufficient to dazzle the natives of Candy, are no better than the colours of a marching regiment.

Loud noise, which seems to enter into all the ideas of grandeur among a barbarous people is never omitted in the train of the monarch. His progress is always attended by a number of performers on various instruments, such as tom-toms, or drums of various sizes, shrill and squalling clarionets, pipes, flagelets, a sort of bagpipes, and pieces of brass and iron jingled by way of triangles. The discordant noise produced by all these, sounded and clashed at once, without the smallest attention to time or harmony, is extremly disagreeable to the ears of a European.

But the most remarkable attendants of the monarch are a set of people furnished with long whips of a peculiar kind, who keep running before the procession with strange gestures like madmen, to clear the way, and announce the approach of the king. The whips are made of hemp, coya, grass, or hair, and consist of a thong or lash from eight to twelve feet long without any handle. The loud noise which the forerunners produce with their whips, as well as the dexterity with which they avoid touching those who come in their way, is truly astonishing; although an European, from the indiscriminate manner in which they appear to deal their lashes, cannot help feeling alarmed for his safety. In all the interviews which the embassy I attended had at the court of Candy, the ceremony of the whip-crackers was never omitted, to the great annoyance of our troops, who were very sulky and displeased on the occasion. Indeed it was impossible for the men under arms to attend to what they were about while these long whips were kept continually brandishing and cracking about their ears; and for my own part, although I was well convinced of the dexterity of those who wielded them, yet I could not help expecting every moment to come in for my share of chastisement.

The civil and military establishment of Candy is adjusted to the despotic form of its government, and promotion and appointment of all sorts depend wholly on the pleasure of the prince. The institution of casts, however, is preserved inviolable, and officers of a certain rank must always be chosen out of a certain class. White men rank with the highest. The regular troops, or standing army, do duty in the interior, and are kept near the person of the king, while the defence of the frontiers is entrusted to the adjoining inhabitants, who compose a sort of militia, and are obliged to keep constant watch over the entrances into the country. The various officers under the king have various privileges according to their rank.

The highest officers of state are the Adigars, or Prime Ministers. They are two in number, and may be said to share all the power of the court between them. I have already mentioned the causes which render the power of the present Chief Adigar so formidable; but even at other times these officers have afforded much cause of fear and jealousy to the monarch. To counteract any dangerous designs which their too preponderating influence might inspire, it is the policy of the king to appoint the two Adigars of different dispositions and opposite factions, and thus prevent an union which might overwhelm him. The distractions which these arring interests must always produce, and the constant and anxious attention which the king must bestow in keeping up a balance between them, form part of the miseries entailed on a despotic monarchy, which cannot subsist without employing such instruments as may every moment be converted to its own destruction.

The Adigars are the supreme judges of the realm; all causes may be brought before them, and it is they who give final judgment. An appeal indeed lies from their sentence to the king himself; but as they alone possess the royal ear, it is both difficult and dangerous to assert this privilege, and every one is more willing to acquiesce in their decision, than to hazard an appeal which is likely to be attended with worse consequences than the grievance he complains of.

The Adigars are possessed of all those privileges and immunities which may be supposed to accompany their unlimited power; and in order to approach as nearly to royalty as possible, they have also their particular badge which is allowed to no other person. Their peculiar distinction consists in a certain number of officers attached to their train, who carry a sort of staves of a particular shape, and a seal of hard clay, which are considered as tokens of the Adigar's commission, and when presented along with any mandate never fail to procure immediate obedience.

The embassies to the European government at Columbo are entrusted to these Prime Ministers; and they are also charged with the reception of our ambassadors. I have had frequent occasion to see both the Adigars at Columbo. They are portly good looking men. The one of them appeared much more attached to our government than the other.

The officers next in rank to the Adigars are the Dissauvas. They are the Governors of the corles or districts, and are besides the principal military commanders. Their business is to attend the king's person when required, to collect the revenues, and see that good order and strict discipline be maintained in their commands. But great as is the authority entrusted to these and the other great officers of state over their fellow subjects, none of them are allowed to bring any one publickly to capital punishment without first bringing the matter before the king, whose exclusive prerogative it is to pronounce sentence of death. The power of the Dissauva Udda, or Commander in chief of the forces, is very great; and this officer, having the complete disposal of the military, often becomes an object of apprehension to the king. While I was at Columbo, it was even said that the king had entirely abolished the office, judging the power attached to it too great to be entrusted in the hands of a single individual. I had, however, afterwards an opportunity of finding this report unfounded from my own personal observation, as the Dissauva Udda accompanied the Adigars to meet Governor North, and was received by the troops under arms. The Dissauvas, as long as they hold their office, are allowed by the king a certain portion of land for their services; and they often besides squeeze the people under their command unmercifully, under pretence of collecting contributions for his Majesty.

These great officers generally reside at court, and personally attend upon the king, who is, perhaps, afraid to allow persons endowed with so much authority to remain in their provinces and have an opportunity of courting popularity. As the Dissauvas, therefore, cannot attend in person, they have inferior officers under them, who act entirely by their orders, either in collecting the king's revenues, or in squeezing the people for the emolument of their patrons. These deputy officers are known by the names of Roterauts, Vitanies, and Courlevidanies, and are resident in the different provinces and districts to which they are appointed. An inferior rank of officers to these is composed of Conganies, Aratjes, &c. who hold the same stations here as among the Cinglese, and fulfil the duties of constables and police officers.

This whole plan of government forms a regular system of oppression, which falls with the severest weight on the lower orders of the people. Few have the courage to appeal against the unjust extortions of the higher ranks, and fewer still meet with any redress. It is the policy of the king, in the true timid spirit of despotism, to prevent any good understanding between his officers and the people they govern; and for this reason he is by no means displeased to observe the former exasperating the latter against themselves by oppression. Although the persons of the peasantry be in some measure protected, yet their property is completely at the mercy of the rapacious officers of the court. They have long since been stript of every thing valuable, and many of them trust to the spontaneous fruits of their forests for a scanty subsistence, rather than cultivate fields whose produce must be shared with their oppressors. If a peasant chances by accident to find a precious stone of value, or is possessed of any thing of superior quality, even the fruit which he gathers, he is compelled to give it up to the king's officers; or if it be of such value that they are afraid to appropriate it to themselves, they compel the unfortunate possessor to travel up with it himself, and at his own charge, to the royal residence, where he is often obliged to remain several days in waiting at the palace-gate before his present is received, and he dares not before then ever think of departure. On this account a Candian peasant on lighting by accident on a precious stone, will either destroy or leave it where it lies, rather than subject himself to the trouble and expence of carrying it to the royal residence.

The principal revenues of the king consist of presents or contributions brought him by the people, or rather irregularly enforced by his officers, two or three times a year. These contributions consist of money, precious stones, ivory, cloth, corn, fruit, honey, wax, arms, and other articles of their own manufacture, such as spears, arrows, pikes, targets, tali-pot leaves, &c.

Fear of the Europeans induces the king to practise the

same policy as the dread of his rapacious officers produces among his subjects. He pretends on all occasions to be very poor, although it is well known that his treasury is well stored with various articles of great value. The presents which he made our government in return for some very valuable ones he received from us, were extremely poor indeed.

The lower classes of the people, however, are not the only persons who feel the burden of supplying the royal treasury. Upon certain festivals, which he observes in great state, all the Mahondrews and principal people are obliged to appear before him, and none must come empty-handed. Before they are admitted to the royal presence, they deposit their gifts at the palace gate, and are then received by the monarch according to the value of their offering. It is dangerous for them to keep back on these occasions, and the expected present is necessary for the security both of their persons and property. The *dackenie,* or gift, is always wrapt up in a white cloth, and carried on the head of him who presents it, even were it no bigger than the size of a nut. A white cloth is particularly chosen, as this is the royal colour, and except on business belonging to the king, is never allowed to be employed.

These stated periods of contribution, however, are not the only extortions practised on the Candian subjects. The moment in which the king's officers understand that any one is possessed of valuables, is the signal for demanding a share for the royal treasury; and artists are frequently employed by the king to make him arms and different works in silver and gold, all at their own expence.

As the government of Candy is completely despotic, every subject is of course ready at the call of the sovreign; and as fear of the Europeans keeps him continually on the alert, all the Candians are held obliged to take arms without distinction at his command. His regular troops, as he calls them, may consist of about twenty thousand men. I was led to form this computation from the circumstance that an army nearly of that number of his regular troops met our embassy near Sittivacca, and continued within three miles of us during the whole time we remained in the country. So great was his jealousy of Europeans, that I am convinced his whole efficient force was on this occasion assembled in our neighbourhood; and besides this regular army, large bodies of the Militia of the country lay around us in every direction.

According to the universal usage of despots, who dare not venture to trust their own subjects, the king always keep about his person a body of Malabars, Malays, and others who are not his own natural subjects, but many of them runaways from the Dutch. As these troops are entirely unconnected with the natives, and depend solely on his favour for protection and preferment, he places his chief confidence in them, and employs them as his constant body guard.

Besides this corps of foreign guards, who do perpetual duty at the palace, about eight thousand of his regular troops and a number of the nobles are kept quartered in the neighbourhood ready to be assembled at a moment's notice. These troops, though called regulars, have neither arms nor cloaths to entitle them to that appellation. They wear what dress they chuse, and arm themselves with any sort of weapons they can procure; so that when assembled, they present merely a grotesque groupe of tatterdemalions. Their armour is altogether of a motley nature; spears, pikes, swords, targets, bows and arrows, matchlocks, with, perhaps, a thousand fusees or muskets and bayonets: all these pieces of armour which I saw were in very bad order, and their whole accoutrements and appearance ridiculous.

The rest of the military force, except on particular occasions, lie scattered throughout the country. Their pay and subsistence consists in a small allowance of rice and salt, a piece of cloth annually given them for dress, an exemption from taxes and all other services, and a small piece of ground to cultivate for their maintenance. When any of the soldiers are guilty of a neglect of duty, or any other criminal offence, his usual punishment is to be compelled to level a piece of hill, or clear the channel of a river. This might seem a very reasonable mode of punishment, and well adapted to the improvement of a country; but lest my readers might think this idea rather too refined for a Candian, I must at the same time inform him, that it always makes part of the punishment to carry the earth and rubbish back to the spot from which they were taken and replace them in their original form. For more trivial offences the soldiers are curtailed of their pay and allowances.

Distrust and jealousy, the constant attendants of arbitrary power, pervade the whole of the military system. The commanders and other officers of the forces are never allowed to correspond, or even to see each other, except when the public exigency requires them to be brought together; and it is the policy of the king to encourage them to watch and act as spies upon each other, to prevent combination among themselves or any intercourse with the Europeans. The last object seems indeed sufficiently guarded against by the continued chain of posts and watches established around the whole outskirts of his dominions. Every inhabitant of the borders is a sentinel; and as many of them have their habitations placed on the tops of trees which overlook the whole country, it is altogether impossible to elude so many obstacles, and get either out of the country or into it by stealth or against their consent. Even in the interior of the Candian dominions the same jealous precautions are observed, and no one is permitted to pass from one district to another without first being examined and producing his passport. This passport consists of a piece of clay stamped with a seal or impression denoting the profession of the bearer: the passport for a military man represents a soldier with a pike or gun on his shoulder; that for a peasant, a labourer with a stick across his shoulder, and a bag or wallet attached to each end of it: the passport of an European has impressed on it the figure of a man with a hat on his head and a sword by his side. These precautions are strictly enforced and completely serve the intended purpose: but it would be needless even in the most jealous prince to throw any more obstacles in the way of communication and intercourse, than is interposed by nature, especially when we consider that the king allows none of the woods to be cleared away, nor any roads to be made through his dominions. His apprehension of intrusion from strangers, except when he is at war with the Europeans, is no better grounded; as even the native Cinglese of the coasts, are so possessed with an opinion of the fatality of the climate in the interior, that they think with terror of approaching it. This we learnt to our cost in the embassy to the Court of Candy, when the Cinglese peasants who were employed in conveying our guns and baggage deserted us in such a manner that we were obliged to leave the greater part behind.

The narrow paths which lead through the woods and mountains of the Candians, are indeed sufficient for all the purposes of the natives, as they universally travel afoot. To ride a horseback is a royal privilege; and a privilege seldom made use of by the monarch himself. There are indeed no horses kept in the interior but those belonging to his Majesty; and even the royal stud is in a very reduced state, as it consists merely of presents from the European governments of the coasts. No horses are reared in the interior; and it is observed they die soon after they are brought there, both from the change of climate, and from the want of proper care and management. The native Candians, both from want of dexterity and activity, are bad servants in any point of view; and in the management of horses, an animal to which they are so little accustomed, they are particularly deficient. Nor is all the prospect of royal bounty and favour sufficient to procure his Majesty the services of Malabar grooms in a country and climate so different from their own.

Where the government is a pure despotism, and every thing depends on the immediate will of the sovereign, there can be no fixed and established laws. The Candians, indeed, boast of an ancient code of written laws, but these remain in the hands of the monarch who is their sole interpreter. Certain ancient customs and rules, however, are supposed to have the authority of fundamental laws; but when we hear of the king himself being amenable to them, it means nothing more than that the breach of them excites such general indignation, as more than once to have given rise to a successful rebellion. His authority supersedes every other decision, and every sentence of death is subject to his revisal.

With regard to courts of law, or regular forms of administering justice, the Candians appear to have scarcely formed any conceptions. Their trials are summary; and their punishments, unless where the king interposes, immediate. Their capital punishments are always attended with some aggravating cruelty; having the criminal dashed to pieces by elephants, pounding him in a large mortar, or impaling him on a stake, are the common modes practised. Where the offence is not adjudged worthy of death, the culprit is condemned to pay a heavy fine, to have his property confiscated, to perform severe tasks of various sorts, such as carrying heavy weights on his back, levelling hills, and raising them up again, &c. Imprisonment is a species of punishment never to be inflicted on a Candian, and only suited to the barbarity of Europeans. This may be alleged as the principal cause of their summary trials and punishments, as they never confine a culprit. Not only a prison, but any species of confinement, seems to convey ideas peculiarly horrible to their imaginations. The Candian ambassadors could not even be prevailed upon to allow the doors of the carriage, sent to convey them to an audience with our Governor, to be shut upon them, as they said it looked like making them prisoners: and the doors were actually obliged to be fastened back in order to remove their objections.

The administration of justice is entrusted to the Dissauvas and Adigars; but in capital cases an appeal lies to the king. As respect is paid not only to the merits of the cause, but to the rank of the offender, it is evident that the administration of justice must be very defective. Presumptive proof is allowed to have great weight, and it is therefore probable that prejudice has still more. Nor can we suppose, where so much depends on the will of individuals, that favour does not often triumph over the love of justice; though indeed the judges, if convicted before the prince of unfair dealing, are without farther ceremony instantly put to death in his presence. Debt is looked upon as a heinous offence in Candy, as well as in all other poor countries where there is little accumulation of wealth in the hands of individuals. In the large fines imposed on debtors and those guilty of personal injuries, the king never fails to come in for his share.

The great safe-guard of justice among the Candians is the natural mildness and honesty of their dispositions, in which they excel all other Indians. In a country so poor, there are indeed few temptations to be dishonest or unjust; and it is perhaps the rarity of crimes which has made the administration of justice be permitted to remain so long defective.

I have now mentioned all the circumstances worthy of notice which I could collect with regard to the natives of Ceylon, who live under the dominion of their native prince. The Candians, shut up as they are from all intercourse with foreign countries, and proud of immemorial independence, might be supposed to enjoy amidst their native mountains and woods a life of tranquillity and happiness not to be looked for among those busy nations whose minds are inflamed by luxury and agitated with the thirst of gain. But this is far from being the case. The oppression of their governors, the constant dread of Europeans, and the superstitious fears arising from the nature of their climate, which continually haunt them, deprive this isolated people of all the enjoyments which seem congenial to their situation. It is to be hoped that our countrymen, by a generous and well-regulated policy, will speedily diminish their sources of unhappiness. Much of the gloom which overhangs the minds of the Candians, took its rise from the oppressive exactions and destructive inroads of the Dutch. After the last and most severe blow which the natives sustained, on being deprived of Portallom, which supplied them with fish, and the still more indispensable article of salt, they formed a resolution to abandon for ever a country which could not even supply them with the necessaries of life, but as the price of slavery. They were not, however, permitted to put this last effort of despair into execution: the Dutch were possessed of every outlet of the island; and the passage to the island of Ramiseram, where they had determined to seek for refuge, was guarded by a strong post which the Europeans had established at Manaar. This post proved an insuperable bar, both to their plan of deserting their native country, and to their receiving any assistance from their friends on the opposite continent.

But although strong posts and guards may prevent the escape of the natives from the island, it is evident that such plans can never render them efficacious agents in its improvement. It will require many years of perseverance in a mild and steady policy to obliterate those prejudices with which imprudent cruelty has inspired them against Europeans. But the advantages which may be derived from their friendship and co-operation, certainly render a new system at least worth the experiment. A mild and liberal policy is more congenial to the feelings of my countrymen; and I am happy to observe that the measures already adopted by our government in Ceylon, are of such a nature as to have greatly conciliated the minds of the natives. The reigning prince has had reason more than once to be gratified with our civilities. About five years ago he married a Malabar princess of his own country and sect, and a near relation of the Rajah of Ramnad. She passed into the island by the way of Manaar: and the king acknowledged his obligations to the officer stationed there for the civilities shewn her in her progress to Candy. Attentions of this nature, with some well-timed presents and concessions, must have more effect both on the prince and people, than all the armies which the former possessors of the island wasted in fruitless wars against them.

CHAPTER XIII.

Description of the Bedahs, or Vaddahs.

THE most singular part of the inhabitants of Ceylon remains yet to be described. It has been supposed that man is so prone to society and civilization, that ignorance of them can alone induce him to remain in a solitary or barbarous state; and yet among the woods and mountains of Ceylon we find a race, who are accustomed to see the luxuries of the Cinglese and the arts of Europeans, yet prefer the savage independence of their wilds, and the precarious subsistence procured by the chace. The origin of the Bedahs, or Vaddahs, who inhabit the deepest recesses of the Ceylonese forests, has never been traced, as no other race can be found in the eastern world which corresponds with them. Conjecture has, indeed, been busy on the occasion, as it usually is where real information is wanting. The Bedahs are generally supposed to have been the aboriginal inhabitants of the island, who, upon being overwhelmed by their Cinglese invaders, preferred the independence of savages to a tame submission. A current tradition, however, assigns them a different origin. It is related that they were cast away on the island, and chose to settle there; but refusing, upon a certain occasion to assist the king in his wars against some foreign enemies, they were driven out from the society of the natives, and forced to take up their abode in the most unfrequented forests. Some imagine that the Bedahs are merely a part of the native Candians, who chose to retain their ancient savage freedom, when the brethren of the plains and vallies submitted to the cultivation of the earth, and the restraints of society. This opinion rests entirely on those Bedahs, who are most known, speaking a broken dialect of the Cinglese. It is, however, by no means ascertained that this is the universal language of the Bedahs; nor is any account of their origin supported by the slightest shadow of proof.

It will not seem strange that the origin of the Bedahs is so little known, when I inform the reader that I had lived a considerable time in the island of Ceylon before I even heard that there was such a race in existence; and numbers residing there to this day know nothing of the fact. The first time I understood that the Bedahs inhabited Ceylon was in consequence of a party of them being surprised by our Sepoys in the beginning of 1798, while up the country against the rebellious Cinglese; they were brought to Columbo, where I had an opportunity of examining their appearance. They seemed to be a race entirely different from the other Ceylonese: their complexions were fairer, and inclining to a copper colour: they were remarkably well made, wore long beards, and their hair tucked up close to the crown of the head; their bodies had scarcely any other covering than what they had received from nature.

Since I left the island, I have been informed by Colonel Champagne that he had an opportunity of seeing some more of these savages. They had been making inroads and causing alarms in the northern part of the island, probably at the instigation of the Dutch, in consequence of which several of them had been apprehended and brought before the Colonel. They were wild and savage in their appearance, and armed with bows and arrows. After enjoining them to live in quiet, Colonel Champagne made them a few presents and then ordered them to be released; upon which they instantly fled away into the woods like deer.

The Bedahs are scattered over the woods in different parts of Ceylon, but are most numerous in the province of Bintan, which lies to the north-east of Candy in the direction of Trincomalee and Batacolo. The tribe found in this quarter acknowledges no authority but that of its own chief and religious men. The Bedahs are completely savage here, and have never entered into any intercourse with the other natives, or scarcely even been seen by them. Those bordering on the district of Jafnapatam, and the tribes who inhabit the west and south-west quarters of the island, between Adam's Peak and the Raygam and Pasdam corles, are the only Bedahs who have been seen by Europeans, and are much less wild and ferocious than those who live in the forests of Bintan.

The Bedahs, as they acknowledge no power but their own chiefs, so they adhere from generation to generation to their own laws and customs without the smallest variation. They subsist entirely by hunting deer and other animals with which their forests supply them. The cultivation of the ground is an art which they never attempt to practise; nor would it indeed be possible for them in the thick woods and wilds which they inhabit, without infinite labour, to prepare the ground for the reception of rice or any other sort of corn. The flesh of the animals which they procure by the chace, and the fruits which grow spontaneously around them, compose their whole food. They sleep either on trees or at the foot of them: and in the latter case, they place thorns and other bushes all around them to keep off wild beasts, or by their rustling to give warning of their approach. As soon as the least noise rouses his apprehension, the Bedah climbs up the tree with the utmost expertness and celerity.

The few of this race who are not altogether so wild, although they do not acknowledge the sovereignty of the king, yet they furnish him with ivory, honey, wax, and deer: and such of them as skirt the European territories, barter these articles with the Cinglese for the simple things which their mode of life requires. To prevent themselves from being surprised or made prisoners, while carrying on this traffic, the method they employ is curious. When they stand in need of cloth, iron, knives, or any other articles of smith's work, they approach by night some town or village, and deposit in a place where it is likely immediately to be discovered, a certain quantity of their goods, along with a talipot leaf expressive of what they want in return. On a following night they repair again to the same place, and generally find their expected reward awaiting them. For although they are easily satisfied, and readily allow the advantage to the person with whom they deal, yet if their requests are treated with neglect, they will not fail to watch their opportunity of doing him a mischief. The Cinglese, as they can afterwards dispose of the articles afforded by the Bedahs, find the traffic profitable; and in some parts frequently go into the woods carrying with them articles of barter. This trade, however, can only be carried on in the manner I have already described; for no native of the woods can be more afraid of approaching a stranger than the Bedahs. A few, as I have already said, will venture even to converse with the other natives; but the wilder class, known by the name of Ramba Vaddahs, are more seldom seen even by stealth than the most timid of the wild animals.

As the Bedahs chiefly live by the produce of the chace, they acquire by habit an astonishing dexterity in this employment. They learn to steal through the bushes so warily and silently, that they often come unperceived within reach of the deer; when they throw their little axes so dexterously that the animal seldom escapes alive. Honey, which is found in great abundance in every part of their woods, forms another article of their food, and also serves the purposes of salt, which it is out of their power to procure. They preserve their flesh in honey, and then place it in the hollow of a tree, or a wooden case well chinamed, till they have occasion to use it. This honey, which they employ much of their time in finding out, and which they barter in considerable quantities with the Candians, is also used by the latter for a variety of purposes. A prevalent idea that they employ it to embalm their dead, makes many people on the coast averse to taste honey from the fear of having it only after it has served a former purpose; and I must confess that from this prejudice, I felt no great inclination to use any wild honey, unless it was brought down in combs.

The dogs of the Bedahs are remarkable for their sagacity, and not only readily trace out game, but also distinguish one species of animals from another. On the approach of any carnivorous animal, or of a stranger, they immediately put their masters upon their guard. These faithful animals are indeed invaluable to them and constitute their chief riches. When their daughters are married, hunting dogs form their portion; and a Bedah is as unwilling to part with his dog as an Arabian with his horse. Some time before the last war broke out between us and Holland, a Dutch officer procured a couple of these dogs, which he carried to Surat, and sold for four hundred rix-dollars.

These Bedahs who venture to converse with the other natives, are represented to be courteous, and in address far beyond their state of civilization. Their religion is little known. They have their inferior deities corresponding to the demons of the Cinglese, and observe certain festivals. On these occasions victuals of various sorts are placed at the root of a tree, and the ceremonies of the festival consist in dancing around them.

These few particulars are all that are at present known of this remarkable people; and in their savage and unconnected state, without arts or policy, there are probably few more circumstances worthy of notice that remain to be known. They are rather an object of curiosity, than either of utility or apprehension to Europeans; for many ages must perhaps pass before they can be either brought to assist in cultivating the island, or united into such a society as might disturb the tranquillity of their neighbours.

CHAPTER XIV.

Animals of Ceylon.

HAVING described the island of Ceylon, and the several races of it's inhabitants, I now proceed to give some account of it's natural productions. From my profession and habits of life, a systematic description of these cannot be expected. I shall therefore in plain and common language, relate what I have myself observed, and what I have learnt from authentic information: those who are in the same predicament with myself, and who are unacquainted with the terms employed by scientifick men, may find such an account at least more readily understood; and those who have studied natural history as a science, will be easily able to refer the facts I advance to a regular system.

At the head of the class of quadrupeds, and superior to those of the same species found in any other part of the world, are the elephants of Ceylon. The number of these noble animals produced there is very great, and nowhere are they found either so docile or so excellent in their shape and appearance. To give any particular description of a species so often described and so universally known, would be superfluous: but as the manner of catching them in Ceylon is considerably different from that practised on the continent of India, some account of it may not be without entertainment to my readers.

For a month or two previous to the elephant-hunt, the natives are employed in enclosing a large space of ground in the midst of a tope of Cocoa-trees, and adjoining, or perhaps encompassing a tank or pond of water. The enclosure consists of large, strong posts, usually of cocoa-wood, driven firmly into the ground, and fastened and connected together by strong ropes and the branches of the contiguous trees interwoven. The inclosure is covered with bushes and boughs, so as to prevent the posts or the ropes from being seen. The way leading into this inclosed space is by long, narrow, and circuitous paths fenced on each side in the manner already described, and approaching in every different direction. Besides these paths, which are sufficiently large to admit the elephant, there are various other very narrow ones to allow the hunters to advance towards him and retreat occasionally without his being able to pursue them. Within the large enclosure are several smaller compartments formed with paths leading into them; and one straight path is prepared at the further end to lead out the elephant when he is secured. The whole has the appearance of one large labyrinth; and its construction displays a very considerable degree of ingenuity.

As soon as all this work, which occupies some time, is finished, the Moodeliers and other principal men among the Cinglese set about collecting the peasants from every quarter; and a vast number of men, women, and children, furnished with drums and other noisy instruments are speedily assembled. The woods are immediately beset on all sides by this multitude; when day light fails them they find their way through the thicks by torchlight, and they are furnished with fire arms to defend themselves from any sudden attack of the beasts of prey which infest the forests. The elephants are by this time reduced to great extremities by thirst, as guards have been for some days previous stationed at all the lakes and ponds of water to frighten them away; and now they find themselves roused from their haunts in all directions by loud noises and the glare of torches. One quarter alone, the enclosure I have described, remains undisturbed, and here they are presented both with a peaceful retreat and plenty of water. To this spot therefore they all repair, and are frequently compelled to hasten their steps by the aproaching noises which continually assail them from the rear. On coming to the entrance of the paths leading to the enclosure, their natural sagacity enables them to perceive the altered appearance of the place: the fences and narrow paths, where so little room is left for their natural exertion, makes them suspect that danger is at hand and a snare laid for them; and they begin to shew every symptom of dread and consternation. No time however is left them for deliberation, nor any opportunity of retreat; from the right and the left, as well as from behind, the noise and clamour of enemies immediately press upon them.

Urged on in this manner, they at length enter the paths, and push forward till they reach the large space of the enclosure. As soon as they are thus secured, tame elephants are sent in after them, and all the avenues shut, except those narrow paths by which the natives are to approach them. The hunters now advance by these in all directions, and use every means to separate the elephants and drive them singly into the smaller compartments which are contained within the large enclosure. On this being effected, the only thing that remains is to secure them with ropes. The tame elephants are here of the most effectual service to the hunters, and greatly assist them in throwing ropes round the legs and neck of the wild animals. As soon as the wild elephant is made fast with ropes, he is led out by the straight path prepared for the purpose, and made fast to the strongest trees on the outside of the labyrinth. The hunters then renew the same process with the rest, till all the elephants within the enclosure are successively secured.

It frequently happens that the elephants when first caught are very unruly and violent; in which case it is necessary to have recourse to the powers and sagacity of the tame ones. The latter, when they perceive their wild brother is unmanageable, fall to jostling him, and belabouring him with their trunks, till such time as they have rendered him perfectly calm and compliant. They are also very assiduous in watching all his motions, and prevent him from making any sudden attack on their keepers.

In 1797, no less than one hundred and seventy-six elephants, taken in this manner, were sent over by Adam's bridge from Ceylon to the continent. On their way I had an opportunity of seeing these immense animals at the Grand Pass beyond Columbo. One of them was exceedingly large and tall, and surpassed in size even the royal elephant in the possession of the Nabob of Arcot, which I saw near his palace of Chepauk. These animals, though so lately taken in a wild state, appeared quite tractable, shewed no symptom of being mischievous, and readily obeyed their keepers.

The superiority of the elephants of Ceylon does not consist in their size, (for they are in general not so tall as those on the continent;) but in their greater hardiness and powers for exertion, in their docility and freedom from vice and passion. The natives are so possessed with the idea of the excellence of their own elephants, as to affirm that the elephants of all other parts of the world make obeisance before those of Ceylon, and thus instinctively acknowledge their superiority.

These lords of the forest, though from their size and strength formidable to all its other inhabitants, themselves live in continual apprehension of a small reptile, against which neither their sagacity nor their prowess can at all defend them. This diminutive creature gets into the trunk of the elephant, and pursues its course till it finally fixes in his head, and by keeping him in continual agony, at length torments the stupendous animal to death. So dreadfully afraid are the elephants of this dangerous enemy, that they use a variety of precautions to prevent his attacks; and never lay their trunks to the ground, except when to gather or separate their food.

The struggles which the elephants make to prevent themselves from being secured, and the violence employed to render them tame, produce a number of accidents of which some of them die while others are rendered completely useless. Not above the half of those driven into the enclosure, or otherwise taken, can be preserved from injury so as to be afterwards brought to sale. The hunt in 1797 was the greatest ever known.

Of those animals applied to domestic purposes, Ceylon produces but few. I have already mentioned that the horse and sheep are not natives of this island, and scarcely can be made to thrive there when imported. The horses which are bred on the small islands beyond Jafnapatam, are a mixture of the Arab and the common horse of the Carnatic. They are mostly used for drawing gigs and other light pleasure vehicles. The Manilla, the Pegu, and the Atcheen horses, are much employed for these purposes, and, though small, are very much esteemed on account of their fast trotting, their strength, and their being capable of enduring a great deal of fatigue. The horses used by the civil and military officers are chiefly Arabs brought by the way of Bombay.

As the expence of importation must be added to the price of sheep and horses, and as a great proportion, particularly of the former, die on being landed in the island, these animals are in consequence much dearer here than in any other part of India. Sheep sometimes fetch ten and even twenty times the price they do on the opposite coast of Coromandel.

In Ceylon, or indeed in any part of India, horses are never employed in servile work, or for drawing burthens. As they are scarcely ever castrated, they are indeed so spirited and vicious as in some degree to be unfitted for these purposes. The care and attendance which they require is also too great to allow their being kept by any but the wealthy for pleasure. Two attendants are constantly attached to each horse: one of them is employed in cutting and fetching him as much grass as he requires to eat; while the other takes care of him, cleans him, feeds him, and makes him ready for his master to mount. The last attendant never quits his horse, but follows him wherever he goes, and is ready on all occasions to take charge of him. I have seen some of these horse-keepers, as they are called, keep up to my horse for twenty or thirty miles together, while I was proceeding at the rate of five or six miles an hour.

The Indian horses are extremely spirited, and often defend their riders against the attack of other animals, and I have myself been indebted to their prowess for my preservation from the fury of a buffalo. It is only when so vicious, as to be perfectly unmanageable, that these animals are ever castrated in this quarter of the world; and in this mutilated state, they decrease greatly in value, as they are then by no means so capable of enduring the heat of the climate, and the violent fatigue which must be occasioned by exertion in these countries. In consequence of this, mares are seldom or ever used; and in particular, on a line of march or where a number of horses are collected together, they are never suffered to come in the way, as they would render the horses outrageous.

The oxen of Ceylon are remarkably small, and in size scarcely exceed our calves of a year old. They are far from being well-shaped, as they have a hump on their shoulders. They are as inferior in quality as in size to the cattle of Bengal and the Coromandel coast; and are to be had for ten or twelve rupees, or rix-dollars, about one pound five shillings sterling. The beef is sometimes however, fat and tolerably good, and forms the chief food of the European soldiers stationed on the island.

These bullocks, though small, are very useful. They are employed in all sorts of work to which they are adapted, in drawing artillery, and conveying burthens which are too large for the coolies to carry. The want of proper roads indeed makes these people be employed to do much of the work which would otherwise be imposed on the oxen. Their common method of carrying burthens is on their heads, or suspended to each end of some pieces of bamboe laid across their shoulders; and it is really astonishing to see what loads they will bear in this manner, even under the fatiguing heat of noon. Though they may find considerable difficulty in lifting the load at first, yet when once set agoing, they will travel at the rate of four or five miles for a whole day. The spring in the pieces of bamboe, by yielding to their motions, greatly facilitates the carriage of the burthen. When the roads will admit of it, and the loads are too heavy for the coolies, the bullocks are employed to draw them in carts of a particular construction, known on the island by the name of *bandies*. These vehicles are very long, narrow, and clumsy. The body of the bandy rests on a strong beam, which projects like the pole of a carriage. To the extreme end of this pole a piece of wood, about six feet long, and very thick, is attached crosswise. Under it are hoops fixed for the necks of the cattle, which are kept fast by pegs. By this means the whole weight of the load rests on the neck and shoulders of the oxen, while they drag the cart along. The sides of the cart are composed of thin boards, of the skins of buffaloes, or split bamboes; while a strong post of wood is placed at each of the four corners to give it a shape and hold these firm. The bottom is either of boards, or interwoven bamboes: the axle-tree and wheels resemble those of the Irish truckles, or cars, being blocks of wood rounded.

Buffaloes, being much larger and stronger than the oxen, are much more frequently employed in drawing burthens. These animals are found in great numbers on the island, both in a wild and tame state, and are all of the same species and appearance. They are fierce and rough, extremely obstinate and untractable, with a wild forbidding countenance. Even such of them as are trained to the draught, and familiarised to the people, never lose their original habits, but are always dangerous to meddle with or to meet in the fields. In shape, they are broad before, and narrow behind, and their legs are thick and short. They always carry their heads low: their horns are black and very thick, shooting out backwards to a considerable length, and bending towards the shoulders. The buffaloes do not employ their horns offensively, in the same manner as our bulls, but first run headlong at their object and trample it under foot; and after this is accomplished, they get down on their knees and endeavour to bring their horns into such a position as to gore their victim. It is always dangerous to meet with these animals, particularly for an European, to whose complexion or dress they have the greatest antipathy. A scarlet coat is the chief object of their resentment, and renders them perfectly outrageous. This unaccountable aversion to red is extremely vexatious to military men. I have myself frequently experienced it, and been obliged to escape as fast as I could from their fury: at one time I was saved only by the spirit of my horse. Their fierceness surpasses that of almost any wild beast, as it can never be totally subdued either by gentle usage, or the sense of fear.

The buffalo is of a dirty grey or mouse colour; the hairs, or rather bristles, are thinly scattered over his thick coarse skin. The flesh and milk, though sometimes used, are very rank and disagreeable. These animals are very dirtily inclined, and are constantly to be seen like hogs wallowing up to the neck in mud and water.

The markets of Ceylon are well supplied with pigs, and they can be always had at very reasonable prices; the smaller ones at about five shillings, and even the largest never sell for more than ten. The pigs here are usually about the size of our small greyish ones.

Few parts of India produce a greater variety of wild animals than Ceylon; and its forests are rendered extremely dangerous by beasts of prey and noxious reptiles of various sizes. Many wild animals are also offered to the use of man; and afford subsistence to the tribes who, like them, range the forests.

Varieties of deer and elks are every where met with in the woods and jungles. One species of deer is particularly calculated to attract attention. It is a very small creature, in size not exceeding our hare; it is called by the Dutch the *moose-deer*, and by the natives *gazelle*. In every thing but in size they are complete deer; and their sides are beautifully spotted, or streaked like the fallow-deer. It is usual for the natives to catch them, and bring them down in cages to our markets, where they are sold at about a shilling apiece. Their flavour is much stronger than that of the hare, and when stewed they are excellent.

Rabbits are not natives of Ceylon, and even if they were introduced, it is probable that they would soon be destroyed by the wild beasts and reptiles, which would every where assail them above ground, and even persecute them in their burrows.

Hares, of exactly the same species with our common hares in Europe, abound in every quarter throughout the island, in greater numbers than I have ever seen elsewhere. About Columbo one may easily shoot a dozen in a few hours.

The wild hog is much more esteemed than the tame. The wild boars add much to the dangers of the Ceylonese forests; they are very large and fierce, and boldly attack those who fall in their way. The natives are particularly afraid of them, and think it an exploit of no small intrepidity to hunt them.

The smaller species of tyger also infests the woods, but seldom ventures to attack a man. The larger kind, called the royal tyger, is not an inhabitant of the island, which is a circumstance extremely fortunate for the natives, as from the woody nature of the country, these ferocious animals would have every opportunity to commit their ravages with impunity on the human species.

The tyger-cat found here is about the size of a lap-dog, and presents both in shape and colour exactly the appearance indicated by its name. It is very wild and extremely difficult to tame, though from its size it is not a dangerous animal.

The leopard is a native of the island.

There are no foxes in Ceylon, but their place is amply supplied by an immense number of jackals. These animals very much resemble the fox, but are much bolder and fiercer. It is always by night that they approach the villages in large packs, making a loud and horrible noise like the screaming of children, which they increase as soon as they have found carrion, or any other sort of prey. It is a striking trait of their savage character, that they continue to keep up this frightful noise, even while they are devouring their food. As soon as the uproar of the jackals is heard, all the dogs of the village, as if by one consent, instinctively sally out to attack them and drive them back into the woods.

The hyena and the bear, though natives of Ceylon, are very rarely met with; a few only being found on the north-east side.

A great variety of monkies are found in swarms over the island; and some of the species are uncommon. The *wanderow* is remarkable for its great white beard, which stretches quite from ear to ear across its black face, while the body is of a dark grey. Another species is distinguished by a black body, and a white triangular beard with a purple face. There is also a large greenish monkey which inhabits the woods here. The *rillow* is a very large species, not less than our larger dogs. It is distinguished by long parted hair lying flat in its forehead. This species is extremely numerous, and a great annoyance to the corn fields and gardens, which they rob in the face of the owner, while they deride him by antick gestures.

A variety of porcupines, racoons, armadilloes, squirrels, and mungooses, are found in Ceylon. The porcupines are easily caught, and are frequently kept tame in the houses.

The squirrels are very destructive to the gardens, which they invade in multitudes and devour vast quantities of the fruit. The black squirrel of Ceylon has the nose red, and is remarkable for being three times as large as our common squirrel, and for having a tail twice as long as its body. The small striped squirrel is very playful, and is constantly seen squeaking and skipping about among the trees.

The Indian ichneumon is a small creature, in appearance between a weazel and a mungoose. It is of infinite use to the natives, from its inveterate enmity to snakes, which would otherwise render every footstep of the traveller dangerous. The proofs of sagacity which I have seen in this little animal are truly surprising, and afford a beautiful instance of the wisdom with which Providence has fitted the powers of every animal to its particular situation on the globe. This diminutive creature, on seeing a snake ever so large, will instantly dart on it and seize it by the throat, provided he finds himself in an open place where he has an opportunity of running to a certain herb, which he knows instinctively to be an antidote against the poison of the bite, if he should happen to receive one. I was present at an experiment tried at Columbo to ascertain the reality of this circumstance. The ichneumon, procured for the purpose, was first shewn the snake in a close room. On being let down to the ground, he did not discover any inclination whatever to attack his enemy, but ran prying about the room to discover if there was any hole or aperture by which he might get out. On finding none, he returned hastily to his master, and placing himself in his bosom, could not by any means be induced to quit it, or face the snake. On being carried out of the house, however, and laid down near his antagonist in an open place, he instantly flew at the snake and soon destroyed it. He then suddenly disappeared for a few minutes, and again returned as soon as he had found the herb and eat of it. This useful instinct impels the animal to have recourse to the herb on all occasions, where it is engaged with a snake, whether poisonous or not. The one employed in this experiment was of the harmless kind, and procured for the purpose.

The flormouse, or flying-fox, like the bat, partakes of the appearance both of the bird and quadruped; and its name is derived from the great resemblance of its head and body to the fox. Its body is about the size of an ordinary cat: the wings when extended measure from the tip of the one to that of the other upwards of six feet; and the length of the animal from the nose, to the tail of which it has barely the name, is about two feet. The flormouse lives in the woods, and perches on the tallest trees. While asleep or inactive these animals suspend themselves by the feet from the branches, and continue to hang in this manner as if they were dead. The night is the season of their activity: at that time they fly about with a horrid noise and devour all the fruit which they can come at. To prevent their ravages, strong nets are thrown over the fruit trees, and a sort of rattle made of pieces of board so contrived as to clap together and frighten them away by its noise.

The flying-foxes also see by day, and often fly about observing where fruit is to be found; but then they defer their attack upon it till night, and generally keep among the thick woods till dark. They are very numerous in this island, and I have often seen them in such flocks as we are accustomed in Europe to see crows about an extensive rookery. It was my intention to have one of this species shipped over to Europe, and for this purpose I had killed one as it hovered over my head in the neighbourhood of Nigumbo; but the smell was so intolerable that it was impossible to preserve it even for the shortest time.

The rats are very numerous and exceedingly troublesome. There are several species besides those common in Europe: the most observable are the blind-rat, the musk-rat, and the bandy-coot. The blind-rat lives in the fields, and burrows in the earth like the mole, chiefly about the banks of rivers. Like the mole it is instinctively warned to shun the surface of the ground by a membrane which closes over its eyes as soon as it becomes exposed to the rays of light: and from this it derives its name.

The bandy-coot is as large as a middling-sized cat, the body very thick and round, and the head greatly resembling that of a hog; it also makes a grunting noise like that animal. When closely pursued or attacked, the bandy-coot becomes very fierce, and turns furiously on its assailants.

The musk-rat, or perfuming shrew, is very small, with a long snout, much extended beyond the under jaw. In running about it makes a squeaking noise like the squirrel, but much shriller and louder. From the intolerable smell of musk which accompanies and remains behind these animals where-ever they go, they are very disagreeable inmates; and there is scarcely a house in Columbo in particular which has not been strongly scented by them in every corner. Many articles are rendered entirely useless by the smell of musk which they communicate in merely running over them. For it is a certain fact, that of so penetrating a nature is their effluvia, that if they even pass over a bottle of wine ever so well corked and sealed up, it becomes so strongly tainted with musk that it cannot be used; and a whole cask may be rendered useless in the same manner.

When I arrived in Ceylon in the latter end of the year 1796, the houses were terribly infested with rats.

This was in a great measure to be attributed to the slovenliness and negligence of the Dutch; for though vanity induced them to keep their rooms for the reception of company sufficiently clean, the other parts of their houses, particularly their go-downs or out-houses for their servants and slaves, were so dirty and full of old lumber as to harbour all sorts of vermin, nor were the dogs and cats of the country of much service in destroying them. Since the residence of the British officers on the island, their terriers have been continually employed in clearing the houses of rats, the number of which have sensibly diminished. More attention is also now paid to the cleanliness of those apartments allotted to the servants, who naturally follow the example of their masters, and are consequently much more cleanly in the service of the English than the Dutch.

The *talgoi* is a species of the ant-eater; and destroys the ants in the same manner as the others, by laying his slimy tongue before their nests, and drawing it back into his mouth as soon as he finds it covered with those insects.

The Birds of Ceylon are a very numerous class. All sorts of our domestic poultry, turkeys excepted, are natives of the island; and there are few birds found in our woods or marshes that do not here abound. Ducks, geese, pheasants, parrots and parroquets are all found in great numbers, both wild and tame.

The *lowrie* or *lory* is a species of parrot, and varies in its size.

Snipes are found in great plenty in the hot season, which is the best time for shooting them. The painted snipe is a very beautiful and striking bird. In size it differs little from our common snipe; only the bill is somewhat shorter, the body and wings are spotted with red, yellow and black spots, which give it a very fine appearance.

The florican is a species of the crane kind, about the size and weight of a large capon, and is esteemed excellent eating. It lives among the woods which skirt the banks of pools or lakes. The neck and body are longish, but not so slender in proportion to their length as those of the crane or heron.

The banks of the rivers and lakes abound with storks, cranes, herons, and water fowls of various descriptions.

Wood-peckers are found with beautiful top-knots of a golden colour.

Pigeons, both wild and tame, form a prominent part of the birds of Ceylon. The most remarkable species is the cinnamon pigeon, so called from being particularly partial to the cinnamon woods. It is of a beautiful green colour, and is as large as our common fowl. This species swarms in Ceylon at all seasons of the year; they are often shot by the Europeans, and are highly esteemed for the table. It is remarkable of these pigeons that they never alight on the ground, but perch on high trees, particularly on the Banyan-tree.

There is another species of pigeon of a greyish colour, which is nearly as large as that described; and the woods every where abound with smaller pigeons of different kinds and various colours.

I have been told that the pelican is a native of this island, but I never saw it. There are a few partridges, of the small red-legged kind, found on the west coasts between Nigumbo and Manaar. Many attempts have been made to propagate the breed more extensively here; and General Macdowal was at particular pains in procuring them from Tutocoreen and other parts on the opposite coast, when they were let loose in the cinnamon gardens to breed.

Among a great variety of smaller birds, we particularly distinguish the honey-bird. It is so called from a particular instinct by which it discovers the honey concealed in trees. As if designed for the service of the human species, this bird continues to flutter about and make a great noise till it has attracted the notice of some person, and induced him to follow the course it points out to him. It then flutters before him, till it has led him to the tree where the bees have lodged their treasure. The man then carries off the honey, leaving a little for the use of the bird, which silently and contentedly watches till it is permitted to enjoy its reward. As soon as it has eaten up its portion, it renews its noise, and goes in quest of another tree, followed by the man, who finds a guide here provided for him by nature.

The crows here, as in every other part of India, are exceedingly impudent and troublesome; and it is found very difficult to exclude them from the houses, which, on account of the heat, are built open and much exposed to such intruders. I have already mentioned some of the vexations I experienced from them while at Columbo. They are so audacious, that, like the harpies of old, they will frequently snatch bread and meat from the dining table, even when it is surrounded with guests. In shape they exactly resemble our common crow, but in size are generally smaller. They abound in every town, fort, and village on the island: as if particularly addicted to the society of man, they are continually seen hopping about among the habitations, and are very rarely to be met with in woods or retired places. These animals, however, though so exceedingly troublesome, and continually on the watch to pick up every thing that comes within their reach, still are not to be considered as an unnecessary pest entailed upon the inhabitants of that part of the globe. The crows, in fact, are very important benefactors to the Indians, and by their utility amply compensate for their troublesome knaveries. As they are all voracious devourers of carrion, and instantly eat up all sorts of dirt, offal, and dead vermin as soon as they appear; they carry off those substances which, if allowed to remain, would in this hot climate produce the most noxious smells, and probably give rise to putrid disorders. On this account the crows are much esteemed by the natives, their mischievous tricks and impudence are put up with, and they are never suffered to be shot or otherwise destroyed.

The kites and vultures are very destructive to the feathered tribes of the forest; but where troops are encamped, are, like the crows, very useful in removing all noisome matters.

The Indian roller is a bird remarkable for the beauty of its plumage: its tail is ornamented with two feathers of singular appearance and remarkable length.

The yellow-crowned thrush, which is here kept in cages, is remarkable for its powers of imitation, and can readily repeat every note which it hears.

Among the smaller birds, the tailor-bird is particularly remarkable for the art with which it constructs its nest. This bird is of a yellow colour, not exceeding three inches in length, and slender in proportion. To prevent the possibility of its little nest being shaken down, it contrives to attach it in such a manner to the leaves of the tree, that both must stand or fall together. The nest is formed of leaves which it picks up from the ground; and it contrives, by means of its slender bill and some fine fibres, which it uses as needle and thread, to sew these leaves to those growing on the tree with great dexterity. Hence it receives the name of the tailor-bird. The lining, which consists of down, adds little to the weight of the nest, which is scarcely felt on the twig that supports it.

Two species of fly-catchers are found in Ceylon. They

are remarkable for the enormous length of their tails, which gives them the appearance of arrows while they dart through the air. In the tail of one of them are two feathers, which exceed the others in length by at least nine inches.

The swallows found here are of the same species as ours. They never quit the island.

Two species of the peacock are produced in Ceylon: the one, which is kept in a tame state, is of the same kind with those known in Europe: the other, which roams at large in its native woods, is of a much larger size, and truly a magnificent bird. It is found all over India, which is its native climate; and adds greatly by its splendid plumage to the beauty of the forests.

The jungle-fowl resembles our common fowl in size, but presents a much more beautiful plumage, and is distinguished by its double spurs.

The reptiles and insects of Ceylon are exceedingly numerous, and several species are very little known. Serpents particularly abound, and are a great annoyance to the inhabitants.

The covra capello or hooded snake is found here from six to fifteen feet long. Its bite is mortal; the natives find the herb pointed out by the ichneumon a remedy, if timely applied. When enraged and preparing to attack, it raises its head and body to the height of three or four feet in a spiral manner, while at the same time the remaining part of the body is coiled up to accelerate and give force to the spring. At this instant it distends from its head a membrane in the form of a hood, from which it receives its name. This hood is a membrane which lies along the forehead and the sides of the neck, and is almost imperceptible till the animal gets into a state of irritation, and is about to attack his foe. When the hood is erected, it completely alters the appearance of the head, and discloses a curious white streak, which runs along the forehead in the shape of a pair of spectacles and sometimes of a horse-shoe. The extension of this membrane seems intended by providence to give warning to all those within this animal's reach, that he is preparing to attack them: without this signal, he would be very dangerous indeed, as his motions afterwards are too rapid to be avoided. I have more than once been an eye-witness to instances where the fatal bite of this snake was escaped from merely by the object of his vengeance timely observing his preparations.

One remarkable characteristic of these dangerous serpents is their fondness for music. Even when newly caught, they seem to listen with pleasure to the notes, and even to writhe themselves into attitudes. The Indian jugglers improve greatly on this instinct; and after taming them, by degrees instruct them even to keep time to their flagelets.

The covra manilla, the most dreadful of all snakes, is about two feet long, and continues from head to tail nearly of the same thickness. Its colour is a reddish black. The bite proves almost instantly fatal, and has never been known to be recovered from. By the goodness of Providence, however, this species is not numerous, and is almost entirely confined to some parts of the interior. Indeed, so rarely is it met with, that I have never conversed with one who had actually examined, or even certainly seen it. The account I have given is taken from the most common reports on the subject.

The whip-snake and grass-snake are both poisonous. They are of a greenish colour and speckled.

The water-snake, the wood-snake, and a few other species usually found among old ruins, are perfectly harmless. They are distinguished from the poisonous kinds, by not raising themselves up to prepare for attack, but keeping their head close to the ground and hissing all the while.

The rock-snake is an immense animal, extending to thirty feet in length. I have myself seen one twenty-two feet long, and about the thickness of a man's thigh: and I was told that much larger ones were to be found in the island. I had a transient glimpse of another as he glided past me through the bushes in the neighbourhood of Columbo; in size he seemed to exceed the one I had formerly seen. The rock-snake inhabits chiefly the rocky banks of rivers. His colour is greyish with broad white streaks. The animals, though formidable from their immense size, are perfectly free from poison. They are, however, destructive to some of the smaller animals, and will devour kids, goats, hogs, poultry, &c. first twisting their tail round their prey, to break its bones and squeeze it to death.

Before I arrived in the island, I had heard many stories of a monstrous snake, so vast in size as to be able to devour tigers and buffaloes, and so daring as even to attack the elephant. I made every inquiry on the spot concerning this terrible animal, but not one of the natives had ever heard of the monster. Probably these fabulous stories took their rise from an exaggerated account of the rock-snake.

Alligators of an immense size infest all the rivers of Ceylon, and render them every where very dangerous: many persons continually fall victims to them. In the year 1799, when Colonel Champagne was lieutenant-governor in the absence of Mr. North, an alligator was sent him down for inspection by one of the principal Cinglese. It was full twenty feet in length, and as thick in the body as a horse. It was killed about thirty miles from Columbo, and required two carts placed one after the other, and drawn by eight bullocks, to transport its immense body, while part of the tail still hung trailing on the ground. On being opened, it was found to have in its belly the head and arm of a black man not yet completely digested. The skin was of a knotty horny texture, like that of a young rhinoceros, and quite impenetrable to a musket ball. In February of the same year, when the escort of the Governor, on his way to meet the Candian ambassador, arrived at Sittivacca, some of the soldiers having gone, after the fatigues of their march, to refresh themselves by bathing in the river which runs through this beautiful and romantick spot, they were alarmed to find the place pre-occupied by a number of alligators. Being present at the time, and happening to have a fowling-piece in my hand, I fired at two and killed them. They were young ones about eight feet in length.

The guana in appearance very much resembles the alligator. It is a very disgusting animal to look at, but is perfectly harmless, and lives in holes in the ground. It is esteemed good food by the natives, and makes excellent curry, or rich soup. The flesh tastes very like that of a rabbit.

An immense number of toads, lizards, blood-suckers, camelions, and a variety of others of the same class abound every where throughout the island; but a particular description of them could afford no entertainment to my readers.

One species, however, has left too deep an impression on my mind to be passed over unnoticed. Besides the leeches employed by apothecaries, to reduce tumours and carry off corrupted blood, there is another species which infests in immense numbers the woods and swampy grounds of Ceylon, particularly in the rainy season, to the great annoyance of every one who passes through them. The leeches of this species are very small, not much larger than a pin; and are of a dark red speckled colour. In their motions they do not crawl like a worm, or like the leeches we are accustomed to see in Europe; but keep constantly springing, by first fixing their head on a place, and then bringing their tail up to it with a sudden jerk, while at the same time their head is thrown forwards for another hold. In this manner they move so exceeding quickly, that before they are perceived, they contrive to get upon one's clothes, when they immediately endeavour by some aperture to find an entrance to the skin. As soon as they reach it, they begin to draw blood; and as they can effect this even through the light clothing worn in this climate, it is almost impossible to pass through the woods and swamps in rainy weather without being covered with blood. On our way to Candy, in marching through the narrow paths among the woods, we were terribly annoyed by these vermin; for whenever any of us sat down or even halted for a moment, we were sure to be immediately attacked by multitudes of them; and before we could get rid of them our gloves and boots were filled with blood. This was attended with no small danger; for if a soldier were, from drunkenness or fatigue, to fall asleep on the ground, he must have perished by bleeding to death. On rising in the morning, I have often found my bed clothes and skin covered with blood in an alarming manner. The Dutch in their marches into the interior at different times lost several of their men; and on our setting out they told us that we should hardly be able to make our way for them. But, though we were terribly annoyed, we all escaped without any serious accident. Other animals, as well as man, are subject to the attacks of these leeches. Horses in particular, from their excessive plunging and kicking to get rid of these creatures when they fasten upon them, render it very unsafe for any one to ride through the woods of the interior.

A species of flying lizard is found here, furnished with membranes extending along its sides in the form of wings, with which it is enabled to take its flight from tree to tree. It is not above nine inches long, and is perfectly harmless, although it is the only animal known which resembles the fabled dragon.

The insects of Ceylon are extremely numerous. There are several species of spiders found, of uncommon size, and poisonous. Flies, beetles, butterflies, muskettoes, cockroaches, with almost every insect known in Europe, are here found, of curious shapes, and ornamented with a variety of colours. Ground-lice and ticks plague the dogs to such a degree as almost makes them mad.

Ants, which are here found of every species, were another pest, in addition to the leeches which we had to encounter in our journey through the woods of Candy; and our clothes and furniture suffered extremely from these vermin. The large red ants, which live on trees, and build their nests among the branches, bite very severely; and one in passing among the trees requires to be very cautious of approaching their habitations, or he will speedily be made to feel the effects of his inadvertency. There are also other varieties of black and red ants of a smaller size, which inhabit rotten trunks and stumps, and are observed in perpetual motion, running up and down the trees. They are perfectly harmless, and though they bite occasionally like those of our own country, yet their bite is attended with very little uneasiness.

There is a very small species of ant which is found in dwelling houses, where it is of very great use in destroying the larger ant, the white ant, and the cock-roach. They speedily devour every thing which is exposed to their ravages; and if one at table accidentally drops a bit of bread, meat, or any sort of food, it instantly appears in motion and animated, from a vast number of these creatures fastening upon it, to carry it off. It is impossible by any contrivance to prevent them from invading the table, and settling in swarms on the bread, sugar, and such things as are particularly agreeable to their palate. It is not uncommon to see a cup of tea, upon being filled out, completely covered with these creatures, floating dead upon it like a scum.

But the most mischievous species of these vermin is the white ant, which is equally destructive in the fields and the dwelling-houses. They build their nests of a very fine clay, which they throw up in large mounds, and carefully prepare for the purpose. It is made into such an excellent cement, that as soon as it is dried up by the rays of the sun, it becomes so hard that it requires great exertion even with a pick-axe to level the heaps. These ant-hills are often from six to eight feet high, and have large openings both at the top and around the sides to serve for entrances and communications. They often serve as a receptacle to much more dangerous animals, such as scorpions, and the covra capello snake; on which account the natives are careful never to lie down or fall asleep near the ant-hills. The white-ants, in the space of one night, will demolish and eat up all the boots, shoes, and bottoms of trunks which come in their way, or are left on the ground. This is never done but by the carelessness of the black servants. In camp, the furniture of the tents is placed on inverted bottles, with their necks planted in the ground, which, on account of the slippery nature of the glass, cannot be climbed up by the ants. In the dwelling-houses, the trunks, chairs, and bed-posts are for the same reason placed in tin vessels full of water. I have frequently seen the large beams of a house almost eaten through by these insects, and ready to tumble down on the heads of the inhabitants.

This destructive instinct, however, is not without the most singular utility, and is made by the Creator to serve the same benevolent purposes, which are conspicuous in every part of his plan. In the immense forests which they inhabit, and which are never subject to the hand of human cultivation, the constant accumulation of decayed timber would in time greatly impede, if not entirely choak vegetation, were not these animals employed by Providence continually to devour it.

Another instinct is also combined with their destructive inclinations, which in a great measure counteracts them, and prevents their injurious effects. Were the white ants, endowed as they are with such powers of destruction, to carry on their operations like other ants in secret, and unobserved by those who were interested to obstruct their progress, there would hardly be a possibility of preserving from their ravages any thing either in the fields or the houses, especially in Ceylon, where they are more numerous and destructive than perhaps any where else. When they intend to move from one settlement to another, or when they have fixed on a piece of wood or some other article which they mean to destroy or effect a lodgement in; before commencing their operations, they first raise a tube or hollow passage for themselves, where they may work, or pass and repass without being seen. This tube, which is about the size of a goose-quill, is made of fine sand, with much despatch and dexterity, and when newly finished appears wet. As soon as it has attained a proper consistency, they fall to devour under its covert with great celerity. So powerful is this instinct, that they will not even pass from the bottom to the top of a house, along the walls or posts, without first preparing their covert way. This contrivance, by which they expect to escape detection, never fails to betray them, and point them out to the observation of their enemies. When these tubes are swept down and destroyed, the ravages of the ants are for that time prevented, as they will never proceed to work without previously renewing their structure.

The black scorpion of Ceylon is a very dangerous insect, and its sting is frequently mortal. This species is about four inches long and from one to two broad over the middle of the body. When running or disturbed, their tail is usually carried on their backs. They bite with their fangs or forceps, and instantly dart the sting, which lies in their tail, into the place they have bitten. Their sting emits a poison resembling milk, but not altogether so white. When these scorpions are attacked by their inveterate enemy the ant, and cannot get rid of him, they sting themselves to death.

The centpied or centipedes, which receives its name from the many legs which shoot out from every part of its body, stings in the same manner as the scorpion, first biting the object, and then darting the sting on its tail into the wound.

There is an immense spider found here, with legs not less than four inches long, and having the body covered with thick black hair. The webs which it makes are strong enough to entangle and hold even small birds which form its usual prey.

There is an insect found here, which resembles an immense overgrown beetle. It is called by us a carpenter, from its boring large holes in timber, of a regular form, and to the depth of several feet, in which when finished it takes up its habitation.

Fish of every sort in great abundance are found in the lakes and rivers of Ceylon, as well as in the surrounding seas. Those found in the fresh water are much more remarkable for their vast numbers than their quality. The mullet however is very good, and perhaps the best of the fresh-water fish. None of the species, as far as I could learn, are peculiar to Ceylon; but all common to the warm latitudes, though differing from the European. One circumstance has often struck me with astonishment, that in every pond or muddy pool, casually supplied with rain water, or even only recently formed, and entirely unconnected with any other water, swarms of fishes are continually found. The only explanation which it appears possible to give of this phenomenon, is that the spawn is by some unknown process carried up with the rain into the skies, and then let down with it upon the earth in a condition immediately to become alive.

Many excellent kinds of fish are caught all around the coasts of the island, and form a principal article both of the traffic and food of the natives.

CHAPTER XIV.

Vegetables of Ceylon.

CEYLON is particularly prolific in plants. Almost all those fruits which are peculiar to India and the countries within the tropical climates, are here found in great abundance and of a superior quality. Except in one or two species, the mangoes of Massegon, and the mandarine orange of China, which has within these last few years been raised at Bombay, this island maintains an undeniable superiority over all our settlements on the continent of India. The climate is remarkably adapted to promote vegetation, and there are few parts where some species of fruit or other does not grow in luxuriance. Most of those fruits, which are natives of the island grow spontaneously in the woods without any culture or care in the rearing; and the only labour required from the peasants is merely to pluck and bring them to market, where they are of course sold at a very low price.

Among the fruits which grow spontaneously in the woods of Ceylon, are found most of those which constitute the most delicious desserts of our European tables: such as pine-apples, oranges, pomegranates, citrons, limes, melons, pumpkins, water-melons, squashes, figs, almonds, mulberries, bilberries, &c. all of which are too well known to require any particular description.

The *mango* is of an oblong cylindrical form, in shape and size resembling an egg. Its taste and flavour are peculiar, and it is reckoned one of the most delicious fruits in India. One remarkable circumstance is, that no one mango resembles another plucked from the same tree in taste or flavour. The pulp, which is extremely juicy and of a stringy texture, is covered with a coat like a peach, but larger and thicker, and easily peeled off. The kernel is very large, and of the same shape as the fruit. In smell the mango resembles the melon, although at times it smells not unlike turpentine. The fruit when ripe is extremely wholesome to eat; and when plucked before arriving at maturity it makes the best pickles and preserves known in that quarter of the world. The mango-tree grows to a vast size, and extends its large and beautiful branches like our oak; but the timber is not applied to any useful purpose.

The *mangusteen* is a fruit very highly esteemed, but one of the rarest in Ceylon, being only found in one or two gardens belonging to Dutch gentlemen. In appearance this fruit resembles the pomegranate, but the pulp is more like that of the mango, and consists of fibres full of juice. It is esteemed an excellent remedy in fluxes.

The *shaddock* or *pumpelmose* often grows to the size of a man's head. In shape it resembles the orange, and is covered with a coat of the same texture, although much softer and thicker. The pulp also resembles that of the orange, only the juicy fibres are proportionably larger. There are two species of shaddock; the one is of a white, and the other of a yellow colour; and they also differ in flavour.

The *tamboe* or *rose apple* is about the size of one of our ordinary apples, and of nearly the same shape, only more oval. It is of a beautiful red and white colour: the pulp is of a softer texture than our apple, and has the taste and smell of a rose, from which it derives its name. It is a very wholesome fruit, cooling and pleasant, though insipid. It contains a large soft kernel nearly half the size of the fruit.

The *cushoo* apple is of a smaller size than the former, soft and full of a very harsh astringent juice which puckers up the lips when applied to them. The nut, which in shape is not unlike a kidney-bean, grows to the end of the apple; and tastes, when roasted, like our chesnuts, but more oily.

The *katapa* somewhat resembles our walnut, but to my taste, has a better flavour.

The *paupa* or *papaya* is of the size of a melon, and has a pulp nearly of the same taste and smell, but so soft as to be divided with a spoon like pudding. Although it is not a fruit of a delicious flavour, yet from its being very wholesome and cooling, it is much eaten. In the inside of the pulp there is a hollow space which contains a quantity of seeds of the colour and size of black pepper, having exactly the taste of water cresses, instead of which I have often used them.

The *custard* apple is so called from the pulp having some resemblance in taste to custard pudding. The pulp is contained in a speckled shell like a fir cone, and has a number of black seeds mixed with its inside, which is nearly of the same consistence as that of the former.

The *tamarind* grows in long green pods like those of our kidney-beans; but of a stringy and spungy texture. It contains a number of kernels, and is very acid, for which quality it is often made use of. The tamarind tree renders the air beneath its shade so unwholesome, that it is a general order with the troops, never to allow horses to be picketed there. This noble tree expands its branches so widely, that assemblies for religious and other purposes have been held under its shade, secure from the influence of the sun. The fruit is extremely refreshing, and very efficacious in fevers and dysenteries.

The *plantain* is a small tree with wood of a soft nature. The leaves are very broad, long and green. As soon as this tree has borne fruit, the trunk dies, and a new one springs up through it from the root. The fruit grows at the top of the tree in bunches, resembling in shape our hog's puddings, from six to twelve inches long, and from ten to twenty in a bunch. It is covered with a coat of a lemon colour, which is easily peeled off; the inside when ripe is of a white or yellowish colour. It has a pleasant flavour, and no quantity eaten of it has been found to injure the stomach. When fried it is delicious, in appearance like fritters, and in taste resembling pancakes. The size of this fruit varies as well as its colour, which is sometimes a beautiful vermilion.

Ceylon produces two species of the bread-fruit tree. One species, the *jacka*, or jack-fruit, grows upon a tree of a very large size, which spreads out its branches around like our chesnut. This fruit is of a very extraordinary appearance, growing to the thickness of a man's waist. It does not, like other fruits, spring from the branches, but issues from the body of the tree itself, or immediately from the root; the latter is preferred. Nothing can exceed the grotesque appearance of the body of the tree when it is stuck all over with these immense protuberances, hanging from short stalks, which, though exceedingly tough and strong, are frequently unable to support their unwieldy burden; the fruit is therefore often obliged to be prevented from falling off by being placed in baskets of cane or cocoa-tree leaves, which are fixed to the trees, and remain there till the fruit is ripe for pulling.

The external coat of the fruit is extremely thick and hard, of a green colour, and full of prickles. The inside of this coat is covered with a soft, white, glutinous substance, which, when touched, adheres to the fingers like bird-lime. When cut, it distils a milky, ropy kind of gum. The eatable pulp is small when compared to the size of the fruit while it is covered with the outer coat. It is divided into different compartments, each containing a kernel or two of the size of a chesnut, but longer. When roasted or boiled, these kernels in taste very much resemble a potatoe. The pulp is not very agreeable to the palate of an European, having a strong smell not unlike turpentine. The only way we could bring ourselves to eat it, was by first soaking it in a glass of salt and water. The natives eat it with much relish; and when they go upon a journey, they generally travel with a bag of the kernels roasted.

Another species which is usually called the *bread-fruit tree,* in the appearance of the fruit, is quite similar to the jacka, only that it is much smaller. The leaves of this tree are large, and of a dark green colour. The fruit is dressed in a variety of different ways, and no less than fifteen different dishes are prepared from it. When sliced and roasted, it is eaten in place of bread; and is often scraped into flour by the natives, and then baked into cakes. These fruits are invaluable preservatives against famine, of which neither their own indolence, the terrors of their enemies, nor the tyranny of their governors are able to deprive the Ceylonese. By regular cultivation, however, their utility might be greatly extended, and their quality improved.

The *cocoa-tree* is of such singular utility not only to the Ceylonese, but to all the natives of India, that I hope a full account of it, and its uses, will not be thought superfluous by my readers, even although it is not by any means peculiar to the island I am describing.

The cocoa-tree grows to a great height, is slender and straight, with the body completely bare, and only the top crowned with a bunch of long green leaves. These leaves may be compared in appearance to a goose-quill: a thick ligament passes through the middle, and long green slips grow out from its sides, in the manner of fern. Under the leaves the nuts appear growing in clusters: each tree bears from two to three dozen. The nut has a rind or outside coat of a green colour, very thick, and composed of fibrous threads. These are so long as to be manufactured into ropes, called coya ropes, and cordage of various descriptions: even cables of the largest size are made of them, and are generally esteemed from being more buoyant in salt water than those made of hemp. These fibres, however, are of too harsh a nature to be manufactured without some previous preparation; and therefore on being taken off, the rind is put into water to swell, and is afterwards beaten, before it is capable of being wrought into cordage.

When this outward rind is removed, if the nut is recently plucked, the shell is found slightly covered with a white pulp which adheres to it. After being kept for some time, however, this pulp dries up and becomes of a brownish colour. On being stript of its external coating, the nut, which when plucked from the tree was as large as a middling sized bowl, is reduced to the size of a twelve or eighteen pound cannon ball. On the smaller end of the nut being opened, we find about a pint of a very cool, refreshing, milky liquor, which forms a delicious drink. To the inside of the shell adheres a coat of about half an inch thick, of a very white substance, in taste resembling a blanched almond. It is frequently eaten in its natural state, but more frequently in curries, mulicatauny, and peppermint water. It is first scraped off the inside of the shell with an instrument I have already described, resembling the rowel of a spur; and then being mixed with water forms a substance like milk.

The oil extracted from the cocoa-nut is highly esteemed among the natives, and indeed is applicable to every useful purpose. It is prepared from the oldest of the nuts, which are first split and left in the sun to dry without any of their inside coating being removed: and when sufficiently dried, they are put into mills prepared for the purpose, and the oil is expressed from them.

It is not, however, the nut alone that affords food and luxuries to man. From the top of the tree where the leaves shoot up, a liquor called *toddy* is procured by incision. A slit is made in this part of the tree with a knife overnight, and a *chatty* or earthen-pot suspended from the branches so as to receive the juice, which immediately begins to distill, and continues to do so till next morning, when the pot is removed. This liquor, when drunk before the heat of the rising sun has caused it to ferment, is very wholesome and cooling, and operates as a gentle purgative. But upon being fermented, it becomes intoxicating; and in this state is well known to the European soldiers who use it in large quantities, when they cannot procure the arrack distilled from it. Arrack in Ceylon is solely made from *toddy*, and whole woods of the cocoa-tree are employed for the purpose of procuring it. A barm or yeast arises from this process, equal to that which is procured from our malt liquor employed in the preparation of whisky. The toddy is likewise made into vinegar, and yields a species of coarse black sugar known by the name of *jaggery*.

Nature seems to delight in making the cocoa-tree serve as many useful purposes as possible. At the foot of the tree, and likewise among the branches at the top, grows a coat or web of a very light and porous substance which is manufactured into a very coarse cloth called *grinjakken* or *gunny* cloth. It is used for bags to hold rice, and also for coverings to the cinnamon bales. The grinjakken is also made into a coarse species of paper.

The utility of the cocoa-tree does not end here. When cut down, the trunk furnishes posts to support, and the branches rafters to roof the *bungaloes* or huts of the natives; while the leaves are employed to cover them, and repel the inclemencies of the sun and the storm. Various other purposes are served by the wood of this valuable tree. Besides many domestic uses, it is much employed also in the construction of canoes; and with it the Mosula boats of Madrass are built. In some parts of India this wood is applied to the construction of larger vessels. I have been assured that the king of the Maldive islands sent his ambassadors to the Dutch Governor at Columbo, in a small ship which was entirely built and rigged from the cocoa-tree, while those employed in fitting it out were fed upon the nuts.

It is surprising to see with what dexterity the natives climb those high, straight, and slender trees. They have many ways of facilitating their ascent. Sometimes they tie pieces of the long leaf, twisted together like ropes of hay, around the body of the tree, leaving the distance of about two feet between each piece, and thus forming for themselves a sort of ladder. Frequently they embrace the tree with their feet and then tie both together by a rope passed round the ancles: at the same time they clasp the tree with their hands, and thus ascend, resting alternately on their ancles and their arms. Having gained the top of one tree, their agility and dexterity prevents them from having to renew their toil. By means of the adjoining branches, and some ropes fastened at different places for the purpose, they contrive to pass from one tree to another. I have seen them in this manner collect the toddy from a whole grove of cocoa-trees without once descending; and their feats of agility on these occasions equalled any thing I have seen the most dexterous of our sailors perform among the rigging of a ship, and was scarcely outdone even by the monkeys, the native inhabitants of these groves.

The trees from which the toddy is extracted, being deprived of so much of their juice, produce fruit of a very inferior quality, and much sooner fall into decay.

When we consider the innumerable comforts which this tree affords to the natives of India, it is not to be wondered that they hold it in the highest esteem, and reckon it a most important part of their wealth. When a child is born, it is customary for them to plant a cocoa-tree in memorial of the happy event; and the rings which are left around the trunk by its animal vegetation, serve to mark the number of the recurring birth-days.

Another tree, bearing a fruit as generally used, though by no means equal in utility to that of the cocoa, is the *betel-tree.* I have already mentioned how universally the areka or betel nut is chewed by the natives of India. The leaf usually distinguished by the name of the *betel-leaf* does not, however, grow upon this tree, but from being constantly chewed along with the betel nut, has acquired this appellation. The tree, though remarkably tall and straight, is equally remarkable for its extreme slenderness, being no thicker than the calf of a man's leg, The nuts grow in bunches at the top like those of the cocoa, but are in size no bigger than a nutmeg, and with the same sort of shell. After they are pulled, the Cinglese expose them in the sun to dry, and then split the outside husk, in order to separate it from the nut. The leaves of the betel-tree are from four to six feet in length, and very much resemble those of the cocoa, although of a more delicate texture. From the tree, at the root of the leaves, a substance grows up, and overspreads them like a thick coat. This extraordinary substance resembles a tough leaf or rather a skin: it is used by the natives to hold their victuals, and is of so strong a texture that it retains water or arrack like a bladder; a purpose for which it is generally employed.

The nuts, from their general use, form a great article of trade among the natives. The timber of the tree is used for rafters to houses, and makes excellent lath. It is also employed in pales to fence their grounds.

The plant from which the betel-leaf is procured resembles a vine, and is supported by twining around other trees or poles placed for the purpose. The leaf in shape and colour is not unlike that of the ivy, but larger and rather thicker. As I have already mentioned in a former part of this work, the natives always chew it along with the betel-nut, and also contrive to render the mixture still hotter, by the addition of lime, tobacco, and the most pungent spices.

Ceylon, which has been so long renowned for its spices, produces several sorts of pepper. The *chilly* or red pepper is produced on a shrub. The fruit grows in small oblong pods which are at first green, but upon being pulled and dried, become red; and from them the cayen-pepper is made. The troops on a march have found it of great benefit to cut up some of these chillies in their green state, and qualify the water with them before drinking it.

The *black pepper,* though not peculiar to Ceylon, nor found in so great plenty there as in the Molucca isles, still forms an useful part of its produce. The plant twines around supporters like the vine, and the pepper hangs from it in clusters like grapes. These clusters are at first green, but gradually change to a dark brown; and upon being pulled and dried become black. The husk is separated by a machine framed for the purpose, with a wire bottom twisted together. The *white pepper* is originally the same with the black, and is rendered of that colour by a preparation of chinam applied to it before it is dried, which takes off the black coat with which it is covered.

Cardamoms grow in the south-east part of the island, particularly in the neighbourhood of Matura. The seeds in taste resemble our carraways, and are used for seasoning to various dishes.

The *coffee* produced in Ceylon is of a very good quality, and in flavour resembles the Moka coffee. The *coffee-tree* has been raised in the plantations with the greatest success, and presents a very beautiful appearance.

The *palm* or *palmira* tree resembles the cocoa, but is much inferior to it in utility. The leaves are thicker and shorter than those of the former, and fold up like a fan, in which form they are used by the natives to write on.

A tough whitish skin, like that found on the betel, covers the body of the tree, and is also employed by the natives to hold their liquor. The nut contains a sort of milk; and by incision the body of the tree affords a very pleasant liquor, not so strong or intoxicating as toddy.

The *sugar-tree* is a species of the palm found in several parts of the island. It is a very tall tree, and has around its trunk a number of rings which increase with its growth. It bears a flower distinguished by the variety of its colours. On cutting off the flower, and making an incision in the place from which it sprung, a juice distils which by a slight process of boiling and straining yields as good a sugar as that extracted from the cane, and far superior to the jaggery. The commercial advantages to be derived from the proper cultivation of this plant need not be insisted upon; and experiments will no doubt speedily be made to ascertain whether this tree might not be made a substitute to the cane.

But it is not sugar alone that Ceylon seems destined to afford to the general use of the Western world; the *tea-plant* has also been discovered native in the forests of this island. I have in my possession a letter from an officer in the 80th regt. wherein he states that he had found the real tea-plant in the woods of Ceylon, of a quality equal to any that ever grew in China; and that it was in his power to point out to Government the means of cultivating it in a proper manner. The vast advantages to be derived from the cultivation of the tea-plant in our own dominions, ought at least to prompt a speedy and vigorous experiment on the subject.

The most beautiful species of the palm kind which Ceylon produces is the *talipot-tree.* This tree is very rare in other parts of India and seems a peculiar blessing bestowed by Providence on this island. It grows very tall and straight: the wood is hard, and veined with yellow, and is employed in carpenters' work. The talipot bears a large yellow flower, which, when ripe, bursts with a loud noise, and diffuses a disagreeable and unwholesome smell. It is on this account that the natives will not place their huts near it. The fruit is of a round form, and about the size of a cannon-ball: it contains two nuts of the same shape. But it is from its leaves that the talipot derives its high estimation. These hang downwards from the top, and present a most elegant and grand appearance. The leaf is completely circular, terminating in the most beautiful rays, it folds up into plaits like a fan, which in figure it nearly resembles. In size and thickness it completely surpasses always all other leaves. The breadth of the diameter is from three to four feet, and the length and thickness is in proportion: it is large enough to cover ten men from the inclemency of the weather. It is made into umbrellas of all sizes, and serves equally to protect the natives against the intolerable rays of the sun, and the rains which at particular seasons deluge their country. As it is of such an impenetrable tex-

4

ture as to defy either the sun or the monsoon, it affords a shelter even more secure than their huts. During the violent rains it is not unusual to see the natives prop up one end of a talipot leaf with a stick two or three feet long, and then creep under it for protection. I have already described the manner in which the natives make use of this leaf for writing.

The *banyan* tree, or, as it is frequently called, the *Indian fig-tree,* is a native of Ceylon. It bears no fruit nor blossom, but grows to an immense size, and has some striking peculiarities in its appearance. It first rises to a great height in the air, and then drops its branches downwards. A vast number of roots are then observed to shoot forth from the lower extremities of the branches, where they continue suspended like icicles, till they at last fasten themselves in the earth. From these roots new shoots spring up, which in their turn become trees, and strike their branches into the ground. A whole grove is thus formed from one original stock; and the arches formed by the branches and the numerous interwoven shoots, come in time to have actually the appearance of grottos and excavations. The circumference of the grove arising from one stock has frequently been known to extend to several hundred feet.

It is no wonder that the admirable shelter afforded by this noble tree should have pointed it out to the particular veneration of the inhabitants of the torrid zone. Indeed without the assistance of its impenetrable shade, it is almost impossible that the numerous ceremonies enjoined by their superstition could have been at all performed. It is here therefore that we find the Brahmins and the devotees of their religion continually celebrating their rites. The pagodas are usually erected in the neighbourhood of this friendly shade, as well as the choultries prepared for the accommodation of the weary traveller. It is common for the Indian to take up his abode under this tree, and to remain stretched at his ease in the shade while every thing exposed to the rays of the sun is scorched with the intolerable heat.

The *cotton-tree* of Ceylon grows to a middling height. It is slender and straight, with the branches shooting out near the top. The cotton grows in pods of an oblong shape, about the size of a small pear. When ripe they burst, and the cotton is then seen projecting out of them. In this state they are gathered. Within the pod a number of seeds like black pepper are mixed with the cotton, from which they are separated by little sticks in the form of a cross, which the women turn round very quick with their hands, and during this operation the seeds fall out. The cotton procured from this tree is contaminated with an oily substance, and is not by any means equal in goodness to that which grows on the shrub in other parts of India. It is, however, much used for matrasses and pillows; and coarse cloth, fit for common purposes is made of it. The wood is much employed in making fences.

The *tick-wood* tree, which may be called the oak of Ceylon, is found to be of great value, and is applied to the most useful purposes. Owing to the firm texture of this wood, which is uncommonly hard, it is able both to endure the intense heat of the sun without splitting, and also to resist the attacks of ants and other vermine with which warm climates abound. On these accounts tick-wood is much used for tables, chairs, and other pieces of household furniture, as well as for building vessels, &c. which are much exposed to the rays of the sun. At Bombay it is frequently employed in the construction of ships; and these are found quite as durable and adapted for every service as those made of oak.

Nando-wood is also used in furniture of various sorts; but it is not near so highly esteemed for this or any other purpose as tick-wood.

Satin-wood is very much employed by the Dutch in their tables, chairs, and couches; and when properly finished it has a very handsome appearance.

The most beautiful wood however which the island affords is the *calamander*. The colour is nearly black with white and brownish streaks, which, when it is highly polished, appear with uncommon beauty. The natives employ it much in household furniture and writing desks; but although a considerable quantity of these articles are manufactured, the beauty and elegance of their appearance render the demand still greater, and they are consequently very high-priced.

The *manjapumeram* is remarkable for having a fresh and flourishing appearance during the night, while its boughs begin to droop as soon as the sun appears above the horizon, and do not again raise their heads till he has set. In appearance it resembles the olive; and, according to the Indian poets, is the tree into which their Daphne was metamorphosed on rejecting the embraces of the Sun.

The *morinda* grows in all the watry parts of India. The wood is useless, but the root is employed to dye red.

The *sindric-mal* is a plant employed by the natives to supply the want of clocks; as it has the quality of continuing open from four in the evening till four in the morning, and remaining shut during the other twelve hours. It is said to be customary for the Candians to plant it in their gardens, and in cloudy weather when the height of the sun cannot be seen, as well as when the approach of morn cannot otherwise be discovered, it in some degree supplies the want of a better time-piece.

The *limes* bear a small fruit resembling lemons.

The *manghas-tree* produces a fruit considerably smaller than the mango, and remarkable for a hollow on one side, which has given rise to the tradition that this was the fatal apple tasted by Eve, and that the mark of the bite has continued on it as a testimony to all future ages. The odium thrown upon it by this tradition has occasioned a general belief that it is of a poisonous quality; but it is so no more than any other fruit, and is only fatal when eaten to excess.

The true *ebony*, so remarkable for its weight, and the polish which it takes, is found in great abundance in this island.

Gamboge, well known to painters as affording a rich yellow, is here procured from a large tree which bears a roundish ribbed fruit, of a yellow colour. The gamboge is extracted from the wood of the tree, in the form of a juice which soon becomes solid. It is used in medicine as well as in painting, and acts very powerfully on the intestines both upwards and downwards.

Gum-Lac is found in great plenty on a plant which grows in abundance in different sand-pits throughout the island. It is dissolved in spirits of wine, and then employed in lacquering.

The *sugar-cane* has been introduced into the island, and plantations of it are found in the neighbourhood of Caltura. Some rum is made from it, and the natives are fond of chewing the pulp.

But the most remarkable plant which Ceylon produces is the *nepenthes*, known among the Cinglese by the name of Bandura. It is also called the *penis* plant from its appearance. The leaves are narrow, and from their ends issues a long tendril, which terminates in a long cylindrical tube, closed at the extremity by a valve. This tube, while growing, and in full vigour, seems like a blown bladder, and contains within it about a wine glass of pure limpid water. There is no appearance of any passage for the entrance of this water; but the general way of accounting for the phenomenon is, that it is formed by the dew soaking through the valve. Shortly after being pulled, the head, from the pressure of the water inside, bursts, and the coat soon withers away; but as long as it is able to retain the water, it remains round, distended, and in full vigour. The seeds are small and black, not unlike those of the tulip.

The flowers of Ceylon, though not numerous nor much attended to by the natives, have a most rich and exquisite scent. I have already mentioned a species of *jessamine,* which is worn by the ladies of Ceylon, both on account of its odour and the ornamental appearance of its beautiful white flowers. The scent is too powerful for an European, but is highly esteemed among the natives.

The *champaca* produces flowers of a most elegant saffron colour, with which the native women adorn their hair, and produce a fine contrast to its glossy jet. They are also accustomed to strew it over their beds and furniture.

As the chief food of the natives consists of *rice,* so their principal labour consists in the cultivation of it. It is sown chiefly in the level lands towards the southwest of the island. In the interior, little in proportion is sown, owing to the woods and the steep nature of the country, which prevent the rice from being properly flooded. The manner of cultivating it is as follows: around the fields intended for the reception of the rice small embankments are raised to the height of about three feet, to retain the water, which being then let in upon the grounds levelled on purpose, soon completely inundates them. As soon as the fields begin again to get dry, buffaloes are introduced to tread them over, or they are turned up with a sort of light plough, which I have already described in a former part of this work. The ground, thus prepared, looks like one large tract of mud; and in this state it receives the rice which has previously been steeped in water mixed with the lime of burnt shells. The soil is afterwards levelled, and prevented from caking into lumps by a sort of harrow or rake, which consists simply of a piece of board fixed to a pole, and drawn edgewise along.

As the rice will not thrive without the ground being completely drenched, it is always necessary to have the fields embanked and prepared by the commencement of the rainy season. They usually sow in July and August, and reap in February; although when proper advantage is taken of the monsoons, they have often two crops a year. As from the manner in which their lands are held, it is necessary for them to clear the whole fields at once, they are very careful to manage it so that their whole crop of rice may be ripe at the same time. In bringing this about, they are particularly dexterous; and though they may have several kinds sown, which naturally ripen at different periods, yet by the manner of sowing and the quantity of water which they introduce, they contrive to make the whole crop advance equally.

When the rice is pretty well grown up, the different embankments are laid open, and furrows at the same time are drawn to carry off the water. When it is arrived at maturity, instead of reaping it according to the European custom, they pull it up by the roots, and then lay it out to dry. The rice is trodden by oxen to separate it from the straw, and is afterwards beaten to take off the husk.

Where the rice fields lie on a declivity, very great art and labour are employed to make them retain the water. For this purpose they are laid out in narrow slips one over the other, and each secured by a separate embankment, so as to remind one of a flight of stairs. The higher parts are first flooded. and the water overflowing them proceeds successively to those below. Where the water is not easily dispersed over them, or cannot afterwards be readily removed, it is usual to employ scoops for these purposes. The embankments consist of mud-walls, three feet high, formed with great neatness, and serving for foot paths to the people employed in the culture of the rice, who would otherwise be obliged to wade knee-deep in mud and water.

The flooding of the rice-fields attracts a terrible enemy in the alligator, who frequently contrives to steal in unperceived, and conceal himself among the embankments. The natives are on this account often very much alarmed, and search with great care before they venture among the mud and water.

Besides this superior species of rice, there are several

other inferior kinds, as well as other sorts of grain, which the natives frequently sow on account of their requiring less water. What is commonly called *paddy* is a very inferior grain. *Corocan* is a small seed, like our mustard, which they beat in a mortar, and make into cakes. *Tanna* is a very prolific grain, and hardly requires any cultivation. It requires first to be parched by the fire, and then beaten in a mortar, in order to be unhusked. When boiled, it swells even more than rice; and though rather dry and insipid, it is accounted sufficiently wholesome.

CHAPTER XV.

Cinnamon, the staple commodity of Ceylon.

I Shall conclude my account of the vegetable productions of Ceylon with the most valuable and important article of the whole, the Cinnamon. The length of my residence at Columbo enabled me to observe with my own eyes the whole process of procuring and preparing it for exportation; and the importance of the subject induced me to employ much pains to acquire a complete knowledge of its growth, and the improvements of which this branch of commerce is capable. The subject has indeed been frequently attended to before: Dr. Thunberg in particular from his acquaintance with botany, and his being employed in proving the cinnamon, has been able to give the public much information concerning it; and in order to render this account as complete as possible, I shall not scruple to avail myself occasionally of his assistance.

The principal woods, or gardens, as we call them, where the Cinnamon is procured, lie in the neighbourhood of Columbo. They reach to within half a mile of the fort, and fill the whole surrounding prospect. The grand garden near the town is so extensive as to occupy a tract of country from ten to fifteen miles in length, and stretching along from the north-east to the south of the district. Nature has here concentrated both the beauty and the riches of the island. Nothing can be more delightful to the eye than the prospect which stretches around Columbo. The low cinnamon trees which cover the plain allow the view to reach the groves of evergreens, interspersed with tall clumps, and bounded every where with extensive ranges of cocoa-nut and other large trees. The whole is diversified with small lakes and green marshes, skirted all around with rice and pasture fields. In one part the inter-twining cinnamon trees appear completely to clothe the face of the plain; in another, the openings made by the intersecting footpaths just serve to shew that the thick underwood has been penetrated. One large road, which goes out at the west gate of the fort, and returns by the gate on the south, makes a winding circuit of seven miles among the woods. It is here that the officers and gentlemen belonging to the garrison of Columbo take their morning ride, and enjoy one of the finest scenes in nature.

The soil best adapted for the growth of the cinnamon is a loose white sand. Such is the soil of the cinnamon gardens around Columbo, as well as in many parts around Nigumbo and Caltura, where this spice is found of the same superior quality. What is gathered at Matura and Point de Galle differs very little from this, especially in those parts near the sea, which are most favourable to the growth of cinnamon. The quantity found in the other parts of the island is so trifling, as hardly to deserve notice. Of late years, little is procured from the interior; and what is brought thence is coarser and thicker in the appearance, and of a hot and pungent taste. The interior is not so well adapted by nature for producing this plant; and the exactions and avarice of the Dutch, as we have already mentioned, at length reduced the King of Candy to such desperation, that he resolved to secure himself against their future attacks, by leaving nothing in his dominions which could excite their covetousness. With this view he has, since the last treaty he was forced to make with them, employed every means to prevent the growth and propagation of the cinnamon tree.

As this spice constitutes the wealth of Ceylon, great pains are taken to ascertain its quality, and to propagate the choicest kinds. The prime sort, and that which grows in the gardens around Columbo, is procured from the *laurus cinnamomum.* This is a tree of a small size, from four to ten feet in height: the trunk is slender, and like several of our shrubs, a number of branches and twigs shoot out from it on every side. The wood is soft, light, and porous, in appearance much resembling that of our osier; and when barked it is chiefly fit for fuel, to which use it is commonly converted. It is, however, sometimes sawed into planks, and manufactured into caddies and other pieces of furniture; but its scent does not secure it from the attacks of the worms. A vast number of roots and fibres run out from the root of the tree, and shooting up into slender twigs, form a bush around it.

The leaf a good deal resembles that of the laurel in shape,

but it is not of so deep a green. It has three fibres running lengthwise, but no cross or intersecting fibres, like most other leaves. At its first appearance the leaf is of a scarlet red; but after some time it changes gradually to a green. When chewed, it has the hot taste and smell of cloves.

The blossom is white, and when in full blow seems to cover the woods. It is probably from the great distance at which an object of this colour is seen, that voyagers have been led to affirm that the cinnamon may be smelt far at sea off the island. This assertion is, in fact, a mere fiction, as even in passing through the woods I never could perceive any scent from the tree, except by pulling off some of the leaves or branches. The flower has even less scent than the leaves or a bit of twig.

The cinnamon tree produces a species of fruit resembling an acorn, but not so large, which gets ripe about the latter end of autumn, and is gathered by the natives for the purpose of extracting oil from it. The process they employ is to bruise the fruit, boil it, and skim off the oil: this they use for their hair and body on great occasions, and also for burning in their lamps. When mixed with cocoa-nut oil, it gives extremely good light. The Kings of Candy use it for this purpose, and formerly commanded their subjects to bring them a certain quantity as a yearly tribute. When any ambassadors are sent to these princes, they always burn this oil during the time of audience.

When the tree gets old and decayed, and most of the

branches fit for barking have been stript off, it is customary to set fire to it, and burn it down to the ground; the roots are seen to shoot up again in long straight plants, much better formed than the preceding ones. From these are cut the highly-esteemed cinnamon walking-sticks, which when fresh are of a lively green, resembling holly, but after some time the bark becomes shrivelled, and they have very much the appearance of hazle-sticks. They still, however, retain the taste and smell of cinnamon. The bark of these shoots is extremely valuable, and the practice of cutting them when young for sticks has been found to prove so materially injurious, that it has been totally prohibited since the island came into our possession.

There are several different species of cinnamon trees on the island; at least, trees which in appearance resemble them. Four sorts however are alone barked, and all these are species of the plant I have all along been describing, the *laurus cinnamomum*. Cinnamon is known among the natives by the name of *curundu*, and it is by various epithets joined to this appellation that the several kinds are distinguished. The *rasse curundu*, or honey-cinnamon, is distinguished by its large, broad, thick leaves, and is accounted to have the finest flavour. The *nai curundu*, or snake cinnamon, has also large leaves, and is not greatly inferior in quality to the former. The *capuru curundu*, or camphor cinnamon is an inferior species: its root yields camphor by distillation; or if an incision be made in it, a gummy substance containing camphor distills of itself from the wound. The *cabatte curundu* is an astringent species of cinnamon, harsh to the taste, with rather smaller, leaves than the former sorts. These four are the only species of cinnamon-tree which produces this spice of a good quality, or indeed which are ever allowed to be barked by the servants of government. There are some other varieties which are easily distinguishable. The *saevel curundu* has its bark of a soft, fibrous texture, neither so compact nor so firm as those already mentioned, but easily bending without breaking; when chewed it leaves a slimy mucus in the mouth. The *dawul curundu,* or flat cinnamon, receives its name from the bark, on being dried, not rolling itself together, but remaining flat. The *nica curundu* is distinguished by its long narrow leaves. These are the only species which even from appearance run any risk of being confounded with the proper cinnamon.

Till this island was possessed by the Dutch, cinnamon grew entirely in the wild state; it was even believed by Europeans as well as natives that it was in this state alone it was to be found in perfection, and that upon being planted it never failed to degenerate. The propagation of the tree in the wild state is attributed to the birds, who swallow the berries, but the kernels not dissolving in their stomachs are thrown out, and thus dispersed up and down wherever the birds chance to fly. During the course of the last century, however, experience has shewn that the cultivated cinnamon is every way equal to the wild. The Dutch Governor, Falk, first attempted to rear cinnamon-trees by art in his garden at Pass near Columbo; and soon raised in that spot a plantation of several thousands, which yielded cinnamon of the first quality. After this he employed the same means to extend the cinnamon gardens around Columbo, and reduce them more into regular form. These useful labours have rendered his memory highly esteemed; and he is still remembered on the island as one who preferred the public benefit to his own private interest, the only character fit to preside over a colony. His successors, however, did not follow his example; cutting and collecting the cinnamon seemed to be their only care, and they were at little trouble and expence either to increase or continue the supply. The woods were, therefore, found by us in a neglected and exhausted state; but we were fortunate enough, on taking Columbo, to find stored up there a vast quantity of cinnamon which they had not had an opportunity to send off to Europe. The strictest attention is now paid to the cinnamon gardens by Governor North. Since his arrival, they have been much improved, and enclosed with a broad embankment. He has also caused a new road to be made through them in a different direction from the circular one I have already described, but equally excellent and pleasant.

The plantations, besides yielding cinnamon of an equal quality with that found in the wild state, are infinitely more commodious, from the trees being regularly placed in rows, instead of the people employed in barking being obliged to creep through intricate and pathless woods in search of it.

There are two different seasons in which cinnamon is barked. The greater quantity is prepared during what is called the *grand harvest,* which lasts from April to August. The *little harvest* continues for little more than a month, from November to January. The barking is, however, by no means restricted to these particular seasons; I have observed bark brought in every month of the year.

Each particular district where the cinnamon grows is bound to furnish yearly a certain quantity of cinnamon proportioned to the number of the villages and inhabitants which it contains. The Cinglese, in return for this service, have each a piece of land allotted them rent free. They are also exempted from other government services, and enjoy other privileges in proportion to the quantity which they deliver.

Those who are employed to bark the trees are called *schjalias* by the Dutch, and by us *choliahs.* Over them are placed officers of a superior class, whose business it is to superintend the workmen, to take charge of the woods, and to prevent cattle and improper persons from trespassing there. Besides these, there is a set of officers of a higher cast, called *cinnamon moodeliers,* whose business it is to judge and punish all small offences, and to superintend the different districts and villages where the choliahs reside. Over the whole a head officer is placed, usually known by the Portugese name of Captain *Cannaillé*, which means Captain *Cinnamon.* He is styled by the natives *Corundu Mahabadda*, or Chief of Cinnamon. The chief Moodelier receives all the reports concerning the woods, and the cinnamon affairs in general, from the inferior officers, and transmits them to the Captain, who is accountable only to the Governor.

Under the government of the Dutch the *choliahs* enjoyed very extensive privileges, and were accounted amenable only to their own Moodeliers. From hence they thought themselves entitled to resist the authority of our military officers. In the district of Caltura, where Lieutenant Macdonald commanded, they absolutely refused to acknowledge his authority, and a party of them one day crossing the Caltura river, almost under the Commandant's windows, they shewed their disrespect by maltreating the natives who ferried them over, and throwing several headlong out of the boats into the river, to the imminent danger of their lives. Mr. Macdonald having investigated the circumstance, ordered the offenders to be tied up and flogged, the ordinary punishment in such cases. At the same time he reported what he had done to Governor North, and represented to him the necessity there was of punishing such contempt of subordination. The choliahs on their part complained to the Governor of this encroachment on their privileges, and insisted that they were amenable only to their own chiefs. Governor North, however, was well convinced that the admission of this plea would only pave the way to greater excesses, and that it was impossible to suffer an independent jurisdiction to exist in the heart of his government. He therefore gave his approbation to what Mr. Macdonald had done; and from this decision, the choliahs must now consider themselves as subject to the same jurisdiction with the rest of the natives.

The process of preparing the cinnamon for exportation is conducted as follows. It is the first care of the choliahs to find out a tree of the best quality. This their sagacity and practice easily enables them to do from the leaves and other marks. Such branches as are three years old, and appear proper for the purpose are then lopped off with a large crooked pruning knife. From these branches the outside thin coat of the bark is scraped off with a knife of a peculiar shape, concave on the one side and convex on the other. With the point of this knife the bark is ripped up longwise, and the convex side is then employed in gradually loosening it from the branch till it can be taken off entire. In this state the bark appears in the form of tubes open at one side; the smaller of which are inserted into the larger, and thus spread out to dry. The heat of the sun by quickly drying up the moisture makes the tubes contract still closer, till they at last attain the form in which we see them in Europe. When sufficiently dry the bark is made into bundles of about thirty pounds weight each, and bound up with pieces of split bamboe twigs. These bundles are carried by the choliahs to the cinnamon *go-downs* or store-houses belonging to the company. As they are brought in, each bundle is marked and weighed, and placed in the heap of the particular district or village to which those who brought it belong; each heap being kept separate till the quantity expected from the district be made up. The several processes required in cutting and barking the cinnamon are parcelled out among several classes of choliahs who are employed only to perform their own particular branches; by this subdivision of labour, the service becomes much easier to them, and much more profitable to their employers.

The next step after the cinnamon has been carried into the company's store-houses, is to examine its quality. This task is imposed upon the company's surgeons, and a very disagreeable one it proves to be. It is performed by taking a few sticks out of each bundle, and chewing them successively, as the taste is the only sure method of ascertaining the quality. The cinnamon, by the repetition of this operation, excoriates the tongue and the inside of the mouth; and causes such an intolerable pain as renders it impossible for them to continue the process above two or three days successively. The surgeons are however obliged in their turns to resume it, as they are responsible for the goodness of the cinnamon: it is customary for them to mitigate the pain by eating a piece of bread and butter between whiles.

The best cinnamon is rather pliable, and ought not much

to exceed stout writing paper in thickness. It is of a light yellowish colour; it possesses a sweet taste, not so hot as to occasion pain, and not succeeded by any after-taste. The inferior kind is distinguished by being thicker, of a darker and brownish colour, hot and pungent when chewed, and succeeded by a disagreeable bitter after-taste.

After the quality of the cinnamon has been by this means ascertained, it is made up into large bundles, each about four feet long, and all of the same weight. The weight of each bundle is at the time of packing up eighty-five pounds, although it is marked and reckoned for only eighty pounds; five pounds being allowed for the loss by drying during the voyage. The bundles are firmly bound and packed up in coarse cloths made of strong hemp or from the cocoa-tree; and are then carried on board the ships which touch at Ceylon for that purpose. In stowing the bales, black pepper is sprinkled among them so as to fill up all the interstices, and by this means not only is the cinnamon preserved, but both spices improved; as the pepper, being of a hot and dry quality attracts to itself the moisture of the cinnamon. As the island of Ceylon does not produce within itself a sufficient quantity of pepper for this purpose, the ships which come to carry the cinnamon to Europe, bring along with them a sufficient quantity from the other parts of India, and particularly from the Malabar coast.

After that part of the cinnamon which is fit for exportation has been sent off to Europe, the very refuse of this valuable spice is capable of being converted to use. The fragments and small pieces which happen to be broken off in packing up the bales are collected, and put into large tubs, about a hundred weight into each, with just as much water as is sufficient to cover them completely. This mass is left for six or seven days to macerate, and is afterwards poured by little and little into a copper alembic, to which a slow fire is applied. The water which comes over, called *aqua cinnamoni*, is received in glass vessels of a peculiar construction; it is nearly of the colour of milk, and the oil floats at the top of the glass recipient. The process is slowly and cautiously conducted; one tub being usually distilled off in twenty-four hours. Two commissaries, (who were members of the council of justice in the time of the Dutch,) are appointed to superintend the whole of this process; and one of them is always required to be present to prevent the apothecary, who conducts the distillation, from embezzling any of the oil. After remaining for some time in the recipient, the oil is carefully skimmed off under the eye of the commissaries, and put into large bottles, which are sealed with the government seal, and brought to the governor, by whom they are placed in a chest secured in the same manner. The reason of all these precautions is the great scarcity and value of this oil. It is only made at the company's laboratory at Columbo; and the quantity is much less than can be procured from an equal weight of any other spice. The jealousy of the Dutch has prevented the exact quantity procured from the hundred weight from being ever accurately ascertained. The usual price on the spot was three-fourths of a Dutch ducat; but of late years little has been to be procured at any price. I saw a pint bottle of it set up for sale among the effects of the late Dutch Governor Van Anglebeck; but the upset price, which was upwards of ten pounds sterling, deterred any one from becoming the purchaser. Cinnamon-oil is esteemed an excellent remedy for spasms in the stomach. That extracted from the finer sorts of cinnamon is of a beautiful gold colour, while that from the coarser bark is darker and brownish.

The process for obtaining the oil of cinnamon which I have at present described is that which was put in practice by the Dutch. The manufacture has not been carried on since the island came into our possession, and indeed it can never be resumed with much advantage, or to any considerable extent. The small quantity of oil which the finer cinnamon yields, however valuable, does not fetch a price equal to what the cinnamon itself brings on being exported to Europe; and the oil from the coarser kinds is of a very inferior quality.

After this description of cinnamon, and the processes employed in bringing it to market, it may not be unimportant to enquire how this valuable branch of commerce may be improved or extended. The growth of cinnamon seems to have been confined by nature to the island of

Ceylon; for at Malabar, Batavia, the isle of France, and indeed every other place to which it has been transplanted, it has uniformly degenerated. Even in Ceylon it is found in perfection only on the south-west coast. In the northern parts, and about the harbour of Trincomalee, it cannot be reared; and therefore it must always be sought on that coast which the want of harbours renders most inconvenient for exportation. The season at which the cinnamon is prepared however suits with the time at which the ships touch at Columbo, sufficiently well to prevent any great disadvantage arising from this circumstance. The principal accession which the cinnamon-trade can receive, is from the introduction of an improved method of cultivating the plant. Of late years the rearing it by art has been attended with every success, and the plantations are already in a flourishing state, under the active management of Governor North. Two principal advantages may be derived from an improved system of planting. By carefully selecting cinnamon seeds and plants of the first quality, the whole grounds, which are at present unprofitably occupied with coarser kinds, may be made to produce the finer species. If the system of plantation were once fully established, the cinnamon grounds might be divided into three or four great divisions, one of which should be cut down each year. By this means a successive crop might be obtained, the quantity to be procured exactly calculated upon, and a great waste saved. Improvements might certainly be also introduced into the method of barking and collecting the cinnamon; the present system is very rude, and the labour of those employed very unproductive compared to their number.

These few hints I suggest with diffidence, and leave to the judgment of more skilful persons. My object is gained if I succeed in turning the attention of the public to a concern of national advantage, and in shewing that it is capable of improvement.

CHAPTER XVI.

Minerals of Ceylon.

THE minerals of Ceylon are numerous, and the island has long been particularly famous for its precious stones, of which we find not less than about twenty different sorts. I was enabled to procure specimens of them all, which I brought home with me to Europe, both in a rough and polished state.

The ruby, the topaz, and the diamond of Ceylon or Matura, are not by any means so valuable as those of Golconda or the Brazils. The saphire, amethyst, aqua marine, and tourmalin, are on the contrary equal to those of any other country.

The *diamond* of Ceylon is seldom completely transparent, but generally appears of a milky colour. Burning has the effect of rendering it somewhat purer. It is cut for rings and buttons, in which I have already said the Ceylonese are very expensive. As it is found in great abundance, it is not by any means high-priced here.

The *ruby* is esteemed according to its clearness, the deepness of its red, and its freedom from flaws. These stones are seldom found of any considerable size in Ceylon; and most frequently are no larger than grains of barley.

The *amethysts* are merely pieces of mountain crystal, tinged with a violet colour. They seldom exceed the size of a walnut, but most commonly are found very small. Their value depends upon their size, and the deepness of their colour. It is often diminished by partial colouring, and spots or streaks of different tinges. They are formed, according to their sizes, into buttons of various descriptions.

Stones, known by the name of *tourmalins*, though destitute of any electrical qualities, are found here, of various colours. The *red tourmalin* appears transparent only when it is held up against the light; it then presents a pale red hue. The *blue tourmalin* is simply a slightly coloured quartz. The *green tourmalin*, or *chrysoprase*, is of a beautiful transparent grass colour, and much esteemed. The *yellow* or *topaz tourmalin* generally resembles amber, although it is sometimes found of a deeper colour. It is seldom larger than a pea, but looks very beautiful when set in rings.

The *topaz* is chiefly found in yellowish splinters, and the shades of colour vary considerably.

The *blue saphire* and the *green saphire* are made into buttons and rings. They vary from the palest to the deepest hues; and the blue saphire is frequently unequal in its colour.

White crystal is found in abundance. *Yellow* and *brown crystals*, only differing in colour, are also met with; and the whole are used for buttons and other ornaments.

The *black crystal* is a species of shirl. It presents a

shining surface, but is not transparent. It is too common to be of any great value.

The *cat's eye* is a species of opal, and receives its name from a white sparkling ray in the centre, which still meets the eye whichever way you turn it. This stone is much esteemed by the natives of India, and a perfect one of the size of a nut will fetch sixty rix-dollars and upwards. The rarity and curiosity of the cat's-eye is the cause of its high price. It is much worn in rings by the Indians.

Cornelians, and other stones of the same description, are found in Ceylon in great plenty. Precious stones were formerly an article of revenue, and collected by farmers, who contracted for a particular range with government. This plan, however, has for some years back been given up, as the stones found in the King of Candy's dominions were superior to those of the lower parts of the island, and the Dutch found it the easiest method of procuring them to demand from him a certain quantity as tribute. For some time that Prince was obliged to comply with the mandates of his imperious neighbours, and send them a certain proportion of stones every year. Of late, however, he has shaken off this servitude; and to tempt the avarice of Europeans as little as possible, he has prohibited any more from being collected in his dominions. He does not now allow his subjects, on any account, to barter precious stones with Europeans, or to carry any above a certain value out of his territories, under pain of death. It is even dangerous for a Candian to retain any above a certain value in his possession, as by a royal decree they all belong to the King. I have already mentioned the hardships to which the poor natives are exposed by this arbitrary decree, and that they will often rather privately give or throw valuable stones away, than run the risque of being obliged to carry them up to Candy, and wait, half-starved, at the palace gate, till his Majesty deigns to receive them.

The precious stones are generally sought for among the hills and rocks, and along the banks of rivers, where they are frequently picked up. By the river which passes Sittivacca, and divides the King's country from ours, they are particularly found. The violent rains which frequently fall in the higher parts of the island wash down these stones from the hills; and when the rivers begin to subside, and get clear and low, they are found among the sands of the channels which are then left dry. I have seen the black fellows, whom we usually call stone-merchants, tracking the bed of a river for this purpose, and often with great success.

Those black merchants swarm in great numbers about Columbo. They are a mixture of the different casts and nations of India; few of them are Cinglese or natives of the island. They are constantly seen in numbers hawking about their stones, and besieging the doors of the European Officers and other gentlemen, whom they always find to be their most liberal customers. They present the stones for sale in all different states, both polished and unpolished; but most usually they have them set in rings of various shapes, in breast pins, crosses, and other ornaments of the same description. At particular seasons of the year, the Europeans are obliged to be on their guard against these troublesome fellows, who are almost all perfect vagabonds, and infest the houses with the double purpose of disposing of their wares, and carrying off any loose article that comes in their way.

These fellows are often at a loss for purchasers, and at times a very valuable stone may be got from them for a trifle. But a person requires to be very cautious in dealing with them, as they are apt to impose upon him with pieces of glass or inferior stones, which they cut and assimilate to the more valuable ones with such dexterity, that it requires considerable skill to distinguish the one from the other.

The black merchants often encounter much labour and many dangers in procuring the stones. It is not unusual for them under various pretences to go into the Candian territories, and carry them off privately from the natives at the risk of their lives.

With regard to the pearls, which form so considerable an article of revenue and traffic in Ceylon, I have already given so full an account of them in describing that part of the coast where they are found, that it is unnecessary to add any thing here. As they are whiter than those of the Gulph of Ormus and the coasts of Arabia, they are not so highly esteemed by the natives, who are more partial to those of a yellowish or golden cast.

Lead, tin, and iron ores are found in the interior, but they are never wrought or applied to any purpose.

There were several mines of *quicksilver* wrought by the Dutch in Ceylon. In 1797, Colonel Bobertson found out one at Cotta, about six miles from Columbo. The quantity we procured from it did not exceed six pounds, but it afforded a most useful and seasonable supply to the garrison, as at that particular time all we had was exhausted, and mercury was the principal remedy resorted to in all liver complaints.

Although some quicksilver was still procured from this mine, yet the labour and expence attending it was so great, owing to the want of experienced and skilful workmen, that it was judged proper to give up working it altogether before I left the island. I have since been informed that the undertaking has been resumed at the same place with more success.

In this article of quicksilver we had a remarkable instance of the secrecy with which the Dutch carried on all their transactions in this island; for previous to the discovery of the mine at Cotta, we never knew that this mineral had ever been found here, nor did any of the Dutch inhabitants ever hint the circumstance to us, although they had at different times extracted large quantities. They indeed observed the same policy in every other instance, and never gave us any piece of information which it was in their power to withhold.

I may here introduce an account of some springs possessed of peculiar qualities, which are situated at Cannia, about six miles from the fort of Trincomalee, on the road to Candy. The waters were analysed by Dr. Christie of the 80th regiment, with some other medical gentlemen belonging to the garrison. The result of this analysis, with a copy of which I was favoured, is as follows.

The hot-wells of Cannia are six in number, and of different degrees of heat. They all, however, evidently communicate, for the water in all of them is at an equal distance from the surface of the ground; and a body immersed in one of them raises the height of the water in the other.

As the water also from all the six wells exhibits the same phænomena, there can be little doubt that they all proceed from the same spring.

Upon examining the heat of the different wells with great attention, it was found they varied from 98 to 106½ degrees of Farenheit's thermometer, nearly in proportion to their different depths.

Bubbles of air are seen to rise from the bottom of all the wells, and it was therefore conceived that the water might be acidulous, and impregnated with carbonic acid gas.

It was found, however, that the water did not sparkle in a

glass more than common water, nor did it turn a delicate vegetable colour red; and upon filling a large case bottle with the water, and tying an empty wet bladder to the mouth of it, it was found, after shaking a long time, that no air was disengaged.

It would therefore appear that the water is not impregnated with any air; but that the bubbles are merely common air disengaged from the water by the heat. As the air, however, might be collected with a proper apparatus, its quality may be easily ascertained.

The water has nothing peculiar in its colour, smell, or taste. It is not crude or hard, for it dissolves soap readily and perfectly.

It contains no sulphureous principle; for a piece of polished silver, when immersed in it, contracted no rust nor dark colour.

It contains no acid nor alkali in a disengaged state; for upon mixing a delicate vegetable colour with it, no change to a green or red colour was perceptible.

The water does not contain any selenite, or earthy or alkaline matter combined with vitriolic acid; for upon adding a solution of mercury in nitrous acid to it, no sediment was deposited. Nor does it contain any earthy matter in combination with marine acid, nor any copper, nor zinc, for upon mixing mineral and volatile alkalis with the water, no precipitate was formed.

On mixture with a decoction of galls, the water acquired

a blackish tinge, which shews it to be slightly impregnated with iron.

On mixture with a solution of silver in nitrous acid, some precipitate of luna cornea, muriat of silver, was produced. This shews it to contain a very small portion of sea salt; but not more than the common waters of Trincomalee, on which the solution of silver had the same effect, with this difference, that the precipitate from the water of the hot wells was blackest, probably from the impregnation of iron.

These experiments were made at the wells, with water from those of the highest and of the lowest temperature, on the 4th of July 1798, when the heat of the atmosphere was at 91 degrees. They were also repeated upon the water after it was brought to Trincomalee, with the same result.

From hence it would appear, that the hot wells of Cannia possess few mineral qualities, or any virtues besides their heat, which is of a temperature not unfavourable for hot bathing.

For many complaints, drinking of hot water is recommended, and for this purpose as well as for bathing, a hot spring is always preferable to water heated artificially, because it is always of a fixed degree of temperature.

CHAPTER XVII.

General Observations—Present state of the Island—Improvements—Revenue—Civil and military establishments—Advantages.

I HAVE now laid before my readers every thing worth notice which fell under my observation during my residence in Ceylon; and if my researches on some topics appear to some too limited, it will, I hope, be recollected at the same time that all my other pursuits were of course considered as subordinate to my military duties. I shall conclude my account with a few general observations on the state and value of this new acquisition to the British crown.

The cultivation of Ceylon, as I have observed in a former part of this work, was extremely neglected under the government of the Dutch. For some years previous to our taking possession of it, the unfortunate situation of affairs in the mother country, as it precluded any supplies from being sent from thence, or indeed any attention being paid to the management of distant colonies, may serve as some excuse for this neglect. But even before this period, when the Dutch republic was in its highest degree of prosperity, the little progress made in the cultivation of Ceylon is a proof that the system pursued with regard to it was fundamentally wrong. In the collecting and cultivation of the cinnamon, the staple produce of the island, their whole attention seemed to be absorbed, and all other advantages were overlooked. The impolicy of such a system will easily be perceived from a few observations.

The soil of Ceylon, particularly in those parts bordering on the sea-coast, is well adapted for the production, not only of all those articles which are common to the tropical climates, but of many which are properly natives of Europe. Even the sands and brittle clay which are found scattered up and down in different parts of the island, produce abundantly, and are equal in fertility to the richest earth. This is to be attributed to the uniform and mild temperature of Ceylon, and the frequent rains which supply its fields abundantly with moisture; while on the continent of India vegetation is often destroyed by the excessive droughts and the hot parching winds to which it is subject at different seasons of the year.

So little advantage, however, was taken of this excellent temperature and soil, that Ceylon has never yet produced a sufficient quantity of rice and wheat for its own consumption, although these and other kinds of grain could with proper attention be raised here to as great advantage as at Bengal or Surat. The inattention of the natives to agriculture was partly owing to the abundance of spontaneous productions with which nature supplied them, and the few wants either of clothes or food in this warm climate; their cocoa-trees and jack-fruit being almost of themselves sufficient for all their purposes. The Dutch, however, by a well-directed policy and by holding out proper encouragement, might have in a great measure overcome the indolence naturally arising from these causes, and might have taught them to know and appreciate the comforts and enjoyments arising from industry and affluence.

These measures, however, were either entirely overlooked or culpably neglected by the Dutch governors. But I am happy to add, that there is every appearance of their being speedily carried into execution, with the best effects, by our countrymen. Within the last two or three years a great increase of tillage, and much improvement in the cultivation of rice and paddy have taken place in the south and south-west parts of the island, in consequence of the encouragements held out by government. The advantages to be derived from a perseverance in this policy are incalculable. The money which is every year sent out of the island to purchase grain being retained in it, in consequence of a sufficient quantity of that commodity being produced within itself for its own consumption, would tend to the rapid increase of its wealth, and consequently of its improvement. The excitement of a spirit of industry among the natives might also be productive of advantages which at present it would be difficult to estimate. If they could first be engaged to cultivate their lands, and to taste the comforts arising from industry and property, their own inclinations would speedily lead them to manufactures and commerce.

Another immediate consequence of the progress of cultivation would be the amelioration of the climate, by clearing the country of those thick woods and marshes that serve to form and perpetuate those noxious vapours which have often proved fatal to Europeans, and deterred the natives of the continent from settling in the island.

By the increase of cultivation, other obstacles to settlers would be removed. The high price of provisions on the Island in comparison of what it is on the Continent from whence they are imported, operates greatly to deter manufacturers from quitting the latter for the former. For whatever commercial advantages Ceylon may present, the dearness of provisions must greatly check infant manufactures, and tend in a high degree to prevent their establishment. But if by the progress of cultivation, a sufficiency of provisions could be produced in the island, and a reduction of prices should, in consequence, take place, manufacturers of different descriptions might be more easily tempted, by various advantages, to settle there. And, if by this means, not only provisions, but clothes and other necessaries could be obtained within itself, without having recourse to other countries, Ceylon would soon become independent of the continent of India, and capable of supporting itself without any external assistance.

I have had occasion in the course of this volume to remark that the soil and climate of Ceylon are favourable to the production of some very valuable articles of commerce. Tea, coffee, tobacco, and sugar-cane, have already been cultivated to great advantage. This circumstance was not unknown to the Dutch; but, with a policy of unexampled absurdity, they repressed every attempt to cultivate these articles in this island, fearing it might diminish their value in the other Dutch East India possessions where they were produced. I need not dwell on the advantages both to our commerce and revenue which may be obtained by pursuing a different system. It is not useless to observe that the tea-plant is found in the greatest abundance in the northern parts, which are most unfavourable to other kinds of produce.

I need not here repeat what I have already said with respect to the improvements which must necessarily result from making roads, and thus opening the communication between the different parts of the island. It is, however, but justice to remark, that at the time I left the island, Governor North was busily employed with every object which could tend to its advantage. He was then on the eve of setting out on a tour round the island, for the sake of inspecting its state in person. In this expedition he was to be accompanied by several gentlemen well calculated to examine the various natural productions with skill and accuracy.

The revenue of Ceylon is of course an article of great interest and importance to our government; but from what

I have said of its present state, and the improvement of which it is capable, it is evident that no fair estimate of the future revenue can be formed from its actual state. By the reports of the Dutch board of trade and revenue for Ceylon, it appears that it was from twenty to thirty years back able to defray its own expenditure; and at times the balance was even in favour of the island. The increase of military establishments and expenses, however, which had taken place in consequence of the destructive wars between the Europeans and the natives, joined to that corruption and inattention to public affairs which began gradually to undermine the prosperity of the colony, soon raised the expenditure far beyond the produce of the revenue. In 1777, and the following year, there was a great deficiency. In 1795, the revenue amounted to no more than 611,704 livres; while the charges of the establishment were 1,243,338 livres: so that the expense of Ceylon to Holland was 631,034 livres, or £57,934 sterling. This deficiency was easily made up by the cinnamon, cardamoms, coffee, and other articles sent from the island to Europe, as well as by the profits of the pearl-fishery, and the imposts laid on the several articles imported into Ceylon from other parts of India.

On the introduction of new improvements into the cultivation of the island, the establishment of manufactures, and the consequent influx of wealth, it is not to be doubted, that the revenues levied in the island itself will soon exceed its expenditure. Considerable advantage is also to be expected from an improved mode of taxation and collection: and in fact several additions have already been made to the revenue since the arrival of Governor North.

It must however be observed, that these advantages to the revenue cannot be expected without a considerable previous expense on the part of Government. An example of cultivation must be set to the natives. Such advantages must also be held out to foreign manufacturers as will induce them to quit their own country for this island. By a well-timed liberality on the part of Government, much may speedily be effected; and improvement once begun goes on of its own accord with accelerated rapidity.

The natural strength of the island of Ceylon, and the few points at which it can be safely approached, seem to promise it a great degree of security; yet repeated experience has shewn that they are insufficient, without a considerable military establishment, to protect it completely against a powerful or an enterprising enemy. The force formerly maintained by the Dutch on the island consisted of about three thousand Europeans and about two thousand Malays, Topasses, and native Cinglese. These were dispersed in the various strong posts around the island, in such a manner that no great number could readily be collected upon one point, except at Columbo, where by far the larger proportion of the military establishment was usually stationed. This place had also been greatly strengthened by the Swiss regiment of De Meuron; but unfortunately for the Dutch the term of its services expired at the critical season of danger; and by an unaccountable oversight in policy, this fine body of troops were permitted, on greater advantages being held out to them, to transfer their services to their most dangerous enemies, and to co-operate powerfully in the reduction of their former masters.

This military establishment of the Dutch, which rarely exceeded five thousand men in all, was found sufficient to repel the attacks of the native Princes. It was also capable, from the nature of the country, of completely baffling the attempts of any European force that did not much exceed in number the troops stationed at any particular point. But it is evident, from the great extent of the island, that this small force was obliged to be too much scattered, to be capable of making any effectual resistance against a numerous enemy. When the depth of water on the eastern shore is considered, as well as the facility afforded for landing by the spacious harbour of Trincomalee, it is impossible that a sufficient number of troops for the defence of this quarter could have been spared from the protection of the rich countries, on the south-west, which were menaced by an enemy ready to make a descent from the coast immediately opposite. The difficulty of communication likewise requires the force employed to be the greater, as it is next to impossible to march troops from one side of the island to the other, in time to render each other any effectual support.

But it is not the defence of the island itself alone that should induce us always to maintain a powerful force here. From its situation, it affords the best point for stationing those troops which are destined to protect our several establishments in India, and to act as a constant check on the native princes. On the Coromandel coast in particular, where our possessions have of late been so much extended, troops may arrive from Ceylon in a day or two, and by this means preclude the possibility of our settlements being overrun by surprise before a sufficient force could be collected to oppose the invader. During the disturbances which arose on the borders of Tinivelly and Madura, my attention was forcibly called to this subject by the events which took place there. Owing to the small number of troops stationed at that time in Ceylon, it was found impossible to co-operate from thence with those sent by the company to repress the commotions; and before a sufficient force could be brought together from other quarters for this purpose, several officers and a great number of soldiers were killed and wounded. Had a large force been at that period stationed in Ceylon, the disturbances might have been almost immediately quelled.

Troops may be sent to any of our possessions in the peninsula of India from Ceylon at a less expense, and in much shorter time, than from either of the presidencies of Bombay or Madras. Since we have been in possession of the island, detachments have at various times been sent with great effect to join the troops serving against the Poligars and the Nairs in the Cotiote.

It is impossible to estimate the establishments intended to be placed in Ceylon by government, from their situation when I left the island, as at that time it had not been ceded by treaty to the British crown, nor had circumstances as yet permitted any regular plan of appointments to be fixed upon with regard to it. The force, according to the latest accounts, stationed there, consists of the 19th and 51st regiments, three native battalions, and about 200 of the Bengal artillery, besides the Malays who entered into our service on the capture of the island. The policy of our government in raising native troops who are enured to the climate and acquainted with the country, promises to be productive of the happiest effects, and seems the best that can be employed to secure a distant colony. The officers very properly are Europeans.

The force though perhaps sufficient in times of profound peace for the preservation of tranquillity in the island itself, is by no means fit to be entrusted with the defence of such a valuable colony, and far less to render any effectual assistance to our other possessions in the event of any commotions. The smallest establishment which can be appointed to this must consist of at least three European regiments, and seven or eight battalions of native troops for the garrisons of Trincomalee, Columbo, and Point de Galle alone; without including the fort of Jafnapatam,

Manaar, and the other subordinate posts round the island, which will require to have garrisons proportionate to their importance. There are several posts which it would be necessary to strengthen, and place on a more respectable footing than they are at present, particularly Manaar, Calpenteen, Nigumbo, Caltura and Matura, which the Dutch suffered to fall almost to total decay, but found much reason to repent their neglect on the first attempt made by an enemy at invasion.

Many material improvements have been made in both the military and civil department since the arrival of Governor North on the island, and it is not to be doubted that by a perseverance in the same plans of policy, it will soon, without any additional burthen to the British government, be placed in such a posture of defence as to set any attempts of an enemy at defiance. No motive can be wanting to stimulate our government to place the military establishment there on a respectable footing, while the examples of the Portuguese and Dutch are immediately before our eyes, and while it is evident the successive expulsion of these nations, and the consequent ruin of their empire in that quarter of the world, was owing to the insufficiency of their forces, and the neglect of military discipline.

After the security of the island has been provided for by an adequate military establishment, its tranquillity and prosperity must in a great measure depend upon the arrangement of the civil department, and the proper administration of jutice. While Ceylon remained in the hands of the Dutch, its Governor was absolute with regard to the affairs of the island, but subordinate to the Governor of Batavia, who was considered as Governor-General of all the Dutch settlements in India. The Governor of Ceylon was assisted by a council, composed of the most respectable Dutch gentlemen residing at Columbo. The members of this council were nominated by the Governor, and confirmed in their appointments by the government of Holland.

For the administration of justice, there was a high court established at Columbo, to whom the ultimate decision in all capital cases belonged. At Trincomalee, Jafnapatam, and Point de Galle, there were subordinate civil magistrates, with suitable appointments. In all the inferior forts and stations throughout the island, there were petty courts, called *landraeds,* for the more speedy administration of jutice in matters of less importance. In these the military commanders of the district usually presided. An appeal lay from all these inferior courts to the high court of justice at Columbo.

The whole Dutch civil establishment, independent of the military who acted as civil magistrates, was computed to amount to four hundred and fifty persons, comprehending all who were anywise attached to it. This may seem a small proportion for an island of such magnitude, and from whence such valuable articles of commerce were exported: but according to the computation of the Dutch, Ceylon ranked only as their eighth Indian government.

For some time after we took possession of Ceylon, the government was necessarily a military one, until tranquillity was completely established. From the arrival of Governor North, the civil establishment has its date. He abolished the office of Provost Martial, and the jurisdiction of the military courts, and restored the civil establishment to near the same form it bore under the dominion of the Dutch. He re-established the supreme court of justice at Columbo, with a civil magistrate to superintend the police of the Fort, and another in the Black Town. The various officers necessary for the service of these departments were at the same time appointed; and similar regulations were adopted through the other parts of the island. The petty courts in the distant parts of the country still continue to be presided over by the commanding officer of the nearest post. The government of Ceylon was for some time dependent on that of Madras, but is now only subject to that of the mother country, and entirely unconnected with the East-India Company.

For the better ordering of military affairs, there is a military board established at Columbo. It consists of six members taken from among the commanding officers of the several corps stationed in Ceylon. The commander in chief of the forces in the island is president of this board, the Commandant of Columbo for the time being Vice-president. It has attached to it a secretary, clerks &c. with suitable salaries.

I have now brought my account of Ceylon to a conclusion. After the remarks which have occasionally been interspersed, it would be needless to recapitulate the advantages to be derived from it to this country. As a field for commercial enterprise, as a general depôt for stores and troops, and as a centre of communication with our other East India possessions, there can no other station be pointed out to equal it in that quarter of the world. The measures already taken by Government sufficiently indicate that those in power are well aware of the importance of the acquisition. By perseverance in a wise and moderate policy there is every reason to hope that the natives will speedily be brought to co-operate in our plan of improvements; and that the period is not far distant when we shall look upon Ceylon as not inferior in value to any of our foreign possessions.

The Journal of the Embassy to Candy may serve to throw some light on the situation of the interior; and as I am anxious to give my readers as accurate an idea as possible of every thing regarding the island, I have subjoined a description of the different roads which pass through it, as they were ascertained by a survey very lately made by the Post-master General of Ceylon.

JOURNAL

OF

THE EMBASSY

TO THE

COURT OF CANDY,

In 1800.

GOVERNOR NORTH having determined on sending an embassy to the King of Candy, both with an intention to keep up a friendly intercourse with that Monarch, and also with a view to political objects of importance, General Macdowal, the commander in chief of the forces on the island, whose well known ability and conciliatory manners rendered him every way worthy of being selected on this occasion, was appointed to undertake the commission.

As it was intended that this embassy should be as splendid as possible, and should make a strong impression on the minds of the Candians, by far exceeding any thing of the kind which had hitherto been seen on the island, the Governor, previous to its departure from Columbo, sent his private secretary, Mr. Boyd, to the borders of our territory at Sittivacca, there to meet with the Adigar and the other ministers of his Candian Majesty, in order to make with them the necessary arrangements for its passage through the country, and its reception at court. As the General was to be accompanied by a large escort, it was necessary to quiet the apprehensions, and remove the suspicions of the Candians on this head, as they had always been extremely averse to the introduction of a military force into their country.

This object having been effected, and the necessary arrangements having taken place, the embassy prepared for its departure. The presents destined for the King of Candy had for some time been in readiness, and the detachment from the garrison of Columbo, which was to accompany the General, had been appointed. It consisted of the light company, and four battalion companies of his Majesty's 19th foot, five companies of the 2d battalion of 6th regiment of coast sepoys, five companies of the Malay regiment, a detachment from the Bengal artillery, with four six-pounders and two howitzers, and part of the Madras pioneer and lascar corps.

March 10th. The tenth of March, 1800, being fixed upon for the day of our departure, the General, his staff, and suite, with the above escort, marched from Columbo to Palambahar, about four miles distant, and situated on the right bank of the Mutwal river. Here we encamped in some rice-fields adjoining.

11th. Remained in our encampment waiting for the presents which were still at Columbo. One Maclaren, a private in the 19th regiment, was drowned while bathing in the river. Rain, thunder, and lightning at night. Thermometer at 79°.

12th. Remained in the same place, the presents not being yet arrived, nor a sufficient number of coolies provided to convey the hospital doolies, and provisions for the detachment. Some of the natives who had been appointed to look for the body of the man we lost the preceding day, found it near the spot where he had sunk. Slight rain and thunder at night.

13th. Marched about eight miles to Cudavilli, the road lying along the river in a very agreeable manner. Here we encountered a very strong and narrow pass: on our left lay the uncommonly steep banks of the river: our right was skirted by hills covered with thick jungle; and in front appeared a kind of fort or breast-work which had been thrown up by the Cinglese during their rebellion against our government in 1797. This entrenchment, if held by an enemy possessed of any degree of military skill, could not be forced without considerable difficulty, as the approach to it is by a deep hollow defile, lined on each side with bushes, where troops might easily be stationed in such a manner as to annoy the enemy severely without exposing themselves. We had several sepoys killed and wounded here at different times before the rebellious Cinglese could be subdued. A considerable number of years ago, the Dutch had about four hundred of their troops surrounded and cut off near this spot. Our escort encamped about half a mile beyond the pass, in an open plain, nearly surrounded by the river, which winds here in a variety of directions. The situation of Cudavilli is delightfully romantic.

14th. Halted this day. From Columbo we learnt that the 51st regt. from Madras had arrived there and disembarked in order to form part of the garrison. Rain, thunder and lightning at night.

15th. Marched twelve miles to Gurrawaddi, a very pretty place situated in a pleasant and romantic country, with several high and steep hills in the neighbourhood. An extensive choultry, or house for the accommodation of travellers was built here by the Dutch: at present it is much out of repair. A Cinglese village and a small circular fort or rather intrenchment, lie close by the river which is here broad and rapid. During the disturbances in 1797, the 35th battalion of Madras Sepoys occupied this post for several months, and during that period lost many of their men from the fire of the rebels who concealed themselves in the neighbouring thickets.——This day a private of the 19th regt. while washing his trowsers on the brink of the river was suddenly seized and dragged down by an alligator. Rain with severe thunder and lightning at night.

16th. Halted. We now began to experience the difference of climate here and at Columbo. Heavy fogs and dews at night, succeeded by excessively hot and sultry weather by day; the height of the thermometer being 92 at noon.—— Rain thunder and lightning at night.

17th. About two o'clock the General ordered the guns with two companies of Sepoys and the pioneers to proceed about six miles farther; as the next day's march was long, and the fatigues which the men would have to encounter from being exposed to the heat of the sun, would be greatly encreased if they should be obliged to accompany the artillery, which on account of the badness of the roads could proceed but very slowly.

18th. The escort set of very early in the morning, and marched fourteen miles to Sittivacca. The road was exceedingly hilly and difficult, full of ascents and descents, and often obliged to wind among the vallies which intersect the hills, as the impenetrable thickets on each side prevent any passage but by the beaten tract.

Sittivacca presents as beautiful and romantic an appearance as any spot in Ceylon. It is famous for being the chief theatre of intercourse, both friendly and hostile, between the Candians and their European neighbours. Here many bloody battles were fought by the natives against the Portuguese and Dutch; here their treaties, or rather truces, have been repeatedly signed; and this was the spot usually chosen for the interviews of the European with the Native Ambassadors. It is the last station belonging to us in this quarter, and is separated from the King's country only by a large branch of the Mullivaddy river, which winds around here in several directions, and is joined by a branch of the Malivagonga a little below this place.

On the summit of a hill, immediately under which we encamped, stood a large range of buildings defended by an entrenchment, and formerly occupied by the Dutch, but now almost in ruins. The view of the country from this height is truly grand and enchanting. The hills, covered with the thickest woods, are diversified with immense perpendicular ledges of rocks, which rear their stupendous heads above the tallest groves. Through the thickets which cover the valleys, the eye is enabled to trace the windings of the rivers and the green tracts of clear land which imitate their serpentine course.

On our arrival here, the General sent across the river to inform the Adigar, who lay encamped on the opposite side with several thousand Candians, that he intended passing over next day. The thermometer was to day at 96°. The excessive heat of the weather was occasioned by the closeness of the surrounding hills. About three o'clock the General received a message from the Adigar, with leave to pass the river at the time he had appointed. This night we had rain, with thunder and lightning.

19th. About twelve o'clock we struck our tents, and began crossing the river. A vast number of Candians flocked down to the water edge to see our troops, and were not a little astonished at the quickness and facility with which we drew the guns and artillery waggons over. No such appearance had been presented to them for many years before, nor had there ever been such heavy metal introduced into their country.

The ford where we crossed was not more than from three to four feet deep, it being then the dry season. The descent from our side was so great, that the bullocks were obliged to be taken from the waggons, and the troops employed to draw the artillery through the water, while the ammunition was transported on the heads of the lascars and pioneers attached to the guns. We encamped close to the banks of the river at Golobodivilli, where is a Candian village with a choultry, and several ranges of buildings erected on purpose for the reception of the Ambassadors and their trains, when they repair hither to have an interview with the Europeans. The General went to the choultry, where he received a visit from the Adigar, who came preceded by a Candian, carrying the King's letter wrapped up in a white cloth, and bearing it over his head; a mark of profound respect always paid to this, which is the royal colour. The General, in return, delivered Governor North's letter to the Adigar. The heat to day was excessive; thermometer at 98°.

20th. I took the opportunity of our halting this day to go to see the ruins of a temple which lay close by our encampment. It was the first built of stone which I had seen on the island. About four or five feet in height of the walls still remained, with flights of steps all around them. Great pains had been bestowed on its construction; and several inscriptions were still visible on the flags and pillars which formed its basis. Contiguous to it lay a neat village, but entirely deserted, as the women had universally left it on our approach, and the men formed part of the militia which attended the Adigar. About eight o'clock at night, the Adigar came in great state by torch light, to pay a visit of ceremony to the General, when the conference continued for a full hour on complimentary matter. A number of officers who had dined this day with the General were present during the interview. The conversation was carried on standing, and if I may judge from myself, all parties were heartily tired of it, and wished it to be brought to a speedy conclusion. The Adigar promised to send the General five hundred of his people to convey the presents intended for the King of Candy, and to assist the Cinglese peasants in our service in transporting our baggage and provisions: but this promise, if we may judge from the performance, might also be set down among the complimentary matter. Rain, thunder, and lightning at night.

21st. Halted. Sent the pioneers to repair the roads which were represented to be in a very bad condition.

22nd. The Adigar waited on the General in his usual state, being accompanied by several of the chief men and about three hundred of his guards. Their great guns were carried on men's shoulders, being little more than musquets of a very wide bore with blocks of wood attached to the lower end of the barrel near the breech. Those guns, when about to be fired off, are simply placed on the ground, while the muzzle is elevated by the piece of wood I mentioned. Immediately opposite the street leading to the place of audience stood a very fine Banyan-tree, around which a sort of platform had been placed, where the priests of Buddou were accustomed to performed their sacrifices, and the chief people to take their stations at any occasional assembly. As the Adigar and his train were to pass that way, several of our officers and soldiers planted themselves on this elevated situation in order to have the better view of the procession. The Adigar however chancing to observe them above him, expressed great indignation, and desired that they should be ordered down, as no one ought in his presence to be placed higher than himself, who personated a king with whom none is on a level and before whom as the descendent of the golden sun all men should fall prostrate. Before the Adigar were carried several flags and streamers, with people playing on a variety of musical instruments peculiar to their country, and a number of fellows cracking immense whips so as to produce a most stunning noise, while they continued running about like so many madmen. While the General and the Adigar were engaged in conference, I had an opportunity, by means of a Malay Prince who interpreted for me, of conversing with some of the principal Candians, who waited at the outside of the choultry. They seemed a handsomer race of people than our Cinglese; their manners were more courteous, and their conversation more polite. They were as eager to obtain knowledge of our customs, as we were to be informed of theirs; and they examined several articles of our dress with great minuteness. They were not a little surprized on Captain Vilant, of the 19th regiment, sketching off a likeness in a few minutes of one of their chiefs, and presenting it to him. Our watches did not escape their notice, and they were very curious to have the uses explained to them of those extraodinary machines. Upon being offered some little presents, they seemed afraid on account of each other to accept of any thing, lest it should come to the king's knowledge. They informed us that we should find it impossible to bring up our horses and waggons to Candy, which was afterwards found to be really the case. I shall not forget the significant smile which one of them gave on seeing a tumbril pass by: it seemed emphatically to say, "you may as well leave it where it is." The Adigar, on returning from this conference with the General, sent some of his people to fetch the presents which the Governor had destined for his Candian Majesty. They were very valuable, and consisted, among other things, of an elegant state-coach drawn by six horses; a betel dish with ornaments of solid gold which had belonged to the late Tippoo Sultan, and was valued at eight hundred star-pagodas. There were besides presents of rose-water and a variety of fine muslins. After these had been delivered, and we had been joined by two hundred Candians, sent by the Adigar to supply the place of those Cinglese who had deserted us through dread of the climate, at one o'clock we set forward, and marched about three miles further to Apolipitti, a small plain surrounded with very high hills. We had scarcely pitched our tents when torrents of rain began to descend, accompanied by the loudest and most awful peals of thunder that imagination can conceive, while the vivid flashes of lightning succeeded each other so rapidly that the firmament seemed to flame in every direction. This alarming uproar of the elements lasted for upwards of three hours; but although several tents were struck, providentially no lives were lost, nor indeed was the least injury done to any of our troops.

23d. The General ordered the whole body of pioneers and Lascars, accompanied by a company of Europeans and one of Sepoys and Malays, to set about making a road in our front for the artillery, as the paths through which our march lay, besides being exceedingly narrow, was so full of precipices and ravines, that without smoothing the one, and filling up the other, it was absolutely impossible to proceed. The Adigar, on seeing the men at work for this purpose, sent to the General to express his disapprobation of this measure; and remonstrated against any of his master's territory being infringed upon in the slightest degree, though he knew that we must either repair the road, or give up our intention of proceeding further. Every thing indeed shewed that this minister was by no means much inclined to shew us any favour. The whole tract which it was intended we should pursue in our progress to Candy, was marked out by twigs and bushes set up at proper distances. It was well-known that a far easier road than that pointed out to us was known to the Adigar. Had we taken a direction either more to the west or to the south, as the Dutch were accustomed to do, we should have escaped many of those inconveniences to which we were daily subjected. The minister seemed indeed to have pitched upon the most difficult and intricate paths for us, in order that we might suffer the more in our march. The circumspection with which we were constantly watched, shewed how little confidence the Candians reposed in the good faith of Europeans. At the distance of two or three miles from our encampment lay a large body of the king's troops, consisting, as we were informed, of seven thousand men with some elephants. This body we never saw, as they kept a few miles a-head of us the whole way, and were cautious always to remain just out of our view. None of our officers were allowed to approach them, or to have an opportunity of observing their numbers. I attempted to ascertain how far report had been correct in this point; but although I contrived to pass several of their parties unmolested, I was forced to return without having effected my object as prudence forbade me to venture farther alone against their inclinations. Beside the regular troops, the whole inhabitants of this part of the country were assembled in arms, and lay in every direction around us. Some of them often came among us; and whenever any of us walked out from our encampment, we seldom failed to perceive the Candians skulking about the woods in our vicinity. The party sent out in the morning to make the roads, were obliged to return at one o'clock, on account of the rain thunder and lightning which began to be as severe as yesterday.

24th. About eleven o'clock struck our tents to proceed to Ruanelli, or, as it is called by the Candians, the valley of precious stones, ten miles from Apolipitti. The day was most uncommonly hot, the thermometer being at 101°. In addition to this, the road was exceedingly difficult and fatiguing. I had here an opportunity of observing that the Europeans bore the extreme heat much better than the natives. The Bengal artillery men exerted themselves with the greatest perseverance, and the soldiers of the 19th regiment were frequently obliged to assist in dragging the guns through the ravines and defiles. But such was the badness of the roads, that in spite of these efforts, and though the troops and pioneers had been employed two days in clearing away the stumps of trees and pieces of rock which obstructed the passage, we were obliged after all to leave the guns five miles in the rear, with a covering party of two companies of Sepoys, while the Europeans and the rest of the native troops marched on to a very extensive tope of cocoa-trees near Ruanelli, called Resue Orti Palagomby Watty, or the King's Royal Gardens, where we encamped. The leeches infested us in this march to a most alarming degree; most of the soldiers had their legs and different parts of their bodies streaming with blood. On taking off my gloves and boots I found that I had not escaped, for what I had taken to be nothing more than excessive perspiration, now turned out to be the effects of these leeches. The officers and men employed in clearing the jungles presented an appearance absolutely shocking, as they seemed to be completely covered with blood. Nor was it possible by any precaution to prevent the attacks of the leeches, owing to the immense multitudes of them which swarmed among the bushes and the grass. The Dutch always said they were one of the worst enemies they had to encounter. The only serious accident which occurred to us on this day's march was one of the Europeans being struck with a *coup de soleil*, which rendered him for some hours delirious. It was impossible to avoid the heat by marching before sun-rise, as the rain which fell the preceding day had so completely drenched our tents that we were forced to remain till the morning sun had sufficiently dried them. The guns besides could not be conveyed without day-light through the shocking roads we were obliged to pass.

On our march we had several beautiful and picturesque views of the country, which presented a charming variety of thickly wooded hills, intersected with delightful valleys. The grove where we encamped was about two miles in circumference, being bounded on the West by a large, deep, and rapid branch of the Malivagonga, while in front towards Ruanelli, another branch ran in a south-east direction, winding in such a manner, that three sides of the grove were encompassed by water, while the fourth was enclosed by thick hedges of bamboes and betel trees. This extensive cocoa-tree garden lies immediately under very steep and lofty hills, which command a most romantic view of the surrounding country. It forms part of the King's own domains, and is the place where his elephants were usually kept and trained.

Hitherto the river was navigable by our boats, and enabled us to have a large proportion of our stores and provisions conveyed by water, as it run in such a direct line with our march that we encamped close to its banks. From Ruanelli up to Candy it is shallow, rocky, and much narrower, so that boats cannot proceed along it without great difficulty, and those only the small canoes of the natives. From Ruanelli to Columbo, the distance by water is about sixty miles; and such was the rapidity of the current occasioned by the dreadfully heavy falls of rain which happened during our stay here, that a boat could go down to Columbo in eight hours, and for most part of the way, the only exertion required of the boatmen was to keep clear of the rocks, stumps of trees, and sand-banks, which happened to obstruct their course; while in returning to Ruanelli, it usually took nine or ten days of excessive labour. The facility of the conveyance from hence to Columbo by water proved afterwards of the highest utility, on account of our sick; as several of our men, and myself among the rest, were attacked with violent dysenteries and fluxes while we encamped here.

25th. Sent back two companies of the Malays to relieve the Sepoys who had been left to cover the guns. A detachment of the other troops and the corps of pioneers returned with them to assist in the difficult work of getting the artillery forward: for although each gun had a number of bullocks yoked to it, they required a number of men to enable them to make their way through the ravincs and steeps. In the Carnatic and different parts of the continent of India, elephants are employed to obviate any difficulties of this sort which may arise on a march. It is astonishing to observe the sagacity of those animals, who, on observing a gun stuck fast in a rut, or a stop made on meeting with a difficult ascent, will come and render their assistance, by lifting up the wheel with their trunk, or by placing their forehead to the hinder part of the carriage and pushing it along. Such assistance was very much wanted on our present march, as the bullocks of Ceylon are much inferior both in size and strength to those of the continent, nor can the united force of a number of those smaller animals be applied so as to produce an effect equal to a few of these larger and better trained oxen. About two o'clock the artillery came up and formed on the right of the tents occupied by the European troops. The weather for the last two days was uncommonly hot, the thermometer being to day as high as 102° at noon.

26th. Remained in our encampment. A number of the coolies supplied by the moodeliers around Columbo, Nigumbo, and Caltura, deserted. Before we could proceed, the General found it necessary to send to Mr. North for others to replace them. The Adigar and his people lay at about two miles from us on the opposite side of the river.

Within a mile of the place where we were encamped, and towards Columbo, rose a hill of a most uncommon and striking appearance. It was situated in the midst of immense and steep rocks, interspersed with plantains and cocoa-trees, reared there by the hand of nature. Under one of these rocks lay a cavern, in which was a temple dedicated to the god Buddou. The accounts which I had heard of this place induced me to seize the first opportunity of visiting it. After crossing a little well-watered plain, you come to the foot of a perpendicular rock, of a very great height, surrounded by others of an inferior size. The ascent to the cavern is about forty feet, and is made by a narrow winding path composed of fragments of rock and stumps of trees. On arriving at the entrance of the cavern, the wild appearance which it presents, the ascent by which it is gained, and the scene which surrounds it, present together a groupe of objects which rivet the eye, and produce an effect on the mind much easier to be conceived than described. On entering the temple, which is a very low and long apartment cut out of the rock, the first object which presented itself was an immense figure of a man carved in wood, and upwards of twenty feet in length. A bed and pillow had been hewn for him out of the rock; and here he lay on his right side, with his right hand supporting his head. His hair was frizzled like that of a negroe; and his serene and placid countenance was dawbed all over with red paint. The inside of the temple was rudely painted with streaks of red and black. It was attended by two priests, who permitted us to enter without any difficulty; nor did they insist on our taking off our shoes, a custom which they generally oblige visitors to observe. Their duty was to wait at the temple, and never to allow the lamp burned before the image to be extinguished. Another reason perhaps operated as powerfully as the rules of their order to enforce their constant attendance; which was, to receive the offerings of the votaries who continually flock to this temple. Our detachment afforded very welcome visitors, as every one who went thither always left some money, fruit, or rice, for the service of the god. The natives who repair hither for the purposes of devotion are constantly obliged to contribute either money, rice, cloth, or some other commodity of value. From the numerous votaries who frequent this temple, the priests are reputed to possess great riches; and the king, who never fails to come in for his share of every thing, accordingly taxes them very highly. I doubt not that his Majesty would be well-pleased that his priests should frequently have such liberal visitors as they found our troops during our stay at Ruanelli. Adjoining the temple where the image was placed, were two other apartments where the priests resided at those hours when their attendance on Buddou was not requisite.

This day it began to rain violently about two o'clock, accompanied with severe peals of thunder succeeding each other almost without an interval. Sent down to Columbo four sick men of the 19th regt.

27th. Remained in the same place. The early part of the day uncommonly hot, with terrible thunder and lightning about the usual hour. The evening was very cold: the dews which fell at night were uncommonly heavy, and did not disperse till the sun broke through next morning in his full heat. Several coolies lost.

28th. The heat of the day very great: thermometer at 104°. Distant thunder and lightning. The General continued to wait for coolies to replace those who had deserted; nor was it indeed possible to proceed without a favourable change in the weather.

29th. Morning very hot. Captain Kennedy who commanded the detachment of the 19th having been very ill since our arrival here, was sent by water to Columbo, where he died in a fortnight after. About three o'clock it commenced a heavy rain, which continued incessantly for ten hours with severe thunder and lightning.

30th. The same weather as yesterday, with the storm of as long continuance. During our stay here several messages passed between the General and the Adigar, who lay about the distance of two miles across the river. The natives seemed very much displeased at our bringing artillery into their country, or stirring beyond the limits of our camp, although permission had been obtained from the court of Candy to have this embassy more splendid and numerous than any which had preceded it, and although orders had been issued to give us the most friendly reception. It was indeed reported, that the King found himself at that time in rather a precarious situation, from the internal divisions and factions among his subjects; which made him wish that the escort attending the embassy should be as strong as possible. But the Adigar, who was a man of great power and intrigue, and, as we had reason to suspect, not very friendly to the English, had sufficient influence to over-rule several of the King's orders, and in many instances to counteract his intentions.

The weather continuing still unfavourable, and there being no prospect of procuring a sufficient number of people to carry the provisions and stores requisite for the whole escort, while the roads which lay between us and Candy were so dreadfully bad as to render any attempt to proceed with our baggage and artillery almost impracticable; the General was induced by these circumstances to leave the artillery with the Europeans and the greater part of the native troops at this encampment, and to proceed to Candy escorted by two companies of Sepoys and the same number of the Malay regiment. Accordingly he gave out that he would cross the river next day, and appointed Colonel Torrens to command here in his absence. During upwards of a month that the detachment which he left behind remained encamped at Re Sue Orti Palagamby Watty, very few days passed without the most heavy falls of rain, attended with close and violent peals of thunder and lightning. This weather, which almost constantly closed the evening, and was followed by thick damp fogs at night, succeeded by excessive heat in the early part of the day, produced such a rapid change of temperature as was attended with the most pernicious effects to the health of the troops. Dysenteries, fluxes, and liver complaints, became frequent; and the jungle fever, which often proves fatal where the person attacked has not an opportunity of being immediately removed to the sea air, began to make its appearance. The woods around the encampment were also so close, that no one could stir out of the camp without the greatest risque of losing himself in their mazes. Two soldiers happening to walk out one day, were in this manner unable to regain the camp, and remained in the woods a day and night exposed to all the inclemency of such weather as I have described: nor would they in all probability ever have been recovered, had not several parties been sent out in different directions, with orders to fire from time to time, in hopes that the stragglers would hear the report of the musquets. This had the desired effect, and these poor fellows were at last brought to the camp, after having undergone the terrible apprehension of being doomed to end their days in a dreary forest.

Having procured the Adigar's leave to make shooting excursions, and also people acquainted with the country to conduct us, we had an opportunity of seeing several of their villages, most of which we found totally deserted by their inhabitants. On the approach of a red coat, the alarm was instantly given, and the natives, men, women, and children, fled directly into the woods. It was not till after some time that we could persuade a few of them to remain in their habitations: but I never saw any thing in the figure of a woman from the time I entered the Candian territory to the moment of my quitting it. We found it very difficult to procure hogs, fowls, and fruits from the natives, although such articles were in great abundance in the country. This not a little surprised us, as the King's officers had expressly issued orders directing us to be supplied with every sort of necessaries. We were more disposed to attribute this to the country people themselves than to any deceit on the part of the court. The Candians, indeed, particularly the lower orders, shewed little inclination to have any connexion with us. Their dread and hatred of Europeans, occasioned by the numberless aggressions of the Portuguese and Dutch, had become too rooted to be easily removed. To this we are to attribute that distrust and dislike towards us, which they took every opportunity of shewing. No sooner were tidings brought them that we had set forward on our route from Columbo to Sittivacca, than they immediately began to assemble in great numbers on their frontiers, under the idea that we were approaching with hostile intentions. A message from the King however removed their apprehensions on this head; and at the same time those militia received orders immediately to join the regular troops, and in no wise to obstruct or molest us in our march through the Candian territory.

Several kinds of precious stones and metallic substances are found in the environs of Ruanelli; and among the sand and gravel lining the banks of the river which ran in the front of our encampment, I picked up several pieces of very fine crystals, of different colours, which seemed to have been washed down from the neighbouring hills. On the opposite side of the river lies a valley encompassed with more gentle and less woody hills, than those on our side, called Ruanelli, or the place of precious stones. Here they were formerly found in considerable plenty; but since the impositions of his European conquerors, the King does not permit them to be dug up or looked for. The black people, Malabars, and others, who belonged to our detachment, were daily employed in searching among the sands of the river. General Macdowal shewed me a great variety of stones, and other curiosities, which these people had brought him. Among these I observed a black shining substance, resembling a petrified shell, with which the Candians ornament their umbrellas made from the talipot tree.

31st. General Macdowal, attended by the escort of Malays and Sepoys which I have already mentioned, and accompanied also by the officers of his staff and suite, and such gentlemen of the detachment as expressed a desire to see the capital, passed the river about eleven o'clock, and proceeded about two miles further to a place where stands a choultry and a pagoda. The rain commenced again about the same time as on the preceding days.

April 1st. Remained in the same place, preparing for the march of next day. Rain, thunder, and lightning.

2d. Moved on about eight miles to Edimalpani. The country was, on this day's march, more open, and less difficult than that we encountered on our approach to Ruanelli.

3d. Halted. Severe storm, as formerly.

4th. Marched twelve miles to Atipitti. The road very difficult and steep. The country, however, was much more open, and the air much cooler than hitherto experienced.

5th. Proceeded six miles to Wolgoagoudi, which signifies, the ground of holes and caverns. It receives its name from a number of cavities in the rocks and hills with which this part of the country abounds. The road here was still worse to pass than on the preceding day. The air was much clearer and cooler than on the frontiers; and the weather now began to become more settled.

6th. Moved on to Ganna Tenna, or, the place of fire; so called from several volcanic eruptions which formerly took place here. In many parts of the interior, volcanoes have at different times burst forth; and the hills seem in a high degree to possess the principle of those eruptions, whatever it may be. Iron and other ores might be procured in various places through this tract, but the Candians, for many years past, have paid no attention to discovering or working any of the veins. I observed the surfaces of several rocks which gave strong indications of metallic ores; and the water issuing from them frequently presented that thick scum and crust which is usually supposed to indicate the presence of some metal. The country around Ganna Tenna was more open, rocky and barren than any we had hitherto traversed; and it seemed continually to advance in height as it approached Candy. This last march was very difficult, as it had to wind round several hills by narrow intricate paths. The steep ascents and descents which every now and then occurred, proved extremely fatiguing. In some of the valleys were cultivated spots where rice, paddy, and other sorts of grain were raised, as they were well-watered by the streams that poured down from the rocks and mountains.

7th. Halted to refresh the troops after the fatigue of yesterday's march.

8th. Marched nine miles to Ganaroa, a high mountain.

The road here was very steep, being up two very high hills. The country seemed more cultivated than any we had yet traversed. The air was more serene and cool, particularly at night; there was less of the noxious fogs and damps than is usually experienced in the lower parts of the country. At the foot of the mountain where the escort now halted, lies a beautiful valley watered by the Malivagonga. The view from Ganaroa is extremely grand, and takes in a vast range of hills, covered with thick woods and jungle, and intersected with valleys presenting here and there some fertile spots cultivated by the Candians. The ruins of an old fort and a temple lie close to the spot where the troops rested.

9th. Halted. Messages passed between the Adigar and the General, previous to the latter proceeding to Candy, which lay at a small distance.

10th. Removed to a spot near the Malivagonga, and encamped opposite the hill on which Candy is situated. A large body of Candians were posted on the other side of river in view of the General's encampment. No intercouse was allowed to be carried on between them and our people; nor any of the escort allowed to quit the camp or examine the country in the neighbourhood. The interviews and correspondence between the Adigar and the General were all conducted with the utmost solemnity, and with all those punctilious ceremonies which according to their ideas are matters of the highest importance.

The attendants, and indeed the whole of the natives, seemed to be actuated by the same mysterious taciturnity; so that little information was to be collected from them about the King or his politics.

The General was now arrived at that place where it was determined he should reside while he transacted the business of his embassy. It might now seem that he had overcome the chief difficulties that lay in his way; and that the fatigues of his tedious march would have been compensated by a frank reception and ready admittance into the royal presence. But it was the study of the Candians to impress the Ambassador with the highest ideas of their dignity, and their condescension in receiving overtures from an European government. With this view, so many ceremonies attended each introduction into the royal presence, that little business could be transacted; and such a space was allowed to elapse between each interview, that the General was only admitted to three during his stay here, which was from the tenth of April to the third of May.

But previous to any interview, it was found no easy matter to adjust the ceremonies of introduction. It had been customary for the Kings of Candy to demand prostration, and several other degrading tokens of submission from the ambassadors introduced to them. The Dutch ambassadors had always submitted to be introduced into the capital blindfold, and to prostrate themselves before the Monarch. In a former war, when Trincomalee was taken by us from the Dutch, proposals were sent to the King to assist him in expelling his enemies out of the island, and to form a treaty of alliance with him. After the envoy entrusted with this business had arrived at Candy, the King would not receive him standing; and the envoy, not having instructions how to act in such a case, declined the interview till he could hear from Madras; by which means so much time elapsed, that the object of the embassy was by intervening circumstances entirely defeated, and the envoy returned without being presented. Even after the British had shewn their power by the capture of Columbo and the expulsion of the Dutch, the Candian Monarch would not recede from his lofty pretensions; and Mr. Andrews, the British East India Company's chief civil servant, who was sent upon a mission to Candy shortly after we had taken possession of the island, was obliged to kneel on being admitted to the royal presence. Nay, to such an extravagant pitch do the natives carry their ideas of the indispensable nature of this royal prerogative, that when Trincomalee was in the last war taken by our troops under General Stewart, and when the King was in consequence prevailed upon to send ambassadors to Madras, these persons very modestly desired Lord Hobart to prostrate himself before them, and to receive the King's letter on his knees. This request, however, his Lordship declined to comply with; but returned for answer, that as they were so much in the habit of kneeling, and so fond of prostration, a custom which his countrymen never adopted, their best plan to prevent the omission of this essential ceremony, would be to prostrate themselves before him who held the supreme authority there: and this alternative, after they found his Lordship would not submit to the other, they actually assented to.

General Macdowal, understanding that this ceremony was expected at his introduction, previously informed his Majesty, by means of the Adigar, that he could not on any account submit to it. The King made many objections to receiving him into his presence, unless he would consent first to prostrate himself and then to remain kneeling during the royal audience. The General, however, positively refused compliance, and informed the minister that his Sovereign acknowledged the superiority of no Potentate upon earth; and that sooner than degrade his Sovereign in the person of his representative, he would return to Columbo without being presented. The King, not daring to come to an open breach with us, upon this waved his prerogative; but in order to reconcile this derogation from his dignity to his own feelings, he informed the General that it was his royal will to dispense in his case with the usual ceremonies required of ambassadors at their introduction, as the General came from his brother the King of Great-Britain, whose great power and strength he acknowledged to be far above that of the Dutch or the East-India Company.

This important matter having been adjusted in this manner, and the time appointed for the first audience being come, the

Adigar, with a numerous attendance, lighted by a great blaze of torches (for audience is always given here by night) came to the edge of the river to conduct the General to the royal presence. The General on his part crossed the river in the boats which were in readiness, attended by his staff and the gentlemen belonging to the embassy, with an escort consisting of a subaltern and fifty Sepoys. He was then conducted by the Adigar about a mile and a half to the King's palace. The road thither was up a steep hill, with narrow crooked paths. The capital was surrounded by thick thorny hedges, with gates of the same, called by the natives *caravetties*. The caravetty nearest Candy has a rampart and breast-work, on which some of their artillery was occasionally mounted. The resistance which it could make to the approach of a regular army is, however, very trifling: Candy is indebted for its principal fortifications to nature.

The way up to the city was very fatiguing, and the escort was not a little incommoded by the crowd of natives who eagerly pressed to gaze at them. This circumstance and the glare of the torches prevented the General's retinue from having an accurate view of the city. The embassy on entering it passed through one long broad street to the palace. The houses, though low huts of themselves, appeared greatly elevated from being built upon high banks on each side of the street, which forms a kind of area below. At the further end of this street is a high wall enclosing the gardens which belong to the palace. After a short turn here to the left, the palace appeared standing on the right. In front of it was a flight of stone steps, and a viranda or balcony, in which a number of the King's guards and several of the chief men in waiting were stationed. After passing this, and descending by another flight of steps, a large square surrounded by a high wall afforded a station for some more of the guards. At the opposite side stood a large arched gate-way, leading into an inner court where the King and his principal officers of state have their residence. In this inner division the King kept his own body guards, who were composed of Malays and Malabars. These troops are armed with swords, spears, and shields; and on them the King seems to place his chief dependence in the event of any sudden commotion or alarm.

On the right hand of this inner court stood an open arch, through which was the entrance to the hall of audience. This state room was a long viranda with alternate arches and pillars along its sides. From this structure, as well as from the appearance of the roof and ceiling, it bore a considerable resemblance to the aisle of a church. The pillars and arches were adorned with muslin flowers, and ornaments made of the plantain leaf, which had a very pretty effect. At the further end of the hall, and under one of the larger arches, was placed a kind of platform or throne, covered with a carpet, and surrounded with steps. Here the King sat in state. A small partition raised in front concealed his feet and the lower part of his body from view. Below the arches on each side of the hall, the courtiers were seen, some prostrate, others sitting in silence and cross-legged like a parcel of taylors on a shop-board. The General was led up with much ceremony and gravity by the Adigar, and the next chief officer present, and placed along with the Adigar on the uppermost step of the throne.

Although the rest of the hall was well lighted, that part where the King sat was contrived to be made more obscure than the rest, with a view of impressing a greater awe on those who approached him. He was in appearance a young man, very black, with a light beard. He was by no means so portly or well-looking as the Adigar and several other of the officers around him. He was dressed in a robe of very fine muslin embroidered with gold, fitted close at the breast with several folds drawn round the waist, and flowing down from thence like a lady's gown. His arms were bare from the elbows downwards. On his fingers he wore a number of very broad rings set with precious stones of different sorts, while a number of gold chains were suspended round his neck over a stiff frilled piece of muslin resembling a Queen Elizabeth's ruff. His head was covered with a turban of muslin spangled with gold, and surmounted by a crown of gold, an ornament by which he is distinguished from all the other Asiatick princes, who are prohibited by their religion from wearing this badge of royalty, and whose ornaments, when they use any, consist simply of a sprig or feather of precious stones. His waist was encircled with a rich sash, to which was suspended a short curved dagger or sabre, the handle richly ornamented, and the scabbard of gold fillagree-work. In appearance his Majesty much resembled the figures we are accustomed to see of King Henry VIII. The Adigar, from his superior size, might indeed be said to do so still more: very little difference in dress was discernible between him and his sovereign, except that the minister did not carry a crown; although his turban also was surmounted by something like a ducal coronet.

After General Macdowal had been presented in form to his Majesty, and a numerous string of ceremonies had been gone through, the King proceeded to inquire about the health of his Britannick Majesty, and the state of our affairs; to all which questions the General returned such answers as propriety dictated. The conversation was carried on with the most profound gravity and reserve. Even the most trifling circumstances were mentioned in whispers, with as much ceremony and importance as if the fate of kingdoms depended upon them. The King directed his speech to the Adigar, who stood on the step below the throne, and who repeated his Majesty's words to the Maha Moodelier, who had come up with the embassy as Cinglese interpreter. The latter in his turn gave it in Portuguese to Monsieur Joinville, who had also been sent up by Governor North to interpret from that language, and who repeated it in French to General Macdowal. Thus the conversation was carried on by five different persons, and in three different languages; the General's answers returning by the same channel which had conveyed his Majesty's questions.

The tedious length to which such a conference must have been protracted, may be easily conceived, and though it lasted near three hours, this first interview was entirely occupied with complimentary matters. During the conference, rose-water was frequently sprinkled around from curiously wrought vessels of gold; and perfumes were handed about on salvers of gold and silver fillagree-work. The oppressive heat of the room however, joined to the powerful exhalations of the scented oils burned in the lamps, and the rank smell of cocoa-nut oil with which the natives present were universally anointed, overcame the effects of all these precautions, and almost stifled the European gentlemen who were allowed to remain at one end of the hall where the General's guard was stationed. During the audience, the rain poured down in torrents without intermission; and continued to do so until the General was on his march back to the camp, where he arrived about five in the morning, quite exhausted with fatigue.

After this audience, some days were permitted to elapse before another could be obtained; as it is a standing maxim with the Candians never to hurry forward affairs, or to betray any symptom of anxiety for their being brought to a conclusion. I am convinced that their adherence to this principle on the present occasion cost them no small share of uneasiness; as their suspicions of us were too violent to allow their minds to enjoy any rest while we continued in their country.

At the second audience the General introduced the business of the embassy, and made those demands which he was authorised to do on behalf of Great Britain. Concerning the nature of those demands, and the answers returned to them, I do not consider myself at liberty to give any statement, as they were matters of private negociation. One circumstance however was publicly talked of as having been laid before his Candian Majesty by the General on this occasion. It was a request made on the part of our government, that that prince would allow a road to be made and a communication to be opened from Trincomalee to Columbo, through his territories, a little to the north of Candy. This would have been a matter of vast convenience and importance to our government, as hitherto the tapals or letter-bags had to be conveyed by a circuitous route along the sea-coast by Manaar and Jafnapatam, and double the distance of that proposed through the Candian territories. The King however would on no account accede to this proposal; but expressed his decided aversion to any intercourse or connexion existing between his subjects and the Europeans. At the same time, however, he expressed a desire to live on amicable terms with the British, whose power he acknowledged to be far superior to that of the Dutch. Whatever further transpired with regard to the objects of the embassy was too much the result of conjecture to be set down in an authentic narrative.

Between this audience and the next audience for the purpose of taking leave, several messages and conversations took place between General Macdowal and the Adigar on political topics. The greatest precaution was employed by the Candians to prevent any intercourse between those of our escort, particularly the Malays and Malabars, and those in the King's service. Our soldiers who attended the General to the court were prevented by every possible means from conversing with the natives. In spite of these precautions, however, several pieces of information were procured which may be turned to advantage hereafter. Several Malays in the King's service found an opportunity of expressing their sorrow at not having it in their power to return to Columbo with their old companions. Most of those Malays had been slaves to the Dutch, and had on account of ill treatment made their escape to the Candian territories. They would have gladly returned to their former masters, and submitted to any punishment for their desertion, rather than live in continual apprehension from the caprices of a despotic and barbarous court.

At the audience for taking leave, the King put a gold chain round the General's neck, and presented him with a sword and an embroidered belt and scabbard. He also gave him a ring set with different sorts of precious stones, and an elephant. These, even when added to the presents sent to Governor North by the King, were of small value in comparison of those his Candian Majesty received from our government. To the officers who accompanied the King were distributed a gold chain, a ring, and some tortoise shells of little value; and the soldiers were merely presented with a piece of coarse cloth. Nor was the escort even supplied with provisions while at the Candian court; a piece of hospitality which was expected, and which on former occasions it had been usual to confer. A small quantity of rice and paddy of an inferior sort, with a few sweet meats dealt with a very sparing hand, were all the gifts which our troops derived from Candian hospitality.

The General, after taking his final leave of his Majesty, and having obtained orders for departure, commenced his route on the 2nd of May for the camp at Ruanelli, and arrived there on the 6th. Next day he set out with his staff for Columbo, leaving directions with Colonel Torrens to march the detachment back as soon as the escort he had carried up with him to Candy were sufficiently refreshed from their fatigues.

On the tenth of May the whole detachment set off to Sittivacca where they encamped that night.

11th. Marched to Gurrawaddi.

12th. Halted this day, being Sunday.

13th. Proceeded to Cuddavilli.

14th. Marched to Columbo, where the detachment, after being allowed a few days to refresh themselves, returned to Garrison duty.

TABLE OF ROADS IN CEYLON.

I. THE Road along the Coast of the Island of Ceylon, commencing at Trincomalee, and proceeding by Jafnapatam, Manaar, Columbo, Point de Galle, Matura, and Baticolo, with the names and distances of the different stations and resting places on the road, both for passengers travelling, and the people employed to convey the tapal or letter-bags, chiefly taken from a very late survey made by the Postmaster of Ceylon.

The distances are set down in country leagues as reckoned by the natives, which are about six English miles each league—the natives divide their leagues into two *camouchies,* which means the changing between Palankeen - bearers to ease themselves in 'turn when carrying passengers. The distances are calculated in country leagues according to the custom of the country people, for the benefit of travellers, as they will be the better able to judge of the distance they advance on the road. The hours are also set down here which are allowed to the Tapal Peons to go from one station to another, and deliver the letter-bag. All the under-named places are where people are stationed to forward the packets; and stretch all around the island, except the tract between Baticolo and Trincomalee.

From Trincomalee to Manaar.

From where to where.	Country Leagues.	Hours for the Tapal	Remarks on the Road.
Trincomalee to Lavelly...	1½	3	Sandy, very thick wood, hilly, with elephant jungle
Lavelly to Couchavelly....	2½	3½	Rather good, very woody
Couchavelly to Terriate...	2½	3½	Much the same; wild hogs and buffaloes
	6½	10	

From where to where.	Country Leagues.	Hours for the Tapal	Remarks on the Roads.
Trincomalee to Terriate, brought over........	6½	10	
Terriate to Cokelaye......	2½	4	Rather sandy, and water to cross
Cockelaye to Vattouvè....	2½	4	Water to cross, rather hilly and woody, tolerable
*Vattouvé to Mulativoe...	2½	4	Woody, but rather good; wild animals numerous
	14	22	
Malativoe to Matulé.....	1½	3	Rather sandy and woody
Matulé to Chiondicalaw...	2½	4	Sandy, water to cross, woody; road muddy
Chiondicalaw to Beschouter	2½	4	Sandy; cultivated; palmiras at each side
Beschouter to Klalie......	2½	4	Ditto, Ditto, Ditto
Klalie to Chavacherry ...	1	2	Rather sandy, cultivated with palmiras
Chavacherry to Jafnapatam	2	3	Ditto, ditto, but good road, cultivated ditto
	26	42	
Jafnapatam to Calamonie..	1½	2	The sea to cross, sandy } On a line with this part are the small islands and commencement of the gulph of Manaar
Calamonie to Pounaveen..	3	4½	Sandy, with palmiras..
Pounaveen to Bavatongy..	2	2½	Sandy and woody } The country round wild and full of buffaloes, wild hogs, and elephants
Bavatongy to Polveracotta	1½	2	Ditto, ditto, good road
Polveracotta to Palliar.. .	1½	2½	Ditto, ditto, indifferent
Palliar to Elpocarrie......	1½	2½	Ditto, ditto
†Elpocarrie to Vertativoe.	1	2	Ditto, ditto
Vertativoe to Mantotte....	2½	4	Ditto, ditto
‡Mantotte to Manaar....	1	2	Ditto, water to cross to Manaar island
From Trincomalee to Manaar..........	41½	66	

* This ends the district of Trincomalee. † Ends Jafnapatam district.

‡ Mantotte to Bengalle, 1—2.

From Mantolle you leave the road to Columbo, and proceed on your right hand to Manaar by the following road, to the extreme end of the island of Manaar, when you cross over to the continent by Adam's Bridge, at Tulmenar.

From where to where.	Country Leagues	Hours for the Tapal	Remarks on the Roads.
Mannar to Carrichelly....	1	2	Sandy and waste
Carrichelly to Congangelli	1	2	Ditto
Concangelli to Tulmanaar, or Little Manaar.....	1	1½	Rather good; here you cross to Ramisseram island, opposite this
	3	5½	

From Manaar to Columbo.

From where to where.	Country Leagues	Hours for the Tapal	Remarks on the Roads.	
Manaar to Bangalle......	1	2½	Sandy, and water to cross	
Bangalle to Arippo.......	1	2½	Rather sandy, water to cross; a village and choultry. The Moulipatty river runs into the sea here	
Arippo to Callar.... ...	2	3½	Sandy road; pearl banks lie opposite this part	
*Callar to Marchichatty..	1½	2½	Sandy and woody	
Marchichatty to Mardodde	1½	2½	Rather ditto, ditto	
Mardodde to Pomparipo...	1½	2½	Ditto, ditto, ditto	
Pomparipo to Moeroundamvelli...........	1½	2½	Woody and stony; much water, and a great lake near Pomparipo	
Moeroundamvelli to Caredivo...............	1	2	Half good, rest stony, hilly, & woody	Wild animals numerous from Arippo all along this road; and some parts much infested with elephants
Caredivo to Ambellam....	1½	2½	Tolerably good	
Ambellam to Potalum....	1	2	Rather sandy; salt pans: hereabouts the sea flows in far on this flat country	
	13½	25		

* Ends Manaar district, and begins Columbo district; though from this to Chilow more strictly forms one, and from Chilow to Columbo another, both separate, but under the jurisdiction of Columbo.

From where to where.	Country Leagues	Hours for the Tapal	Remarks on the Roads.	
From Manaar to Ambellam, brought over....	13½	25		
Potalum to Onnavelly....	1½	3	Rather sandy and muddy	Near this is Calpenteen island; a great deal of water in the rainy season; obliged to keep farther up by another road
Onnavelly to Andepanie..	1½	3½	Sandy and muddy	
Andepannie to Karcopannie	2	4	Very sandy	barren wild country, with tracts of thick jungle and cocoa-nut trees; very much infested with elephants
Karcopanie to Chilou.....	¼	1½	Ditto, ditto, water to cross	
Chilou to Toddeway......	1½	3	Ditto, ditto	
Toddeway to Merravellie..	1½	3	Ditto, ditto	
Meravellie to Ullevettie...	1	2½	Ditto, ditto	all this coast from Manaar very flat and sandy
Ullevettie to Kaimellie....	1	2¼	Ditto, ditto	
Kaimellie to Nigumbo....	1	2½	Ditto, except a little near Nigumbo	
Nigumbo to Cordé.....	½	¾	The road very good; fort and village here	
Cordé to Dandigam	1	1½	Very good road	pleasant & shady; most of the way plenty of cocoa-nut trees
Dandigam to Jaillé......	½	1	Ditto, ditto, river to cross, little sandy	
Jaillé to Maabolle........	1	1½	Very good road, little sandy	
Maabolle to Passbetale....	½	¼	Ditto, a very broad river to cross	
Passbetale to Columbo....	½	1	Very good road; and a number of houses scattered along	
Manaar to Columbo, distance is..	29¼	57		

In the rainy season the country between Andepannie and Potalum is all full of water, so that the peninsula of Calpenteen becomes an island; and it is impossible to cross between the two places on account of the mud; in consequence of which the letters and passengers going from Columbo to Manaar, or coming from Manaar to Columbo, must be carried over in a boat from Pomparipo to Calpenteen; and then proceed by the following road to get into the usual road at Andapani; and on from that to Columbo.

From where to where.	Country Leagues	Hours for the Tapal	Remarks on the Roads.
From Pomparipo to Calpenteen..........	2½	3½	Sandy; the sea and water to cross
Calpenteen to Etally......	1½	2½	Sandy (Wild and woody)
Etally to Navacally......	2	3½	Ditto (Wild and woody)
Navacally to Vetapallie....	2	3½	Ditto (Wild and woody)
Vetapallie to Andepannie..	2	3½	Ditto (Wild and woody)
	9½	15½	

Road along the South Coast from Columbo to Point de Galle, Matura, and Baticolo.

Columbo to Galgieste....	¼	1¼	Very sandy and woody; cinnamon growing on the left hand side; shady
Galgieste to Pantura....	2	3	A little sandy, good road; pass through part of the cinnamon gardens; river to cross
Pantura to Caltura......	2	3	Very good shady road; cocoa-nut trees the whole way; a broad river to cross; a fort and village
	4¼	7¼	

This Road is reckoned 28 English miles; it is an exceedingly cool and pleasant road to travel: I have myself walked in seven hours from Caltura to Columbo, without being much fatigued.

Columbo to Caltura......	4¼	7	The fort and village, with the country beautiful, and well cultivated
Caltura to Barbareen....	1½	2½	Shady; good road; rather sandy; cultivated; cocoa-trees
Barbareen to Bentotte....	1	1½	Water to cross; good road, rather hilly; cocoa trees; oysters sold here
	7¼	11	

From where to where.	Country Leagues	Hours for the Tapal	Remarks.
From Columbo to Bentotte, brought over....	$7\frac{1}{4}$	11	
Bentotte to Gossgoddé....	$1\frac{1}{2}$	2	Good road; hilly; cocoa-nut trees
Gossgoddé to Amblamgoddé..............	1	2	Ditto, ditto, ditto, water to cross
Amblamgoddé to Ecotté..	$1\frac{1}{2}$	2	Ditto, ditto, ditto, rather sandy, do.
Ecotte to Gendura......	$1\frac{1}{2}$	2	Ditto, ditto, ditto
Gendura to Ponté Gallé..	1	$1\frac{1}{2}$	Good, but rather sandy; water to cross
	$13\frac{1}{4}$	$20\frac{1}{4}$	
Galle to Wakgalmodere. .	$\frac{1}{2}$	1	This road shady here and there, with sandy tracts, and a little cinnamon growing near the coast; two broad rivers to cross; game and wild animals numerous
To Cattecoeroende.......	1	$1\frac{1}{2}$	
To Gay a Pané.	1	$1\frac{1}{2}$	
Gay a Pané to Beligamé. .	$\frac{1}{4}$	$1\frac{1}{4}$	
To Gravetté............	$1\frac{1}{2}$	$2\frac{1}{2}$	
Gravette to Matura......	$\frac{1}{2}$	1	
	19	$29\frac{1}{2}$	
	English Miles		
Matura to Tangalee......	12	0	The Road from Matura to Baticolo lies through a very wild part of the country, difficult to travel on account of the wild beasts; and dangerous from the natives of the island, called Vaddahs, who live in the woods about this east part of Ceylon, which renders it necessary to have military escorts The road is equally dangerous, and unfrequented by Europeans, from Baticolo to Trincomalee
Rainneg and Tallavillie..	20	0	
Ambentotte and Boundelli	24	0	
Patetoupanie and Tate Ri..	25	0	
Patepoutanie and Kouman e	18	0	
Mattiagamgattoa to Baticolo..............	24	0	
About English miles......	123	No Tapal	

This Track round the island may ascertain its circumference with considerable accuracy; and nearly corresponds to what Ceylon is usually supposed to be, which is about nine hundred miles, allowing for the greater extent nearer the sea, which takes in bays and projections of land along the coast.

7

	English miles.
Trincomalee to Manaar...	250
Manaar to Columbo......	160
Columbo to Baticolo......	220
	630
A space between Baticolo and Trincomalee; difference between its utmost projection and the road set down here..	70

II. Road from Columbo to Candy, taken by General M'Dowal.

	English miles.	
Columbo to Cudavilli................	10	A level and pleasant road
Cudavilli to Gurrawaddie............	11	More hilly; though tolerable
Gurrawaddie to Sittivacca............	14	Hilly and difficult
Sittivacca to Apolipitti..............	4	A level road
Apolipitti to Ruanelli..	8	Difficult, full of hills and narrow defiles
Ruanelli to Edimalpani..............	10	Nearly the same
Edimalpani to Atipitti................	12	Very difficult
Atipitti to Wolgoagoddi............	6	Ditto, ditto
Wolgoagoddi to Ganna Tenna........	8	Exceeding steep hills to ascend
Ganna Tenna to Gannaroa..........	9	A very steep hill in the way
Gannaroa to Candy................	3	The ascent to Candy very steep
	95	

III. Road from Trincomalee to Candy, taken by Mr. Boyd.

The route Mr. Boyd took from Candy to Trincomalee; the only one taken by the English..........	
From Candy to Gunnoor, this I take to be Gannaroa, where General M'Dowal halted.............	5

	English miles.	
Gunnoor to Osspoot	16	This road is by Mr. Boyd's account exceeding difficult, and many parts dangerous on account of the elephants. From what I could learn, I understood the distance between Candy and Trincomalee not to exceed 120 miles, and from Columbo to Candy about 90. I have not a doubt but the Candians took Mr. Boyd the longest and most difficult ways, particularly for the last two or three days' march, as they evidently brought him round into the Columbo road at Gunnoor
Osspoot to Allaway	18	
Allaway to Nallendy Caravetty	18	
Nallendy Caravetty to Choultry plain.	5	
From Choultry plain to Gona	18	
From Gona to the Rock River	16	
From Rock River to Wishtegall	5	
From Wishtegall to Pulian Caravetty	20	
From Pulian Caravetty to Permaumado	10	
Permaumado to Tertolay	10	
Tertolay to Tumbela Caumun	16	
Tumbela Caumun to Copputorey	6	
Copputorey to Trincomalee	9	
	167	

Should events hereafter render it necessary for the English to proceed to Candy in a hostile manner, there are other roads much shorter and less difficult than those described; between Chilow and Putalom is a road the Dutch once took, and another between Caltura and Point de Galle, by which the distance is not above 70 or 80 miles.

FINIS.